CONTRIBUTING TO ECLIPSE

the eclipse series

SERIES EDITORS Erich Gamma ▪ Lee Nackman ▪ John Wiegand

Eclipse is a universal tool platform, an open extensible integrated development environment (IDE) for anything and nothing in particular. Eclipse represents one of the most exciting initiatives hatched from the world of application development in a long time, and it has the considerable support of the leading companies and organizations in the technology sector. Eclipse is gaining widespread acceptance in both the commercial and academic arenas.

The Eclipse Series from Addison-Wesley is the definitive series of books dedicated to the Eclipse platform. Books in the series promise to bring you the key technical information you need to analyze Eclipse, high-quality insight into this powerful technology, and the practical advice you need to build tools to support this evolutionary Open Source platform. Leading experts Erich Gamma, Lee Nackman, and John Wiegand are the series editors.

Titles in the Eclipse Series

Kent Beck and Erich Gamma, *Contributing to Eclipse,* 0-321-20575-8

Frank Budinsky, David Steinberg, Ed Merks, Ray Ellersick, and Timothy J. Grose, *Eclipse Modeling Framework,* 0-131-42542-0

Eric Clayberg and Dan Rubel, *Eclipse: Building Commercial-Quality Plug-Ins,* 0-321-22847-2

CONTRIBUTING TO ECLIPSE

Principles, Patterns, and Plug-Ins

Erich Gamma
Kent Beck

⩓ Addison-Wesley

*Boston • San Francisco • New York
London • Munich • Paris • Madrid
Capetown • Sydney • Tokyo • Singapore • Mexico City*

Many of the designations used by manufacturers and sellers to distinguish their products are claimed as trademarks. Where those designations appear in this book, and Addison-Wesley was aware of a trademark claim, the designations have been printed with initial capital letters or in all capitals.

The authors and publisher have taken care in the preparation of this book, but make no expressed or implied warranty of any kind and assume no responsibility for errors or omissions. No liability is assumed for incidental or consequential damages in connection with or arising out of the use of the information or programs contained herein.

The publisher offers discounts on this book when ordered in quantity for bulk purchases and special sales. For more information, please contact:

U.S. Corporate and Government Sales
(800) 382-3419
corpsales@pearsontechgroup.com

For sales outside of the U.S., please contact:

International Sales
(317) 581-3793
international@pearsontechgroup.com

Visit Addison-Wesley on the Web: www.awprofessional.com

Library of Congress Cataloging-in-Publication Data
Gamma, Erich.
    Contributing to Eclipse : principles, patterns, and plug-ins / Erich
Gamma, Kent Beck.
        p. cm.
    ISBN 0-321-20575-8 (alk. paper)
    1. Computer software—Development. I. Beck, Kent. II. Title.

    QA76.76.D47G355 2003
    005.1—dc22

                                        2003020914

ISBN 0-321-20575-8
Text printed on recycled paper
First printing, October 2003
1 2 3 4 5 6 7 8 9 10—CRS—0706050403

To my sunshine Karin, Jeremy, and Jill
—E.G

Behind every book is a network of people and relationships that are invisible to the reader except as they affect the quality of what you are reading. My most important relationship is with my wife, Cindee. She gave me love and support when it was most difficult, encouraged me, worked many hours on the book itself, appreciated the good and pointed out opportunities for improvement, and supported our kids while I worked. You'll never see what she did, but without her, I couldn't have contributed to this book. Thank you, Cindee.
—K.B.

Contents

Foreword

Eclipse is a many-splendored thing. Eclipse is a technology, an extensible platform for tool integration, and a wide range of tools built on that platform. Eclipse is an open source project that delivers this technology. And Eclipse is a community that contributes to the open source project and also produces commercial Eclipse-based tools. The community itself is diverse, ranging from users of Eclipse-based products, to tool writers building extensions, to researchers exploring new ways of using Eclipse.

Eclipse is an ambitious undertaking. It provides a platform that allows diverse tools to interoperate, often in ways that the tool writers did not initially imagine. To make this aim a reality, we use an open, merit-based, collaborative development process—high-quality contributions are accepted from anyone. As the Contribution Rule reminds us, "Everything is a contribution." And with many contributions, the possibilities are endless.

The Eclipse Platform is composed of numerous plug-ins, and if you cast your net more widely, you will discover a plethora of additional plug-ins. *Contributing to Eclipse* enables you to jump into this expanding ecosystem and become a tool writer yourself. It is a guide through the initial barrier to entry, giving you the tools to explore the Eclipse landscape and venture out on your own. A fully worked example takes you step by step through the evolution of a plug-in—from initial implementation to product-ready software. In addition, this book defines Rules for extending Eclipse, so your plug-ins are "done right." Eclipse-literate readers will appreciate this book too: Its instruction confirms your accumulated understanding and it provides new insights into areas where you are less experienced. Chapters end with forwarding pointers to additional material so you can dive deeper.

These authors know what they are talking about. Erich is the authoritative source on the Java development tooling. In addition to leading this effort, he has been influential in the evolution and maturation of the Eclipse Platform.

Kent has a deep understanding of software development processes and he is a master at providing clarity, simplicity, and understanding. Together, they share their experiences with Eclipse and teach us how our own experiences can be successful. I trust you will enjoy this refreshingly practical book while you absorb its instruction on how to immerse yourself into Eclipse.

On a personal note, Erich and I have been collaborating on IDE technology for several years. The previous efforts were educational stepping stones—sometimes not even completed before we moved on to the next iteration. But we kept learning. With Eclipse, we have a technology that will continue to grow and evolve. Eclipse is worth investing in. Put Eclipse to work for you. I have confidence you will find new ways to contribute to Eclipse!

John Wiegand
Eclipse Platform Lead
IBM
September 2003

Preface

Humans need to feel nurtured and cared for. Humans also need to nurture and care for others. Fulfilling the need to nurture and be nurtured is what makes becoming a fully functioning Eclipse programmer so satisfying. This experience is wrapped in all sorts of rational explanations—"productivity," "time-to-market," "leverage." Eclipse is a productive environment in which to work, and contributing to it makes it more so. The right contributions written by the right person can create a highly leveraged reduction in time-to-market. While these explanations are true, though, they aren't the point.

Working in Eclipse feels good to us because our needs are being taken care of by our environment. When we have a programming problem, there is an Eclipse feature that helps us with it. Contributing to Eclipse feels good to us because we know we are adding to that nurturing feeling of nurturing for ourselves and other programmers. When our contributions enable others to make further contributions of their own, a positive feedback loop appears. That positive feedback feels satisfying.

Contributing to Eclipse also has the potential to become an exciting business proposition. You can use Eclipse to ship fully featured products, or you can ship contributions that extend existing products.

Eclipse is powerful—personally, professionally, and socially. But there is a daunting amount of information necessary to join the cycle of contribution. We hope reading this book will help you get over this initial hurdle and begin contributing.

Eclipse is good news and bad news for developers who like writing tools for developers. The good news is that the platform is incredibly powerful and the internal developers have followed all the rules in creating the Eclipse Java development tools. The bad news is that Eclipse has a strong world view. If you want to play nicely in Eclipse's sandbox, you need to learn the rules.

Beginning with Eclipse feels a bit like parachuting blindfolded into Bangkok (this analogy doesn't apply to Thai programmers). When you land you know you need food and shelter, but how are you going to get it? How can you map your clear desires onto the resources available?

Overcoming this feeling of dislocation is the primary goal of *Contributing to Eclipse*. If you parachuted into Bangkok with a guide, you could say, "I'm hungry," and your guide would say, "Here's the kind of place you can get a meal." Similarly, we can listen to, "I want to build such and so," and tell you, "This should be its own perspective, that is an object contribution, and you'll need a new editor for that."

When you are finished with this book, you won't have a complete map of Eclipse, but you'll know at least one place to get each of your basic needs met. You will also know the rules through which you can play well with others. It's as if we draw you a map of Bangkok marked with six streets, a restaurant, and a hotel. You won't know everything, but you'll know enough to survive, and enough to learn more.

When you learn Eclipse, you'll spend much more time reading code than writing code. You will have to grow accustomed to incredibly productive days in which you spend six hours reading and one hour typing. After you become familiar with Eclipse culture, you'll "just know" how to solve more and more problems. However, you'll always solve problems by copying the structure of solutions to similar problems, whether by mimicking Eclipse structure or the structure of your own previous efforts.

As we walk together through our example, we won't pretend that we perfectly remember all the details. Instead, we'll show you how we found structure to mimic. Learning to effectively use Eclipse's search facilities is part of becoming an Eclipse contributor.

This book is not intended for beginners just learning to use Eclipse. We assume a familiarity with the vocabulary of Eclipse—views, editors, and so on. Once you've used Eclipse for a while, you are likely to come up with ideas for extending it. That's when this book comes into play.

When we laid out *Contributing to Eclipse,* we had a daunting stack of concepts to cover. If we tried to tell you about all 2,000 ideas in Eclipse, though, we would have a book that would cut off the circulation to your lower extremities. In deference to your feet, we've chosen the 50 things that we think are most important for getting you started. Many chapters conclude with "Forward Pointers," places in the code where you can explore the extension of the concepts covered in the chapter. When we teach Eclipse, this is exactly the structure we use—"Why don't you look at the `org.eclipse.core.runtime` manifest?"

Once there was a doctoral student who had to take a qualifying exam about fruit. He only had enough time, though, to learn about cucumbers.

When the time came for the exam, the first question was, "Tell us about the tomato." "You see," he said, "the tomato, like the cucumber, is actually a fruit. The cucumber is 80 percent water, has a disease-resistant skin, and is used in salads." Every question that came up, he answered with cucumber facts.

We know cucumbers. Except in our case, there are two cucumbers: patterns and JUnit. You'll find pattern-y advice throughout the book. In fact, we were uncomfortable with writing until we started writing the Rules. Once we had the concept of Rules, we could proceed happily. The Rules are really patterns in a micro format.

JUnit, our second cucumber, is the basis for the running example. We wrote JUnit in a few hours in a plane over the Atlantic in 1997. Since then, it seems much of our technical lives have revolved around it. JUnit is fertile ground for an Eclipse example because the core—running tests—is simple but the implications—the presentation of tests and results—have barely been explored.

We did want to warn you, though, that if you're tired of hearing about patterns and JUnit, this is probably not the book for you.

Conventions Used in This Book

The following formatting conventions are used throughout the book:

Bold—Used for the names of user-interface elements, including menus, buttons, tabs, and text boxes.

Italic—Used for filenames and URLs. Also, new terms are italicized for emphasis.

`Courier`—Used for all code samples and for in-text references to code elements. Plug-in names and elements of XML files also appear in this font.

`Courier Bold`—Used to emphasize portions of code samples, in particular insertions or changes.

~~`Courier Strikethrough`~~—Used in code samples to indicate where text should be deleted.

In the example presented in Parts II and III, we use the following icons to indicate our current activity:

 Searching—Shown when we search and explore the Eclipse code.

 Mimicking—Shown when we present code and XML markup from Eclipse.

 Testing—Shown when we present code from a JUnit test.

Online Examples

The Web site for this book is located at *www.awprofessional.com/titles/ 0321205758*. A snapshot of all the source code developed throughout this book can be downloaded from there. The site will also provide an errata list and other news related to the book.

To use the examples, the Eclipse SDK (Version 2.1.1) is required. You can find a build of the Eclipse SDK for your platform by visiting *www.eclipse.org/ downloads/*.

Acknowledgments

Throughout the writing of *Contributing to Eclipse* we have received the enthusiastic, detailed, and only occasionally annoying support of a fabulous community of reviewers. The first time we incorporated a comment from a reviewer we tried to remember to add his or her name to the following list. If we've forgotten to add you, please remind us, and we'll get your name in the next printing. The reviewers whose names we caught were: Frank Sauer, Jan Schulz, Dave W, Bob Foster, Binyan, Jeff Duska, Tom Ayerst, Richard Kuo, Wirianto Djunaidi, Don Estberg, Andreas Guther, Vincent Massol, John Pickler, The Silicon Valley Patterns Group, Russ Rufer, Tracy Bialik, John Brewer, Jerry Lewis, Jeff Miller, Patrick Manion, Carol Thistlethwaite, Pei-wei Wu, Chris Lopez, Ken Hejmanowski, Walter Vannini, Azad Bolour, Thomas Roche, Phil Goodwin, Carsten Heyl, Ed Burnette, Joe Bowbeer, David Loeffler, Jim Sawyer, Alex Blewitt, Laurent Bendel, Tom Killa, Bill Schauweker, Jan Ploski, Jan Looney, Rich Smith, Andy Farley, Debbie Utley, Ivan Moore, Geoff Gibbs, Mark Barkan, Florian Hawlitzek, Steve Blass, Mayuresh Kadu, Ricardo Lecheta, Stefan Baramov, Arne Hänle, Peter Friese, Randy Gordon, Frank Sauer, Andy Yang, Eric Pieters, Tobias Widmer, Bernard Gaffney, James Howe, Matt Dickie, Lee R. Nackman, and Wim Engels.

Joel Rosi-Schwartz and Betty Rosi-Schwartz also reviewed the manuscript. Bard Bloom effectively pointed out weak spots in Circle Zero. Any remaining errors are our responsibility.

Our special thanks to the committers of Eclipse.org, who gave us timely and thorough technical feedback. We received in-depth manuscript-wide feedback (more than once) from André Weinand, Dirk Bäumer, John Wiegand, and Kai-Uwe Mätzel. The essays in Circle Three were reviewed by Jim des Rivières, Nick Edgar, Philippe Mulet, and Steve Northover. Daniel Megert and Martin Äschlimann checked the source and text for details.

Mike Hendrickson and Eric Evans provided timely technical assistance.

Kent would like to especially thank Erich for putting in the extra effort it took to get this book finished. I enjoy our professional relationship more than I can say.

We would like to thank Cindee Andres for working tirelessly to improve the quality of our prose. Our thanks also to Joëlle Andres-Beck for focusing her attention on our book and finding the forward pointers problem.

Finally, we would like to thank our publication team—Lynda D'Arcangelo, Tyrrell Albaugh, and John Fuller. Mike Hendrickson encouraged us to get the book started. Our editors, John Wait and John Neidhart, stepped in to give us support when we needed it most. The marketing team, led by Chris Guzikowski, deftly communicated the vision of this book to buyers.

CHAPTER 1

The Big Picture

The typical relationship between the programmer and the programming environment is one where the environment nurtures the programmer. In return for this support, the programmer works within the constraints created by the environment.

In the early seventies, Smalltalk was written with a different philosophy. Every user of every application was considered a potential programmer. The classic example is, you could be editing a document and decide you didn't like how the editor worked. Pressing a button would show you the inner workings of the document editor and provide you with tools to change the editor's behavior.

User-as-programmer may seem far-fetched, but Smalltalk saw many cases where non-programming professionals wrote applications uniquely suited to their own needs by learning programming a little at a time and by example. The key to enabling user programming is to structure the environment to encourage learning, giving the user a little payoff for a little investment and a little more payoff for a little more investment.

Eclipse structures the computing experience similarly. Its goals are much the same as the goals of Smalltalk: Give the users an empowering computing experience and provide a learning environment as a path to greater power. In Eclipse, moving up the pyramid requires investment and will be attempted by fewer people (see Figure 1.1).

○ **Users**—Daily Eclipse users. Currently this is restricted to programmers, but there is no reason in principle why Eclipse couldn't be used to structure other computing work.

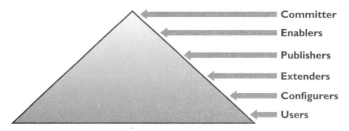

Figure 1.1   Increasing Commitment and Reward

○ **Configurers**—Users who customize their experience of Eclipse, either by rearranging perspectives, setting preferences, or deciding which views to show. Configuration is limited to changes envisioned by the original programmer.

○ **Extenders**—Programmers who make changes not envisioned by the original Eclipse programmers. Eclipse provides a rich set of places to "plug in" new functionality, because Eclipse itself is built entirely by plugging in functionality.

○ **Publishers**—Once you've written something useful, other folks may want it, too. Eclipse is consciously structured so you can easily bundle together extensions so others can load them.

○ **Enablers**—Eclipse is built out of "places-to-plug-functionality-in" (extension points) and "functionality-to-be-plugged-in" (extensions). Once you have published a contribution, the next step is to enable others to extend it in ways you don't foresee. You do this by publishing your extension points.

○ **Committers**—Eclipse is an open source project. If there is a change you want to make that is outside the scope of the available extension points, you can change the source code itself. Getting your changes incorporated into the global Eclipse release requires that you gain the trust of the existing community of committers. Becoming a committer is outside the scope of this book, although we will look at lots of the Eclipse source code so you can get an idea of what would be involved.

We can also map these levels onto a circle as shown in Figure 1.2.

What makes this circle interesting is the final arrow, from Enabler back to User. In Eclipse, you don't just invest more and more and receive more and more. When you take the step to become an enabler with your own extension points, you create for yourself the opportunity to be nourished by the work of others. Sometime later, someone may extend your contribution in ways you

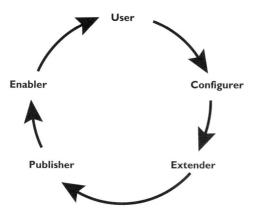

Figure 1.2   The Contribution Circle

find useful. By creating and sharing your own extension points you can get the benefit of their work without further effort on your part.

We intend for this book to be your guide around the Contribution Circle.

1.1   Book Goals

We've been talking about writing a book together for nearly a decade. We share an interest in software design, in the design of software for widespread adaptation (frameworks), and in discovering the "universal" rules that lie behind design. We first met at Bruce Anderson's Architecture Handbook workshop at OOPSLA-93 in Washington, D.C, where we began discussing software design. We discovered that, while we generally shared a common aesthetic of design, we disagreed in enough interesting ways to fuel years of debate and joint exploration. The chance to write this book gave us a good reason to continue and deepen our discussion of design.

We want to help you around the Contribution Circle as far as you want to go. For you to learn your way around the circle to become a enabler, we need to help you learn two things:

○ *About Eclipse.* There is far more to Eclipse than would fit into any ten books, but there are some basic concepts and details you simply cannot live without. By following the examples here, you will see these basics in action.

○ *Learning about Eclipse.* We aren't going to pretend that we have memorized all the details of Eclipse. When we program in Eclipse, we search for examples from which to copy. As we develop our code, we'll tell you how we found our examples.

○ *Design principles*. Okay, this is our secret third agenda. As we go along, we'll tell you about the underlying principles of design behind the structure of Eclipse in particular, but also behind platforms of all kinds.

Pedagogical Structure

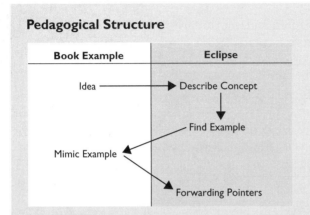

When we want to describe an Eclipse concept, we will always place it in the context of our example application. We'll start with the idea of what feature we want to add, describe the general concept in Eclipse that fits the idea best, show an example in Eclipse that uses that concept, show how the concept is used in our example, then give forwarding pointers to other places in Eclipse you can look for more examples. This is how we develop in Eclipse ourselves, by copying examples, so it's good practice to see it here.

The book is organized as four concentric circles, each taking you around the Contribution Circle in increasing detail.

1. Circle Zero, Chapter 2 and Chapter 3, gets you set up for plug-in development and takes you as quickly as possible from a tiny plug-in idea to its implementation.

2. Circle One, Chapter 4 through Chapter 12, introduces the content of our plug-in and running test cases, and makes and deploys the simplest possible test-running plug-in.

3. Circle Two, Chapter 13 through Chapter 30, takes the basic test-running plug-in and adds all the capabilities expected of Eclipse contributions, acquiring an interesting twist of metaphor halfway through.

4. Circle Three, Chapter 31 through Chapter 37, tours Eclipse designer-to-designer, highlighting areas of Eclipse worth exploring early. These essays use design and implementation patterns as their basic vocabulary, showing how the patterns play out in a variety of contexts.

1.2 Plug-In

Because this chapter and the following chapters constitute a complete circle, we should have a little bit of background about the plug-in architecture of Eclipse. Eclipse is a collection of places-to-plug-things-in (extension points) and things-plugged-in (extensions). The powerstrip is a kind of extension point. Multiple extensions (in this case, power plugs) can plug into it, and although the extensions are different shapes and have different purposes, they all must share a common interface.

1.3 Eclipse in a Nutshell

Here is a bit of the Eclipse architecture to get you started. Then we will start programming. We get back to some key architectural elements of Eclipse in Circle Three. If you are more comfortable having an overall picture before looking at details, you may want to read Circle Three now.

Figure 1.3 shows the three layers of Eclipse.

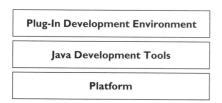

Figure 1.3 The Three Layers of Eclipse

○ **Platform**—The Eclipse platform defines the common programming-language-neutral infrastructure.

○ **Java Development Tools (JDT)**—The Java development tools add a full-featured Java IDE to Eclipse.

○ **Plug-In Development Environment (PDE)**—The PDE extends the JDT with support for developing plug-ins.

The platform consists of several key components that are layered into a user interface (UI)-independent core and a UI layer, as shown in Figure 1.4.

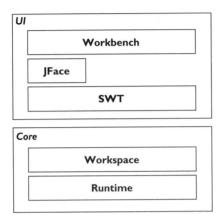

Figure 1.4   Eclipse Architecture Overview

○ **Runtime**—The run-time component defines the plug-in infrastructure. It discovers the available plug-ins on start-up and manages the plug-in loading.

○ **Workspace**—A workspace manages one or more top-level projects. A project consists of file and folders that map onto the underlying file system.

○ **Standard Widget Toolkit (SWT)**—The SWT provides graphics and defines a standard set of widgets.

○ **JFace**—A set of smaller UI frameworks built on top of SWT supporting common UI tasks.

○ **Workbench**—The workbench defines the Eclipse UI paradigm. It centers around editors, views, and perspectives.

Let's take a brief look at the workbench and its components, shown in Figure 1.5.

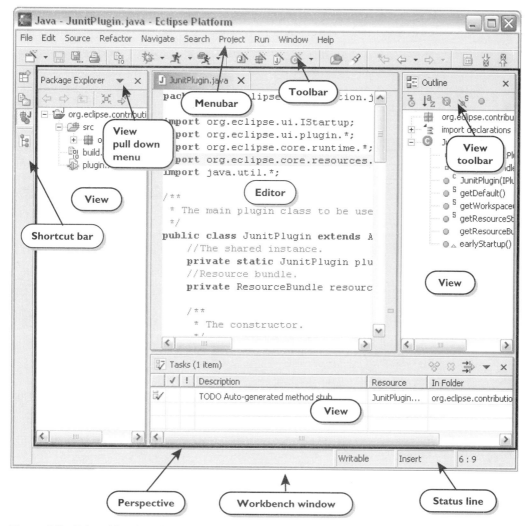

Figure 1.5   Eclipse User Interface Vocabulary

The Eclipse workbench is presented in one or more *windows*. A workbench window contains a set of workbench *parts*. These can be either *views* or *editors*. A *perspective* defines the visual arrangement of the workbench parts.

Finally, since you are about to start extending Eclipse, you should familiarize yourselves with the Eclipse UI guidelines.[1]

---

1. *www.eclipse.org/articles/Article-UI-Guidelines/Index.html*

PART I

Circle Zero: Hello World

This circle will take you through the entire contribution process as quickly as possible. We will skip many details in the name of brevity, but fortunately we have three more circles in which to make up for our haste. Our goal is to get you over the inertia of not having made a contribution. Once you've contributed to Eclipse, you'll be ready to learn to contribute well.

Our example will contribute a button to the toolbar. When we press the button, a dialog will appear announcing, "Hello World." First, though, we need to set Eclipse up for plug-in development.

CHAPTER 2

Setting Up Eclipse for Plug-In Development

Developing plug-ins is a little different than developing vanilla Java applications. First, you need to be able to refer to Eclipse's own internal structure to extend that structure. Second, you will spend much of your early hours as an Eclipse contributor reading source code, so you need access to all the source.

One way to solve these problems is to load the entire source (around one million lines of code) into the workspace. Managing this huge amount of source can expand the memory footprint of Eclipse. However, we will typically only read existing code and not modify or compile it. Fortunately, PDE offers a quick and space-efficient way to set up a workspace where existing plug-ins cannot be modified, but can be browsed. The trick is to represent existing plug-ins as *binary projects*. Binary projects cannot be modified, but are fully searchable for references and declarations.

The distinction is between *working with* and *working on*. A project you are working *with* can be represented as a binary project, saving space. A project you are working *on* must be represented as source.

2.1   Setting Up a Workspace

Here is how to set up a workspace with binary projects for all the plug-ins shipped with Eclipse:

1. If you don't want to pollute your existing workspace, start Eclipse with an empty workspace (use `-data new_workspace_location` on the command line).

2. Switch to the Java perspective by selecting **Window > Open Perspective > Java.**

3. Choose **File > Import... > External Plug-ins and Fragments.** Accept the defaults on the next page. On the third page click **Select All** to import all plug-ins from your host workspace.

4. Click **Finish.** The plug-ins will be imported into binary projects, their build class paths initialized, as shown in Figure 2.1.

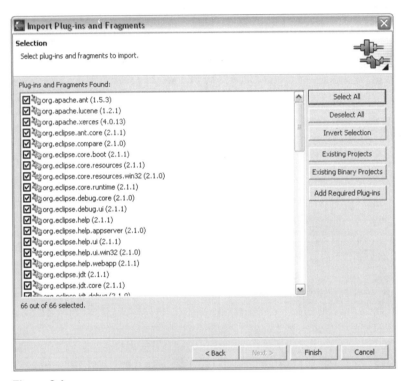

Figure 2.1

2.2 Browsing and Searching Source

You can now browse and search the full Eclipse source. Choose **Navigate > Open Type...** and type in *. You should see thousands of classes. You will have around 60 Eclipse plug-in projects in your workspace.

If you do not want to see these binary projects, hide the binary projects in the **Package Explorer** by turning on a filter for binary projects. Select **Filters** from the **Package Explorer** view pull-down menu, as shown in Figure 2.2 and

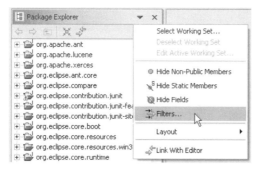

Figure 2.2

select **Binary plug-in and feature projects** in the subsequent dialog, as shown in Figure 2.3.

If you started Eclipse in a clean workspace, the **Package Explorer** will be empty after you invoke the filter because you haven't created any source plug-in projects yet.

One thing to keep in mind when you install a new version of Eclipse: Do not forget to reimport the plug-ins that come with this build. To do so, click the **Existing Binary Projects** button on the import wizard's plug-in selection

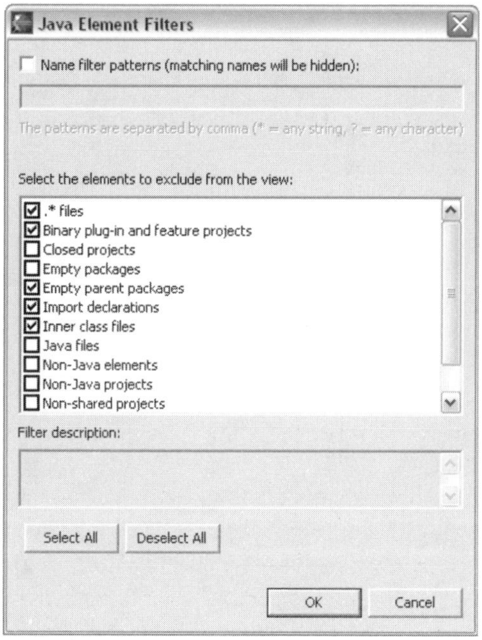

Figure 2.3

page. This will replace your existing binary projects with the code for the new versions.

Now Eclipse is ready to say "hello" to the world.

2.3 Forward Pointers

❍ *Workspace set up with binary projects but linked contents*—If you have a large number of plug-ins and you don't want to create a copy of all plug-ins in your workspace, you can uncheck the **Copy plug-in contents into the workspace location** check box when you import the plug-ins. In this case, PDE creates the plug-in projects in your workspace, but it "links" their contents instead of making a copy.

CHAPTER 3

Hello World

Our "Hello World" plug-in will contribute a button to the toolbar. When the button is pressed, we will pop up a dialog box containing the text "Hello World."

The developers at Eclipse.org share a consistent set of rules for design. Here's the first rule of Eclipse:

CONTRIBUTION RULE   Everything is a contribution.

The whole of Eclipse—the Java development tools, the CVS repository explorer, every single tool—is contributed. That is, none of them is "built into" Eclipse. There is no monolithic tool to which a few things are added. There is a tiny little kernel to which many things are contributed, as shown in Figure 3.1.

As a consequence of making everything a contribution you will have lots of contributions. The Java environment and the Eclipse base together are more than 60 large plug-ins. The IBM WebSphere Application Development environment, for example, adds another 500 plug-ins. Assume that you have a system built out of thousands of contributions. If you want the system to start up this century, you can't do much work per contribution on start-up. In particular, the end user should not pay in start-up time for plug-ins that are installed but not used.

While we speak of performance as being the last thing you should pay attention to in development, performance often has profound impact on the architecture. Eclipse is shaped by the need to process thousands of contributions at start-up, yielding a budget of a few milliseconds each.

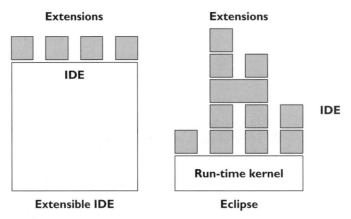

Figure 3.1 Some Extensions Versus All Extensions

Now we come to a dilemma. The logic contained within a contribution can be substantial. The compiled form of this logic, Java class files (collected in a Java Archive [JAR] file), can easily take seconds to load. Making Java classes that are guaranteed to load quickly is more work than most people want to do. If we want to guarantee snappy start-up, we can't load classes. This leads to the Lazy Loading Rule:

> **LAZY LOADING RULE** Contributions are only loaded when they are needed.

Good rule, but how is it implemented?

3.1 Declaration/Implementation Split

If you only know which contributions are present, even if you haven't loaded their implementation you can already give the user a picture of what operations are available. The plug-in architecture implements this split between declaration and implementation by declaring the "shape" of a contribution in an Extensible Markup Language (XML)-based manifest. The implementation of the contribution is in Java (see Figure 3.2).

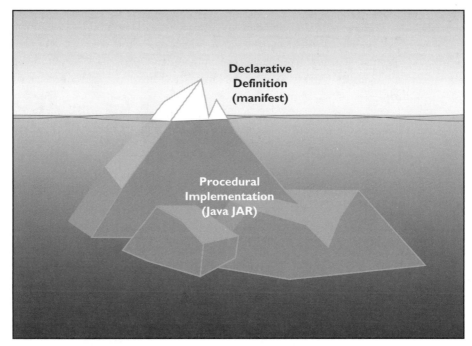

Figure 3.2   The Manifest Describes Your Plug-In's Contribution

The Basic Plug-In Structure

A plug-in is a piece of behavior that is outside the run-time kernel. A plug-in is represented as a directory containing

○   plugin.xml—The manifest, a description of the contributions of the plug-in

○   Resources, like icons (optional)

○   Java code, in a JAR (optional)

The directory structure for the plug-in `org.eclipse.jdt.ui` is shown below.

Name ▲	Size	Type
icons		File Folder
about.html	2 KB	HTML Document
jdt.jar	3,891 KB	Executable Jar File
plugin.properties	26 KB	PROPERTIES File
plugin.xml	102 KB	XML Document

3.2   Hello Button

We want to contribute a button to Eclipse. First we have to create a project. Eclipse has wizards to automate tedious work, but if you haven't done it before, the work is hardly tedious. We'll build our examples as much as possible by hand, then you can use the wizards once you understand what they are doing for you. We'll only use the wizard to give us the basic structure, and we'll explain what it did for us (Figures 3.3–3.7).

1. Open the new wizard.

Figure 3.3

2. Select **Plug-in Project**.

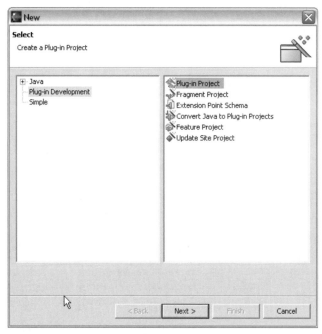

Figure 3.4

3. Define the name of the plug-in project.

Figure 3.5

4. Define the settings related to the plug-in structure.

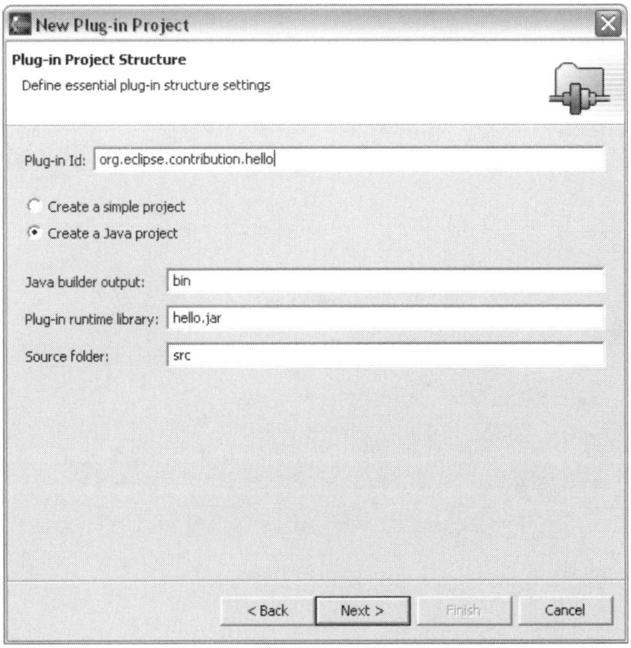

Figure 3.6

5. Create a blank plug-in project without using any of the code generation wizards.

Figure 3.7

Note that on the last step we selected **Create a blank plug-in project** so we could have the joy of filling in as many details as possible by hand. When you click **Finish**, answer **No** to the dialog asking you if you want to switch to the plug-in development perspective. We prefer to do our plug-in development in the Java perspective.

The result is the basic plug-in project structure shown in Figure 3.8.

Figure 3.8   Plug-In Project Structure

We have a nearly empty manifest file describing the appearance and structure of the plug-in, a *build.properties* file that tells the Plug-in Development Environment where to find the source code for building the JAR, and an empty *src* folder.

The manifest file, *plugin.xml* (shown in its entirety in Section 3.3.2), contains the top-level plug-in description. Opening *plugin.xml* will show you the manifest editor, a friendly interface to all the details in the manifest. Since we want to explore the whole manifest, click on the **Source** tab to show the raw XML. You'll see something like this:

org.eclipse.contribution.hello/plugin.xml

```
<plugin
  id="org.eclipse.contribution.hello"
  name="org.eclipse.contribution.hello"
  version="1.0.0">
</plugin>
```

You'll also see a run-time entry in the manifest that defines where Eclipse will look for classes in this plug-in.

IDs in manifests are globally unique. Names, however, are expected to be read by humans. Our first change is to make the name of our plug-in a bit friendlier:

org.eclipse.contribution.hello/plugin.xml

```
<plugin
  id="org.eclipse.contribution.hello"
  name="Hello World"
  version="1.0.0">
```

The version is mandatory because plug-ins can rely on each other (remember that nearly everything is a plug-in) and you can refer to the particular version of a plug-in you depend on.

Plug-In Development Environment (PDE)

Because plug-ins are so important to Eclipse, Eclipse has evolved tools for developing Java projects that are plug-ins. You will see a wizard for creating plug-in projects, specialized editors for the manifest file *(plugin.xml)*, and support for running a second workbench with plug-ins under development.

Running with PDE will be confusing at times because you have to remember whether you are working in the workbench that is editing the plug-in (host workbench) or working in the workbench that is running the plug-in under development (run-time workbench). For example, if you write to `System.out` from inside a plug-in under development, the text appears in the workbench editing the plug-in, not the workbench in which the plug-in is running.

Now we have a plug-in, but it doesn't do anything. We will be able to see it when we start a run-time workbench (see Figure 3.9).

Figure 3.9

Clicking **Run As > Run-time Workbench** will bring up another instance of Eclipse, but this one (the run-time workbench) has our new plug-in loaded. You can verify that our plug-in is present by choosing **Help > About Eclipse Platform > Plug-in Details** in the run-time workbench. Our plug-in is at the top of the list, as shown in Figure 3.10.

	About Eclipse Platform Plug-ins			
Provider	Plug-in Name	Version	Plug-in Id	
	org.eclipse.contribution.hello	1.0.0	org.eclipse.contribution.hello	
Eclipse.org	Ant Build Tool Core	2.1.1	org.eclipse.ant.core	
Eclipse.org	Apache Ant	1.5.3	org.apache.ant	
Eclipse.org	Apache Lucene	1.2.1	org.apache.lucene	
Eclipse.org	Compare Support	2.1.0	org.eclipse.compare	
Eclipse.org	Core Boot	2.1.1	org.eclipse.core.boot	
Eclipse.org	Core Resource Management	2.1.1	org.eclipse.core.resources	
Eclipse.org	Core Runtime	2.1.1	org.eclipse.core.runtime	
Eclipse.org	CVS SSH Core	2.1.1	org.eclipse.team.cvs.ssh	
Eclipse.org	CVS Team Provider Core	2.1.1	org.eclipse.team.cvs.core	
Eclipse.org	CVS Team Provider UI	2.1.1	org.eclipse.team.cvs.ui	
Eclipse.org	Debug Core	2.1.0	org.eclipse.debug.core	
Eclipse.org	Debug UI	2.1.1	org.eclipse.debug.ui	
Eclipse.org	Default Text Editor	2.1.0	org.eclipse.ui.editors	
Eclipse.org	Eclipse Java Development Tools	2.1.1	org.eclipse.jdt	
Eclipse.org	Eclipse Java Development Tools SDK	2.1.1	org.eclipse.jdt.source	
Eclipse.org	Eclipse Java Development User Guide	2.1.0	org.eclipse.jdt.doc.user	
Eclipse.org	Eclipse JDT Plug-in Developer Guide	2.1.0	org.eclipse.jdt.doc.isv	
Eclipse.org	Eclipse Platform	2.1.1	org.eclipse.platform	
Eclipse.org	Eclipse Platform (Windows)	2.1.1	org.eclipse.platform.win32	
Eclipse.org	Eclipse Platform Plug-in Developer Guide	2.1.0	org.eclipse.platform.doc.isv	
Eclipse.org	Eclipse Platform Plug-in Developer Resour...	2.1.1	org.eclipse.platform.source	

More Info   OK

Figure 3.10

Next we need to contribute a button. Here's how we specify our button's appearance:

org.eclipse.contribution.hello/plugin.xml
```
<extension point="org.eclipse.ui.actionSets">
  <actionSet
    id="org.eclipse.contribution.hello.actionSet"
    label="Hello Action Set">
    <action
      id="org.eclipse.contribution.hello.HelloAction"
      label="Hello">
    </action>
  </actionSet>
</extension>
```

Each button is supported by an `Action`, the object that will be invoked when the button is pressed. The buttons in the toolbar are grouped into *action sets*, sets of related actions, as shown in Figure 3.11. For example, the buttons that create Java elements are an action set. The above declaration states that we are contributing a new action set, `point="org.eclipse.ui.actionSets"`, which contains a single action, labelled "Hello". Note once again that the IDs are globally unique but the names of elements are intended for human consumption.

Figure 3.11

When we start a new run-time workbench (clicking the **Running Guy** will rerun what was run previously), we can see our action set in **Window > Customize Perspective... > Other** as shown in Figure 3.12.

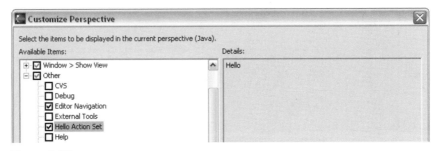

Figure 3.12

Notice that the values of the `label` elements in the declaration are used to present our contribution to the user.

Selecting our action set and clicking **OK** doesn't cause a button to appear. Why? To appear as a button, each action has to be associated with a toolbar path, a hint to Eclipse as to where to put the action. In our case, we don't want to put the action near any other particular actions, so we can make up a toolbar path:

org.eclipse.contribution.hello/plugin.xml
```
<action
  id="org.eclipse.contribution.hello.HelloAction"
  label="Hello"
  toolbarPath="helloGroup">
</action>
```

If there were already actions with the toolbar path `helloGroup`, our Hello action would appear nearby. Since this action is the only one with this toolbar path, our button appears in a group by itself. Because we didn't specify an icon, the button appears as the default red square, as shown in Figure 3.13.

Figure 3.13   Our Button Appears as a Red Square

The button placement behavior leads us to the Sharing Rule:

> **SHARING RULE**   Add, don't replace.

When you contribute to Eclipse, your contributions will be added to the contributions already in place. There isn't a way to replace existing functionality. It's your job to find a way to think of your contribution as an addition to the existing functionality and it's Eclipse's job to harmoniously combine the contributions.

Before we implement the functionality behind the button, notice that we have been able to present our contribution to the user purely declaratively. The manifest defines how the contribution appears; the Java code defines how it behaves.

3.3 Saying "Hello"

We have finished the user-visible appearance of our plug-in. Now it is time to fill in the implementation side, actually opening a dialog containing the string "Hello". According to the Lazy Loading Rule, contributions are only loaded when they are first invoked. Eclipse waits until the button is clicked, then looks for code to invoke. The code is represented as a Java class, so the name of the class has to be part of the definition of the action.

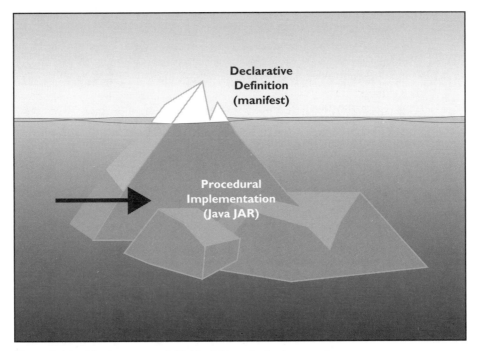

Figure 3.14   The Appearance Is Finished, Now the Implementation

Each action has the name of a Java class associated with it. When the action is invoked, an instance of that class is created to process the button click. The Java class is represented as an element of the action declaration:

org.eclipse.contribution.hello/plugin.xml

```
<action
  id="org.eclipse.contribution.hello.HelloAction"
  label="Hello"
  toolbarPath="helloGroup"
  class="org.eclipse.contribution.hello.HelloAction">
</action>
```

When we start the run-time workbench and click our button, the console in the host workbench (the one where we are developing the plug-in) tells us that the class can't be found:

```
Could not create action delegate for id: org.eclipse.contribution.
hello.HelloAction
Reason:
Plug-in org.eclipse.contribution.hello was unable to load class org.
eclipse.contribution.hello.HelloAction.
```

To make the action work, we need to create a class called `org.eclipse.contribution.hello.HelloAction`. How will the action be invoked? Eclipse needs a protocol common to all actions. This protocol is defined in the interface `IWorkbenchWindowActionDelegate`.[1] As an extender you are required to conform to this interface, the Conformance Rule (see Figure 3.15):

> **CONFORMANCE RULE**   Contributions must conform to expected interfaces.

Before we can define an implementor of `IWorkbenchWindowActionDelegate`, we have to help Eclipse find it from within our plug-in. Eclipse doesn't use the usual classpath mechanism of Java to find classes. Instead, each plug-in has its own class lookup path. This "classpath" is defined by a plug-in declaring which other plug-ins it depends on. At runtime, these prerequisite plug-ins will be searched whenever a class needs to be found. This mechanism is more efficient than Java's classpath, and more predictable, since each plug-in can precisely specify the context in which it is intended to be run.

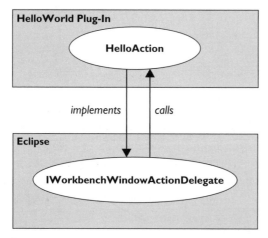

Figure 3.15   Eclipse Calls Our Contribution Through the Expected Interface

---

1. The convention in Eclipse is to name interfaces beginning with an "I."

The interface we want to implement, `IWorkbenchWindowActionDelegate`, is defined in the `org.eclipse.ui` plug-in, so our plug-in needs to depend on it. We add the following to our manifest:

org.eclipse.contribution.hello/plugin.xml
```
<requires>
  <import plugin="org.eclipse.ui"/>
</requires>
```

At this point, we also have to update the build class path. Go to the **Dependency** tab of the manifest editor. Select **Compute Build Path** from the context menu. PDE will now look in `org.eclipse.ui` for classes referenced by our code.

Now we can define our `HelloAction`.

1. Create a package `org.eclipse.contribution.hello` in the source folder `src` of our project.

2. Create the class `HelloAction` implementing the interface `IWorkbench-WindowActionDelegate`.

Eclipse fills in default implementations for the four methods in the signature of `IWorkbenchWindowActionDelegate`:

org.eclipse.contribution.hello/HelloAction
```
public void init(IWorkbenchWindow window) {
}
public void selectionChanged(IAction action, ISelection selection) {
}
public void dispose() {
}
public void run(IAction action) {
}
```

Extension implementations usually have a zero-argument constructor and are declared public because the extension objects will be created by reflection. In this case, we are lucky. Because we inherit from `Object` and define no other constructor, the default constructor is generated automatically. In most cases, we will have to define a zero-argument constructor explicitly.

When we bring up the run-time workbench and click the little red square nothing happens. We want to bring up a dialog with a cheery greeting. We replace the implementation of `HelloAction.run()` with the following:

org.eclipse.contribution.hello/HelloAction
```
public void run(IAction action) {
  MessageDialog.openInformation(null, null,
    "Hello, Eclipse world");
}
```

Spider

In the book we make use of the Spider to draw diagrams of live objects. We contributed Spider while we wrote this book to help us understand and illustrate how Eclipse works. For example, here are some objects behind a `WorkbenchWindow` captured with the Spider:

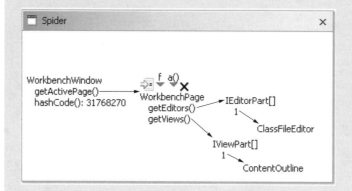

In the Spider diagram we see that a `WorkbenchWindow` has an active `WorkbenchPage` which has a collection of `IEditorParts` and `IViewParts`.

When you click an object in Spider, a set of handles pops-up around the object. In the above example you see four handles attached to the `Work-benchPage`. Clicking a handle allows you to invoke an action on the selected object. From left to right the following handles are shown:

○ Goto source—locates the source of the object's class and opens it in an editor.

○ Expand a field—shows a pop-up menu with all the fields of the object. Selecting a field adds its value to the drawing.

○ Expand an attribute—shows a pop-up menu with all no-argument methods in the object. Selecting a method invokes it and adds the returned value to the drawing.

○ Delete—deletes the object from the drawing

To find a starting point for exploration the Spider provides a Spider Navigator. It shows a set of top-level Eclipse objects that serve as entry points for exploration.

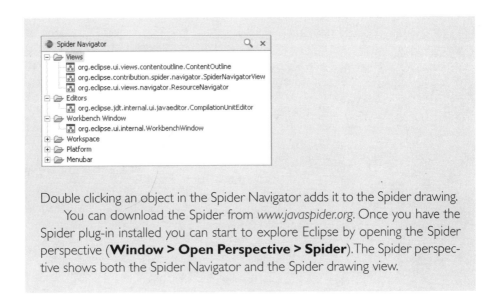

Double clicking an object in the Spider Navigator adds it to the Spider drawing.
You can download the Spider from *www.javaspider.org*. Once you have the
Spider plug-in installed you can start to explore Eclipse by opening the Spider
perspective (**Window > Open Perspective > Spider**). The Spider perspective shows both the Spider Navigator and the Spider drawing view.

Now when we start the run-time workbench and click the button, we see the
message we've been expecting, shown in Figure 3.16.

Figure 3.16

Before leaving our delightful little example, let's see how the Lazy Loading Rule
plays out. Here are the objects of the toolbar item after the HelloAction has been
made visible, but before the button has been clicked. The WWinPluginAction
(for "Workbench Window") is the Proxy for our action (see Figure 3.17).

When we click the button, the proxy creates the delegate and forwards the
request to the delegate, which causes the dialog to appear. Afterwards, our
action delegate has been loaded, as shown in Figure 3.18.

Following the Lazy Loading Rule, our HelloAction class is not loaded
until the first time it is invoked. Then the class is loaded, the instance is created, and the instance is invoked.

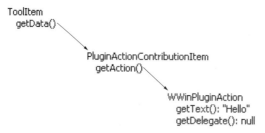

Figure 3.17   The Proxy Action

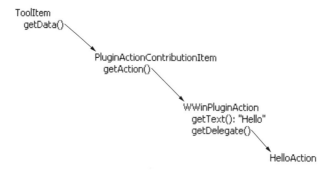

Figure 3.18   After Clicking the Button, the Real Action Has Been Loaded

With a dozen lines of Java and a dozen lines of specification in XML we were able to contribute to Eclipse.

The complete contents of the two files are shown in Section 3.3.1 and Section 3.3.2.

3.3.1   HelloAction.java

```
package org.eclipse.contribution.hello;

import org.eclipse.jface.action.IAction;
import org.eclipse.jface.dialogs.MessageDialog;
import org.eclipse.jface.viewers.ISelection;
import org.eclipse.ui.IWorkbenchWindow;
import org.eclipse.ui.IWorkbenchWindowActionDelegate;

public class HelloAction implements IWorkbenchWindowActionDelegate {

  public void dispose() {
  }

  public void init(IWorkbenchWindow window) {
  }
```

```
public void run(IAction action) {
  MessageDialog.openInformation(null, null,
    "Hello, Eclipse world");
}

public void selectionChanged(IAction action,
  ISelection selection) {
}

}
```

3.3.2   plugin.xml

```xml
<?xml version="1.0" encoding="UTF-8"?>
<plugin
  id="org.eclipse.contribution.hello"
  name="Hello World"
  version="1.0.0">

  <runtime>
    <library name="hello.jar"/>
  </runtime>
  <requires>
    <import plugin="org.eclipse.ui"/>
  </requires>

  <extension
    point="org.eclipse.ui.actionSets">
    <actionSet
      label="Hello Action Set"
      id="org.eclipse.contribution.hello.actionSet">
      <action
        label="Hello"
        class="org.eclipse.contribution.hello.HelloAction"
        toolbarPath="helloGroup"
        id="org.eclipse.contribution.hello.HelloAction">
      </action>
    </actionSet>
  </extension>
</plugin>
```

3.4   Forward Pointers

❍ Plug-ins don't need to contain code. Documentation plug-ins are written as a combination of XML and HTML.

PART II

Circle One:
Basic Plug-In

Chapter 3, Hello World, completed your first trip around the Contribution Circle but left out lots of parts. In this circle we will make a realistic pass around the circle, but for a little bit of functionality. We will implement the world's simplest testing interface: a menu item to run tests and a dialog box to display results. Before we're done with the circle, we will package our menu item, our little test runner, and the dialog box for easy consumption. The chapters are:

❍ *Der Plan*—We create a new environment for running tests.

○ *Contributing a Menu Item to Run Tests*—We add a menu item to run tests.

○ *Implementing the Menu Item Behavior*—We run the tests.

○ *Displaying the Results*—We tell the user whether the tests passed or failed.

○ *Defining an Extension Point*—We generalize our solution into a generic way to add test-running functionality to Eclipse.

○ *Notifying Extensions*—Once we have an extension point we need to invoke it.

○ *Publishing*—We get our contribution ready for others.

○ *Closing Circle One*—We review what we've done in this section.

CHAPTER 4

Der Plan

The best way to tell you about Eclipse is to walk you through the development of an example. As we explained with the cucumber story in the preface, it should be no surprise that we'll use JUnit as our example. What is JUnit?

JUnit is a simple framework for writing automated tests. What makes JUnit interesting as an example is that it is a programming tool written by programmers for programmers, our prototypical Eclipse extension. Also, it is simple so we won't have to explain a lot of stuff that isn't Eclipse-related. While the user interfaces for JUnit to date have all been simple, there are many features we can imagine wanting to add, so JUnit has possibilities (some of which we uncovered in the course of writing this book).

4.1 JUnit by Example

The goals of JUnit with regard to testing are:

- *Tests are easy to write*—Writing tests should take no more time than the testing activities they replace.

- *Tests are automated*—The tests must run and verify results without any human intervention.

- *Tests are composable*—We want to run my tests and your tests together easily.

- *Tests are isolated*—The success or failure of one test cannot have any effect on the success or failure of other tests.

Here is an example of a test for `java.util.ArrayList`. Tests are written as subclasses of `TestCase`.

```java
public class ArrayListTest extends junit.framework.TestCase {
}
```

A test is implemented as a method starting with "test" that takes no arguments:

```java
public void testAddElement() {
  List list= new ArrayList();
  assertFalse(list.contains("junit"));
  list.add("junit");
  assertTrue(list.contains("junit"));
}
```

The expected results are verified by calling assert methods like `assert-True()`. The assert methods are inherited from `TestCase`.

Each test runs in its own setup. The setup for multiple tests is defined in the method `setUp()`. When writing multiple tests for `ArrayList` we extract the list creation into the `setUp()` method and store the list in an instance variable:

```java
public class ArrayListTest extends TestCase {
  private List list;
  protected void setUp() {
    list= new ArrayList();
  }
  public void testAddElement() {
    assertFalse(list.contains("junit"));
    list.add("junit");
    assertTrue(list.contains("junit"));
  }
}
```

Now we can write additional tests:

```java
public void testRemoveElement() {
  list.add("junit");
  assertTrue(list.contains("junit"));
  list.remove("junit");
  assertFalse(list.contains("junit"));
}
```

A test runner runs your tests. A test runner integrated into Eclipse allows you to run tests conveniently from inside Eclipse. When we run the above tests with the integrated Eclipse JUnit test runner, we see what's shown in Figure 4.1.

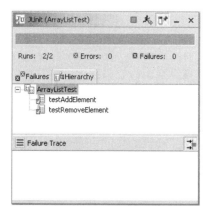

Figure 4.1

4.2   JUnit Integration

At first, our Eclipse/JUnit integration will be simple. In keeping with the cucumber story, not only will we use JUnit as the functionality to be accessed, we will use JUnit itself to develop our plug-in. Instead of the metacircular, self-referential style of the example in *Test-Driven Development: By Example*,[1] we will use the version of JUnit built into Eclipse. In particular, we will use the extension of JUnit for testing plug-ins, PDE JUnit.

The first circle will take you through the development of the JUnit engine. The second circle will add all the bits and pieces that go into making a complete Eclipse contribution. The contributions add up to a new way to think about tests during the development process, and each bit shows you a useful corner of Eclipse.

---

1. K. Beck, *Test-Driven Development: By Example*, Addison-Wesley, Boston, 2003.

CHAPTER 5

Contributing a Menu Item to Run Tests

What we'll see in this chapter:

○ Contributing an action that shows up in the context menu of a selected object

○ Implementing the contribution by looking at an example

We'd like to get the minimal user interface possible for our example, just to have something complete running. Here is where we will start:

1. Choose a test case class in the **Package Explorer.**

2. Pop-up a context menu.

3. Select **Run Test.**

4. Run the tests.

5. Pop up a dialog with the results of running all the tests in the type.

Create a new plug-in project named `org.eclipse.contribution.junit`. Use the default plug-in structure, but uncheck the **Generate code for the class** button on the final page. You will have to delete the line `class="org. eclipse.contribution.junit.JUnitPlugin"` from *plugin.xml,* as the manifest generation code assumes there will be a plug-in class.

Next, we need to say how the contribution will appear to the user: as a menu item available when a type is selected. When programming in Eclipse, always begin by finding a similar application and copying its structure, the Monkey See/Monkey Do Rule:

MONKEY SEE/MONKEY DO RULE   Always start by copying the structure of a similar plug-in.

When You Need a Plug-In Class

Every plug-in is represented by an instance of a plug-in class. The plug-in class Singleton has hook methods for the life cycle of the plug-in. You can load resources when the plug-in is first loaded. You can clean up when the plug-in is terminated (e.g., when Eclipse is closed). The plug-in is also the source for shared information like preferences, images, and persistent dialog settings.

The plug-in we're defining here doesn't perform any life-cycle actions like loading images so far, nor does it need any shared information. We rely on the default plug-in class. Later if we need a plug-in class, we will define one.

Let's say you want to add a menu item that displays when a class is selected and the user pops up the context menu. You need to create an Object Contribution. Object Contributions are specific to the selected object. Applying Monkey See/Monkey Do, where can we find some examples of object contributions? `Org.eclipse.ui` is where the extension point is defined for pop-up menus.

 If you know the name of the extension point, you can search the on-line help for the name of the extension point, or you can use the plug-in search to find its uses or definition, as shown in Figure 5.1.

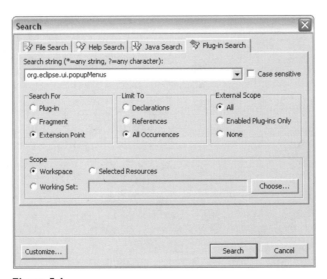

Figure 5.1

Another way to search for examples is by looking at the extension points defined in existing manifest files. Since the `popupMenus` extension point is defined by the `org.eclipse.ui` plug-in we open its *plugin.xml* file in the manifest editor. If you have filtered out binary projects from the **Package Explorer** then you first need to remove the **Binary plug-in and feature projects** filter to get access to binary projects and their manifest files. On the **Extension Points** tab of the manifest editor we can see the extension points defined in this plug-in and (more to our purpose here) where they are used, as shown in Figure 5.2.

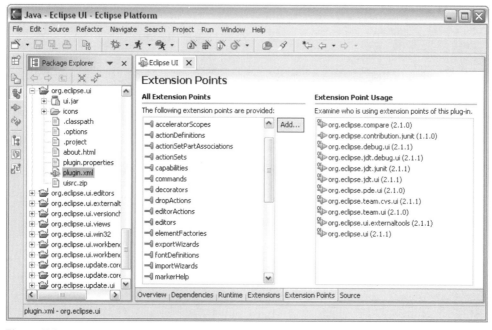

Figure 5.2

Selecting an extension point in the left pane shows its usages in the right pane. We therefore select the `popupMenus` extension point to find its usages. The first usage is in the `org.eclipse.compare` plug-in. By double-clicking on the usage of the extension point, we open the corresponding manifest file and we can see how to declare an extension to the pop-up menus. The whole extension is more complicated than we need, but this part of it seems relevant:

org.eclipse.compare/plugin.xml
```
<extension point="org.eclipse.ui.popupMenus">
  <objectContribution
    id="org.eclipse.compare.AddFromHistoryAction"
```

```
    objectClass="org.eclipse.core.resources.IContainer"
      adaptable="true">
    <action
      id="addFromHistoryAction"
      label="%addFromHistoryAction.label"
      tooltip="%addFromHistoryAction.tooltip"
      menubarPath="replaceWithMenu"
      enablesFor="1"
      class="org.eclipse.compare.internal.AddFromHistoryAction">
    </action>
  </objectContribution>
</extension>
```

Ignore most of this for now. When copying an example, you are looking for structure, much of which you'll typically delete because it doesn't apply, or at least not yet. Here are the bits we know we need to add to *plugin.xml* (looking at the on-line help, **Platform Plug-in Developer Guide > Reference > Extension Points Reference > Workbench > org.eclipse.ui.popupMenus,** for a reminder):

org.eclipse.contribution.junit/plugin.xml
```
<extension point="org.eclipse.ui.popupMenus">
  <objectContribution
    id="org.eclipse.contribution.junit.runtest"
    objectClass="org.eclipse.jdt.core.IType">
    <action
      id="org.eclipse.contribution.junit.runtest.action"
      label="Run Test"
      enablesFor="1">
    </action>
  </objectContribution>
</extension>
```

By adding the above XML to our manifest, `org.eclipse.contribution. junit/plugin.xml`, we declare a pop-up menu item (see Table 5.1 for a description of the elements and attributes).

What is the `IType` referred to in the contribution? Eclipse (actually JDT in the plug-in `org.eclipse.jdt.core`) defines a set of interfaces representing the elements of a Java program. There you will find types representing projects, packages, compilation units and, in this case, types (classes and interfaces).

Now we can run the plug-in. We expect the menu item to show up, but to be non-functional. If it doesn't show up, make sure you've entered the correct fully qualified type name for `IType`. Select a type (not just the compilation unit), pop up the menu, and voilà (see Figure 5.3). You'll have to create or import a project in the run-time workspace so you have a type to select.

In general, when you make a contribution, you need to limit its availability to cases where it would help. You don't want a context menu with 200

Table 5.1   Declaring a Pop-up Menu Item Contribution

org.eclipse.contribution.junit/plugin.xml	Description
`<extension point="org.eclipse.ui.popupMenus">`	This says that we will extend a pop-up menu.
`<objectContribution`	We extend it for all objects of a given type.
`id="org.eclipse.contribution.junit.runtest"`	Unique ID.
`objectClass="org.eclipse.jdt.core.IType">`	All selected ITypes will have this item.
`<action`	This is the menu item.
`id="org.eclipse.contribution.junit.` `runtest.action"`	Unique ID.
`label="Run Test"`	How the item will appear in the menu.
`enablesFor="1">`	The item is only enabled when there is exactly one element selected.

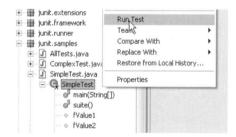

Figure 5.3

items, most of which wouldn't actually work with the current selection. This is the Relevance Rule:

RELEVANCE RULE   Contribute only when you can successfully operate.

Object contributions are a bit optimistic by nature. Our **Run Test** item will show up for any type, not just test cases. The tradeoff is that if the filter for whether the menu item appears is only on the type of the selected object, the plug-in code does not need to be loaded until the menu item is actually clicked. The manifest file is declarative, so it can't be the home for logic.

Although such a coarse filter might seem too optimistic, it works well in practice.

Notice that we have violated the Relevance Rule by having **Run Test** show up for types that don't have any tests. Sometimes rules are in conflict. Here, the conflicting rule is the Lazy Loading Rule. The only way to determine if **Run Test** is really relevant is to run the plug-in. We satisfy the Lazy Loading Rule at the expense of the Relevance Rule. Designers break the right rule at the right time.

Selecting the test gives us a polite error message, as shown in Figure 5.4.

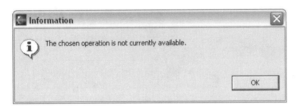

Figure 5.4

This reminds us that we need to define a class for the action to invoke, which we'll do in the next chapter. This polite, non-catastrophic behavior in the face of error leads us to the Safe Platform Rule:

SAFE PLATFORM RULE   As the provider of an extension point, you must protect yourself against misbehavior on the part of extenders.

You'll be responsible for satisfying the Safe Platform Rule when you implement your own extension points. Before moving on, let's review:

- ○ We contributed an action labelled "Run Test" to all Java elements of type `IType`. So far we only have the menu item, not its implementation.

- ○ We began working on our action by finding an example of a similar action in Eclipse. When we implement the logic of the action, we will also start with a similar action implementation.

5.1 Forward Pointers

- ○ You can specify where items appear. See users of the `menubarPath` attribute for examples. (Use file search for all *plugin.xml* files for `menubarPath`.)

○ *Internationalization*—Labels beginning with "%" will be used as a key into *plugin.properties* file. Replacing this file allows you to change the language of the plug-in. (Use file search for all *plugin.properties* files.)

○ *More precise contributions*—The object contribution offers an optional `nameFilter` attribute. Its value is a name pattern (e.g., "*Test.java"). The most sophisticated filters are written with boolean expressions (search on-line help for "action expression").

CHAPTER 6

Implementing the Menu Item Behavior

In this chapter, we will see

- ❍ How the workbench lazily creates the `Action` used in our plug-in
- ❍ How an `Action` operates
- ❍ Plug-in dependency and build classpath management

The class we are about to define will take a selected type, run the tests in that type, and display the results.

One of the consequences of the Lazy Loading Rule is that the logic of the action won't be available when the user first sees the action in the user interface. All that exists before our action has been selected is a generic proxy for the menu item's action. The generic proxy action in the workbench (an example of the Proxy pattern) uses the information in the manifest to decide whether an item should appear for a particular selection, how the item should appear, and whether the item should be enabled.

Figure 6.1 shows the objects implementing our new menu item. The `ObjectPluginAction` is the proxy for the action we're about to implement.

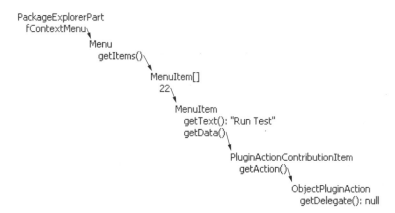

Figure 6.1   The Proxy Menu Action

What object in the new JUnit plug-in should be invoked when the menu item is selected? We need to specify the class of the object in the manifest. Here is our example from Chapter 5:

org.eclipse.compare/plugin.xml
```
<action
  id="addFromHistoryAction"
  label="%addFromHistoryAction.label"
  tooltip="%addFromHistoryAction.tooltip"
  menubarPath="replaceWithMenu"
  enablesFor="1"
  class="org.eclipse.compare.internal.AddFromHistoryAction">
</action>
```

When the menu item is selected, the action proxy will create an instance of AddFromHistoryAction. The action delegate will be passed the current selection and then told to run. The Conformance Rule tells us that the action must implement to an expected interface. But what interface must the action implement? One way to find out is to look in the online documentation. For each extension point there is an API Information section that tells you what interfaces you must conform to.

How does AddFromHistoryAction implement the necessary interface? In Hello World, the interface was IWorkbenchWindowDelegate. When contributing an action to an object, the action should conform to the IObject-ActionDelegate interface:

org.eclipse.ui/IObjectActionDelegate
```
public interface IObjectActionDelegate {
  public void run(IAction action);
  public void selectionChanged(IAction action,
    ISelection selection);
```

```
public void setActivePart(IAction action, IWorkbenchPart part);
}
```

org.eclipse.compare.internal/AddFromHistoryAction
public class **AddFromHistoryAction** implements **IObjectActionDelegate...**

The Shadow World

On startup, the platform builds a shadow of all the plug-ins by reading all the manifest files into a plug-in registry. The plug-ins haven't been loaded, only their declarative representatives. The contents of this shadow world are available to you through the class Platform and its method getPluginRegistry().

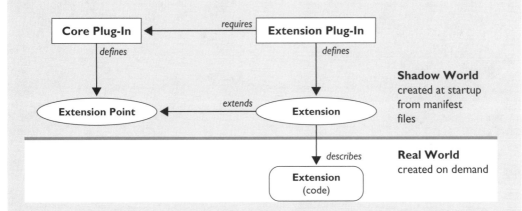

You can see and explore the shadow world by opening the PDE **Plug-in Registry** view with **Window > Show View > Other... > PDE Runtime > Plug-in Registry**.

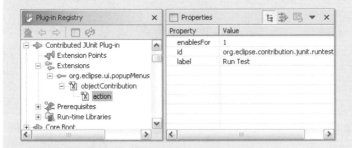

The above image shows that our JUnit plug-in extends the popupMenus extension point. The **Properties** view shows the details of the extension.

`AddFromHistoryAction` stores the selection in `selectionChanged`, because the selection is not passed to `run()`:

org.eclipse.compare.internal/AddFromHistoryAction
```
public void selectionChanged(IAction a, ISelection s) {
  fSelection= s;
}
```

The work of the `AddFromHistoryAction` occurs in `run()`. The details don't concern us here, just the fact that the selection is used:

org.eclipse.compare.internal/AddFromHistoryAction
```
public void run(IAction action) {
  ...fSelection...
}
```

Applying the Monkey See/Monkey Do Rule to copy the structure for our application, we need to first specify which class should be created as a delegate for the Run Test action. In the manifest, we need to provide the name of the class:

org.eclipse.contribution.junit/plugin.xml
```
<action
  id="org.eclipse.contribution.junit.runtest.action"
  label="Run Test"
  enablesFor="1"
  class="org.eclipse.contribution.junit.RunTestAction">
</action>
```

The `RunTestAction` needs to implement `IObjectActionDelegate`:

org.eclipse.contribution.junit/RunTestAction
```
public class RunTestAction implements IObjectActionDelegate {
}
```

We select `RunTestAction` and fill in stubs for `IObjectActionDelegate` using the **Source > Implement/Override Methods...** command.

Starting a run-time workbench lets us select our new menu item without causing an error. Once we've selected the menu item, the delegate for the item is filled in, as shown in Figure 6.2.

The first part of implementing the action is to save the selection whenever it changes:

org.eclipse.contribution.junit/RunTestAction
```
ISelection selection;
public void selectionChanged(IAction action, ISelection selection) {
  this.selection= selection;
}
```

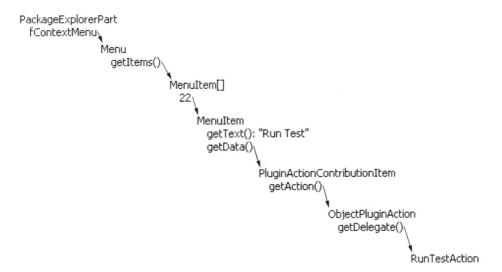

Figure 6.2   The Real Action Has Been Loaded

The run() code we are about to write needs to refer to IType, a type defined in the Java Core plug-in org.eclipse.jdt.core. As a consequence, we have to add this plug-in to our required plug-in list in the manifest. To do so we add an import of org.eclipse.jdt.core to the requires section of the manifest:

org.eclipse.contribution.junit/plugin.xml
```
<requires>
  <import plugin="org.eclipse.core.resources"/>
  <import plugin="org.eclipse.ui"/>
  <import plugin="org.eclipse.jdt.core"/>
</requires>
```

The Eclipse Java compiler has a class path it uses to look for classes and each project has its own build class path. For plug-in projects, the build class path can be derived from the prerequisite plug-ins. PDE can therefore help you compute this path. This is the purpose of the preference **Plug-In Development > Java Build Path Control.**

If you check **While modifying dependencies in plug-in manifest editor,** when you save the change above, PDE will update the build class path automatically to include the project org.eclipse.jdt.core. Alternatively, you can always manually update the build class path with **Update Classpath...** in the project's context menu in the **Package Explorer.**

In Eclipse Java development, you edit the build class path through the project properties. If you do this when developing plug-ins, you can easily

Verifying That Your Plug-In Is Loaded Lazily

To verify that you are following the Lazy Loading Rule, you should check from time to time that your plug-in isn't being loaded until you actually use it. This isn't a big problem for our plug-in at the moment, but it will be as we use more sophisticated features. Plug-in activation happens as a silent side-effect of creating objects or invoking methods, so it's easy to accidentally load your plug-in.

The simplest way to check plug-in activation is to set a breakpoint in the plug-in's `startup()` method. However, to trace the start-up of the all plug-ins, Eclipse has built-in tracing support. To trace plug-in activation, turn on tracing for the `org.eclipse.core.runtime` plug-in. This is the plug-in that loads other plug-ins. We enable three tracing switches: `debug`, `loader/debug`, and `loader/debug/activateplugin`:

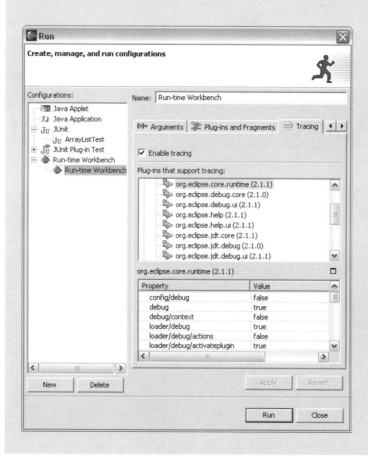

Now start the run-time workbench. You'll see the tracing messages in the console describing the basic Eclipse plug-ins being loaded:

```
Loader [org.eclipse.ui.workbench_2.1.0]^1b26af3 Attempting to
    activate org.eclipse.ui.workbench
Loader [org.eclipse.jface_2.1.0]^1b26af3 Attempting to
    activate org.eclipse.jface
Loader [org.eclipse.jface_2.1.0]^1b26af3 Exit activation for
    org.eclipse.jface
...
```

When we choose our new menu item, we see the trace message for our plug-in:

```
Loader [org.eclipse.contribution.junit_1.0.0]^1b26af3
    Attempting to activate org.eclipse.contribution.junit
Loader [org.eclipse.contribution.junit_1.0.0]^1b26af3 Exit
    activation for org.eclipse.contribution.junit
```

create a situation where the plug-in compiles because the build class path is complete, but it doesn't run because the plug-in prerequisites are wrong. The plug-in prerequisites define the run-time class path. When developing plug-ins, always edit the build class path through the manifest.

Once we've changed the required plug-ins, we have to recompute the build path. Click the **Dependencies** tab in the manifest editor and choose **Compute Build Path** in the context menu for the right-hand pane.

The real "action" happens in run() and here is its code:

org.eclipse.contribution.junit/RunTestAction
```
public void run(IAction action) {
  if (! (selection instanceof IStructuredSelection))
    return;
  IStructuredSelection structured=
      (IStructuredSelection) selection;
  IType type= (IType) structured.getFirstElement();
  // TODO need a run(type) method
}
```

Our version of run() only works if called after the selection has been set to a IStructuredSelection (instead of, say, a text selection). The guard clause ignores other selections. In general, selections can contain multiple entries, but because of the enablesFor="1" line in the manifest, we are guaranteed we will have a single selection (as long as no one else is using our action directly).

How Eclipse Finds Your Classes at Runtime

In Eclipse each plug-in has its own class loader and has its own class look-up path that is derived from the imported plug-ins. A separate class loader gives each plug-in a separate name space for its classes. The class loader also is responsible for triggering the activation of a plug-in. When a plug-in class loader loads the first class from a plug-in, then the plug-in is activated and the plug-in's `startup()` method is called.

The classes are looked-up in the following order:

1. *The plug-in class loader's parents*—The immediate parent of a plug-in class loader is the Eclipse boot class loader. It provides access to the Eclipse boot classes (`boot.jar`). The parent of the boot class loader is the standard Java system class loader, which terminates the parent chain. Notice that the application class loader, which loads classes from the system's `CLASSPATH` variable is not part of this chain. This means classes on the system class path are never found by Eclipse. Plug-ins are the only way to surface additional classes. The following spider diagram illustrates the parent chain:

```
PluginDescriptor
  toString(): "org.eclipse.contribution.junit_1.0.0"
  loader
          PluginClassLoader
            getParent()
                      URLClassLoader
                        getParent(): null
                        getURLs()
                                  URL[]
                                    0
        URL
          file: "C:/2.1.1/eclipse/plugins/org.eclipse.core.boot_2.1.1/boot.jar"
```

2. *The plug-in's class loader itself*—It finds the classes contributed by the plug-in as specified in the run-time section of the *plugin.xml* manifest.

```
PluginDescriptor
  toString(): "org.eclipse.contribution.junit_1.0.0"
  loader
          PluginClassLoader
            getURLs()
                      URL[]
                        0
        URL
          file: "C:/2.1.1/eclipse/plugins/org.eclipse.contribution.junit_1.0.0/junit.jar"
```

3. *The plug-in class loaders of the imported/prerequisite plug-ins*—A delegating URL class loader is used internally to forward the class lookup to the imported plug-ins.

```
PluginDescriptor
   toString(): "org.eclipse.contribution.junit_1.0.0"
   loader
           PluginClassLoader
              imports
                       DelegatingURLClassLoader$DelegateLoader[]
                       0
                       1   DelegatingURLClassLoader$DelegateLoader
                              loader

                                 PluginClassLoader
                                    debugId(): "org.eclipse.core.resources_2.1.1"
                       DelegatingURLClassLoader$DelegateLoader
                          loader

                             PluginClassLoader
                                debugId(): "org.eclipse.ui_2.1.1"
```

Then we get the `IType` out of the selection. We are guaranteed we will have an `IType` selected because of the `objectClass="org.eclipse.jdt.core.IType"` line in the manifest. We run the tests in the `IType` using a to-be-implemented `run(type)` method. We insert a "TODO" comment to fill this in later. This reminder shows up in both the **Tasks** view and the vertical ruler on the left of the editor.

With these class-path-related changes our code compiles, but we have to get back to our "TODO" comment and implement a method to run tests. First we need to find a home for this behavior. Support for running tests is a key function of the plug-in and we want to define it in a central location. A plug-in's plug-in class is such a location. The plug-in class plays a similar role to the top-level application class in a standalone application. In particular, a plug-in class provides the plug-in life-cycle methods `startup()` and `shutdown()`. You can override them to participate in the activation and deactivation of a plug-in. The ground rule is to put as little code as possible in these methods and instead use lazy initialization to conform to the Lazy Loading Rule. Before we can run tests, we have to create a plug-in class.

The first duty of the plug-in class is to be accessible to the other classes in the plug-in. It's a home for shared information. Out we pull handy-dandy

Singleton.[1] Yes, it creates a "global" variable, but here the whole purpose of the class is to share information between objects. The actual scope of the information is only within the plug-in, not the whole system.

The simplest plug-in superclass is `org.eclipse.core.runtime.Plugin`. The other plug-in base class candidate is `org.eclipse.ui.plugin.Abstract-UIPlugin`. It provides additional support for implementing UI functionality. Because we don't need this now, we'll use the simple plug-in class. The Singleton is implemented by saving the one instance that Eclipse is guaranteed to create.

org.eclipse.contribution.junit/JUnitPlugin
```
public class JUnitPlugin extends Plugin {
  private static JUnitPlugin instance;

  public JUnitPlugin(IPluginDescriptor descriptor) {
    super(descriptor);
    instance= this;
  }

  public static JUnitPlugin getPlugin() {
    return instance;
  }
}
```

When we create the plug-in class, we have to update the manifest so our new kind of plug-in object is created when the plug-in is loaded. We forget to do this from time to time, which leads to some pretty strange behavior: `instance` is still null and you get a `NullPointerException`. Why? Because the platform takes care of instantiating a plug-in for us. Unless we tell it a particular plug-in class to create, it just creates a generic plug-in.

org.eclipse.contribution.junit/plugin.xml
```
<plugin
  id="org.eclipse.contribution.junit"
  name="JUnit Plug-in"
  version="1.0.0"
  class="org.eclipse.contribution.junit.JUnitPlugin">
```

Finally, we need a little stub for running tests:

org.eclipse.contribution.junit/JUnitPlugin
```
public void run(IType type) {
  // TODO run the tests in the given type
}
```

---

1. E. Gamma, R. Helm, R. Johnson, and J. Vlissides. *Design Patterns: Elements of Reusable Object-Oriented Software*. Addison-Wesley, Reading, MA, 1995.

Our menu item will run now, but it won't do anything. We'll implement displaying test results in the next chapter. First, reviewing:

❍ We saw that our `RunAction` wasn't created until the menu item was selected.

❍ We saw how the selection is passed as part of `selectionChanged()`, but used in `run()`. These are the only two methods needed to act as the action behind a menu item.

❍ We introduced the plug-in class.

6.1 Forward Pointers

❍ *Dynamic enablement and label changes*—Once your plug-in is loaded, you can update the enablement state or the label precisely from code. To do so, you get the generic `IAction` passed in to both `ActionDelegate` methods.

❍ *Contributing a set of actions in a submenu*—To do so, you describe a menu contribution with a path, which you then use for contributing actions:

```
<menu
  id="aSubMenu"
  path="additions"
  label="A Submenu">
  <separator name="someGroup"/>
</menu>
```

❍ *Other examples of the Lazy Loading Rule*—Preference pages are also loaded lazily. Look carefully. The first time you click on a preference node, there is a brief pause while Eclipse loads the preference page. Subsequently the page loads instantly.

CHAPTER 7

Displaying the Results

We left the last chapter having invoked the tests. In this chapter, we will

- Design the protocol for collecting test results
- Outline what it takes to actually run the tests
- Display the test results

How are we going to display the results? The JUnit plug-in class should know nothing about how results are displayed. So, what if the plug-in class broadcasts the results of tests that are running?

The Observer pattern is useful when you have loosely coupled communication patterns:

- You don't care in what order the receivers receive the messages.
- You don't have to return any results to the sender.
- You don't know *a priori* how many objects will want to receive the message (see Figure 7.1).

These conditions hold in our case. Tests will run and various observers will respond to notifications of progress (see Figure 7.2). The role of the Observer will be played by our `RunTestAction` at first, later also by a view, a tabular report view, and so on. The Observer Interface will contain the set of progress messages: "The tests are starting," "The tests are done," "A test has started," and "A test has failed."

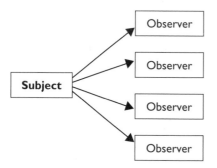

Figure 7.1   One Subject Notifies Several Observers

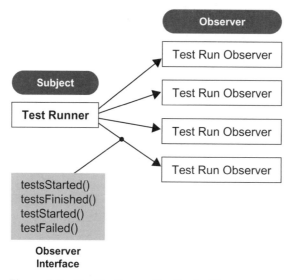

Figure 7.2   One TestRunner Notifies Its Observers

How would this look in the code we've written so far?

1. Before we ask the JUnit plug-in to run the tests, we should connect a listener to the plug-in. The plug-in acts as a Subject in the Observer pattern.

2. The listener will be notified as tests run.

3. When the last test runs, the listener will pop up a dialog containing the results.

4. We will disconnect the listener.

First, we need to change the calling sequence in the action. Before we run tests, we need to register a listener, and afterward we need to unregister a listener. What object should play the part of the listener? A clever solution is to have our `ActionDelegate` also implement `ITestRunListener`. However, this requires us to make the listener methods public in `RunTestAction`, and we don't really want to publicize the test listener methods as part of the action. Instead, we'll implement the listener as a static inner class. Let's start with the code to register the listener in the run() method:

org.eclipse.contribution.junit/RunTestAction
```
public void run(IAction action) {
  if (! (selection instanceof IStructuredSelection))
    return;
  IStructuredSelection structured= (IStructuredSelection) selection;
  IType type= (IType) structured.getFirstElement();
  ITestRunListener listener= new Listener();
  JUnitPlugin.getPlugin().addTestListener(listener);
  JUnitPlugin.getPlugin().run(type);
  JUnitPlugin.getPlugin().removeTestListener(listener);
}
```

The listener will need to respond to the progress of the tests. We'll represent the messages being broadcast as an interface:

org.eclipse.contribution.junit/ITestRunListener
```
public interface ITestRunListener {
  void testsStarted(int testCount);
  void testsFinished();
  void testStarted(String klass, String method);
  void testFailed(String klass, String method, String trace);
}
```

Next we implement the `Listener` as a static inner class in `RunTestAction`. If we want to pop up a dialog with "Pass" or "Fail" when the tests finish, we need to set a flag when the tests start and clear it if a test ever fails:

org.eclipse.contribution.junit/RunTestAction$Listener
```
public static class Listener implements ITestRunListener {
  private boolean passed= true;
  public void testsStarted(int testCount) {
  }
  public void testsFinished() {
    String message= passed ? "Pass" : "Fail";
    MessageDialog.openInformation(null, "Test Results", message);
  }
  public void testStarted(String klass, String method) {
  }
  public void testFailed(String klass, String method,
      String trace) {
    passed= false;
  }
}
```

We really should have passed in a parent shell as the first parameter to the
`MessageDialog`, so the dialog shows up relative to the workbench window.
For now, this is good enough.

We need to implement adding and removing the test listeners:

org.eclipse.contribution.junit/JUnitPlugin
```
private List listeners= new ArrayList();

public void addTestListener(ITestRunListener listener) {
  listeners.add(listener);
}

public void removeTestListener(ITestRunListener listener) {
  listeners.remove(listener);
}
```

We will create a `TestRunner` to run our tests for us. For now, we can't imagine
how your understanding of Eclipse would be helped by seeing the details of
starting a new virtual machine and communicating with it via sockets. See
Appendix A for the details. If you are following along in Eclipse, add the code
for `TestRunner` and `SocketTestRunner` now. You will also need to add `org.
eclipse.jdt.launching`, `org.eclipse.debug.core`, and `org.junit` as
required plug-ins.

With the `TestRunner` in place we can go back to the "TODO" comment
in `JUnitPlugin.run()` and implement the method body:

org.eclipse.contribution.junit/JUnitPlugin
```
public void run(IType type) throws CoreException {
  new TestRunner().run(type);
}
```

Our `TestRunner` will call back to the `JUnitPlugin` to ask it to broadcast
progress to all the listeners. Here is the simple version of these four methods:

org.eclipse.contribution.junit/JUnitPlugin
```
  public void fireTestsStarted(int count) {
  for (Iterator all= getListeners().iterator(); all.hasNext();) {
    ITestRunListener each= (ITestRunListener) all.next();
    each.testsStarted(count);
  }
}
public void fireTestsFinished() {
  for (Iterator all= getListeners().iterator(); all.hasNext();) {
    ITestRunListener each= (ITestRunListener) all.next();
    each.testsFinished();
  }
}
public void fireTestStarted(String klass, String methodName) {
  for (Iterator all= getListeners().iterator(); all.hasNext();) {
```

```
      ITestRunListener each= (ITestRunListener) all.next();
      each.testStarted(klass, methodName);
   }
}
public void fireTestFailed(
   String klass, String method, String trace) {
  for (Iterator all= getListeners().iterator(); all.hasNext();) {
    ITestRunListener each= (ITestRunListener) all.next();
    each.testFailed(klass, method, trace);
  }
}
```

For now, `getListener()` is a simple accessor for the `listeners` field.

We've implemented the listener mechanism, but we did it the usual dynamic Java way. In Eclipse, as much as possible you invite others to share in the benefits of your plug-ins. We'd like to make it easy for others to register their own test listeners. In the next chapter, we'll see how to do that. Reviewing, we

❍ Designed a listener-based protocol for collecting test results

❍ Displayed results using a listener inside our menu action

❍ Implemented adding and removing listeners in the plug-in class

7.1   Forward Pointers

❍ JFace provides a utility class `org.eclipse.jface.util.ListenerList`. You can use it to maintain a list of listeners.

CHAPTER 8

Defining an Extension Point

One early reviewer commented, "I just want to know how to write plug-ins. I don't really want to learn how to declare new extension points. There are hundreds of plug-ins out there and almost none of them enable new extension points." Eclipse is great fun for writing little plug-ins, but if you aren't declaring new extension points, you're missing out on much of the power of the platform. When children are taught to ice skate in Switzerland, they begin skating forwards and backwards the first day. Skating backwards is just never scary if that's how you learn. We believe creating extension points doesn't need to be scary, but you need to start creating extension points early. Once you get good at creating extension points, building upon your work will be easier for you and for others.

Our goal for this chapter is to invite others (and ourselves) to present test results. In this chapter, you'll see

○ Designing and defining an extension point

○ Defining a contribution interface

○ Defining an extension

We have a simple, dialog-based interface, but we can't be sure it is the one and only best way to present results.

INVITATION RULE Whenever possible, let others contribute to your contributions.

How can we open up our system so others can also display results? If we didn't want to change our code, we could implement an extension point, but continue to use dynamic listener protocol. If the rules are different for different clients, though, we miss the chance for valuable feedback.

FAIR PLAY RULE   All clients play by the same rules, even me.

Eclipse has few exceptions to the Fair Play Rule. Even the workbench itself is loaded as an extension. If you want to run a completely different application on top of the platform core runtime, you can define your own extension to the application extension point (`org.eclipse.core.runtime.applications`). If we're going to play fair, we should convert what we have already to use our new extension point.

Eclipse enables people solving a problem many different ways. When contributing to Eclipse, you don't build monolithic functionality. Instead, you create opportunities for extension, and you provide some extensions yourself. Invariably, you also use your own extensions.

Now that we have the basic test-running functionality, we want to open it up. To define and use an extension point, we have to do the following:

❍ Design the extension point.

❍ Define the extension point in the manifest.

❍ Write code to load the extensions to that point.

❍ Invoke the extensions (safely) at the appropriate time.

Object-oriented frameworks are designed, as is Eclipse, to be used by being extended. One problem with object-based frameworks is that every public method is a potential point for extension. If you're successful and people use your framework, you quickly find that you have no freedom to grow the framework further. Every method has potentially been extended, so you can't change anything. As Martin Fowler says, we should distinguish between public and published methods.[1] Published methods are intended for use by others, public methods are merely visible. Eclipse institutionalizes this distinction.

EXPLICIT EXTENSION RULE   Declare explicitly where a platform can be extended.

Extension points are declared in the plug-in manifest. Being good little monkeys, we'd like an example from which to copy. Where can we find a sim-

---

1. See Martin Fowler, *Public versus Published Interfaces*, IEEE Software, March/April 2002.

ilar extension point? We'd like to browse all extension points. We often use the on-line help (see Figure 8.1).

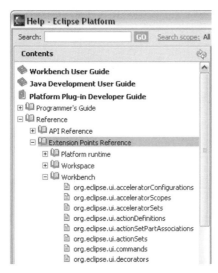

Figure 8.1

Looking around we find `org.eclipse.ui.views`. The example given in the help looks like this:

```
<extension point="org.eclipse.ui.views">
  ...
  <view
    id="com.xyz.views.XYZView"
    name="XYZ View"
    category="com.xyz.views.XYZviews"
    class="com.xyz.views.XYZView"
    icon="icons/XYZ.gif">
  </view>
</extension>
```

In general, an extension point should accept many extensions. The rule is:

DIVERSITY RULE   Extension points accept multiple extensions.

The Diversity Rule is a consequence of the Sharing Rule. If someone adds an extension to an extension point, it should not affect your ability to add another extension to the same point. It's when designing and implementing an extension point that you have to take the Diversity Rule into account. The extensions themselves should never care about the presence or absence of other extensions.

Why isn't a run-time listener good enough? When we popped up the dialog to display the results, we added and removed the listener dynamically. However, we'd also like to create plug-ins that would respond to the running of all tests. For example, imagine a plug-in that counts all tests being run and sends a message to a central server to count all the tests run by everyone in a community. Such a plug-in would not be activated and deactivated dynamically. It would register as an extension and then be activated on demand, the first time a test was run (Lazy Loading Rule).

Mimicking the structure of the `views` extension point, we should have an overall extension point for test listeners with elements, each representing a single class of listener. What should the name of the extension point be? Everywhere the extension point name is used it will be fully qualified, so we don't need to make the name itself unambiguous. We can just call it `listener`. The Diversity Rule implies that the name should be plural, so we get `listeners`. So, in use, the extension point should look something like the following:

```
<extension point="org.eclipse.contribution.junit.listeners">
  <listener
    class="org.eclipse.contribution.junit.RunTestAction$Listener">
  </listener>
</extension>
```

This extension declaration says that when an extension point named `listeners` is invoked, an instance of `RunTestAction$Listener` should be created (by convention, this attribute is always called `class`). In our case we have a static inner class, so we have to qualify the name with "$". Class names in this form are common but not standard. If we wanted to be perfectly portable, we would promote our inner class to a top-level class. Our `listeners` needs to follow the Conformance Rule and implement `ITestRunListener`.

One thing to consider when designing extension points is how to help Eclipse be even lazier loading implementors of the extension point. We can imagine implementing a special extension point that is only notified when a test fails. Extenders would not have to be loaded as long as all the tests succeed. The tradeoff is you don't want tons of extension points that don't do much by themselves. In this case, we can't imagine how we would use an extension point that is notified on test failure but doesn't care about success, so we lump the notifications together in a single extension point. We would only make this kind of refinement if it was possible to typically not load a plug-in at all. Here that's not the case—tests will fail.

Diagnosing Plug-Ins

Sometimes when you have trouble with plug-ins, the problem is really in the internals of the plug-in logic. For these problems, the usual debugging methods suffice: running the workbench under the debugger and setting breakpoints, print statements, and test-driven development. What if the problem is in the manifest?

For these errors you have three primary resources:

○ The PDE manifest editor validates the contents of the manifest when you build your project. PDE runs a special builder (more about builders later) that validates that, for example, all the extension points you reference have been declared.

○ The **Error Log** view in the run-time workbench shows errors explicitly logged by plug-ins. View the log by choosing **Window > Show View > Other... > PDE Runtime > Error Log.** Double clicking an error gives you a chance to see both the conditions under which you created the run-time workbench, and (under **Status Details**) the details of the error, such as the stack trace of any exceptions.

○ The console in the host workbench prints text written to `System.out`. In extreme situations you can fall back on `println` debugging.

PDE tells us that the extension point `org.eclipse.contribution.junit.listeners` is not defined, as shown in Figure 8.2.

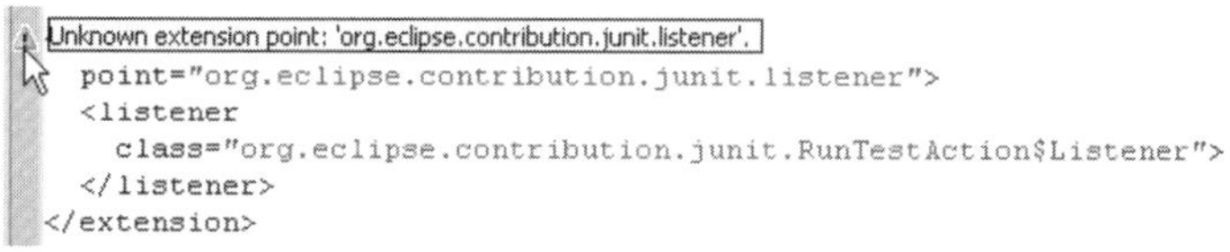

```
Unknown extension point: 'org.eclipse.contribution.junit.listener'.
  point="org.eclipse.contribution.junit.listener">
  <listener
    class="org.eclipse.contribution.junit.RunTestAction$Listener">
  </listener>
</extension>
```

Figure 8.2

How do we declare an extension point? First, we need to find the declaration of our example, as shown in Figure 8.3.

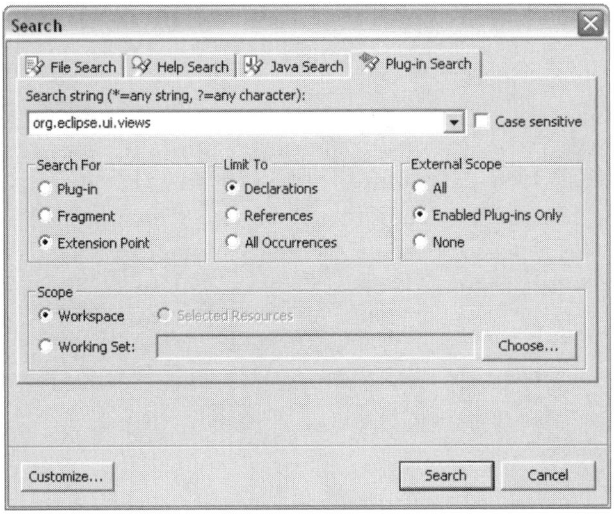

Figure 8.3

This leads us to the following declaration (in the **Source** tab):

org.eclipse.ui/plugin.xml
```
<extension-point id="views" name="%ExtPoint.views" schema="schema/
views.mxsd"/>
```

A point that often trips us is that the only difference between the declaration of an extension point and a use of that point is the dash "-". Be careful when defining new extension points, or use the PDE tools to edit the manifest file. Notice that the `id` in the declaration has no unique prefix. Eclipse prepends the plug-in `id` as a prefix for all extension points. Extensions, however, must use the fully qualified `id`. You always declare an extension point within a particular plug-in. When you use it, however, you could be in the same plug-in, or in a completely different plug-in.

The name of an extension point is used by PDE to display the extension point to a user. The name above is internationalized, a topic we'll cover in Circle Two.

Mimicking the `views` extension point declaration, we need to declare our `listeners` extension point as:

org.eclipse.contribution.junit/plugin.xml
```
<extension-point id="listeners" name="Test Listeners"/>
```

Say we want our result dialog to pop up whenever tests are run. (This is a horrible user-interface long-term, but it serves to demonstrate the topic of this chapter.)

The Fair Play Rule suggests we should use the same mechanism for our code that we offer to clients. We should notify all extensions the same way.

When should we load the extensions? One simple answer is to load them when Eclipse starts up. However, if all plug-ins loaded all extensions at startup, startup would be proportional to the number of installed plug-ins. The better solution is to lazily load the extensions the first time they need to be notified.

The getter method lazily computes the listeners as follows:

org.eclipse.contribution.junit/JUnitPlugin
```
private List listeners; // Don't initialize
private List getListeners() {
  if (listeners == null)
    listeners= computeListeners();
  return listeners;
}
```

How do you load extensions? It took us about five minutes to find a good example. Extension points are read in using many different idioms in Eclipse. What eventually helped us was that we guessed there would be a class called something like `ExtensionPoint`. Since we have all the types accessible in our workspace through the binary projects, we can use type searching to find similar types, as shown in Figure 8.4.

Figure 8.4

We don't want to start looking with ExtensionPoint, because it lives in an internal package. IExtensionPoint is in a published package (no "internal" in the package name), so we can begin looking at its clients.

When following the Monkey See/Monkey Do Rule, you'll often spend five or ten minutes at a time reading code. It's easy to interpret this as wasted time. You're learning all the time you're reading. In a year, your fluidity with Eclipse will increase to the point that you only occasionally have to spend extended stretches reading. In the meantime, you are getting functionality working and integrated into Eclipse.

The example we came to that is close to what we want to do is in Tool-Factory (we've removed some extraneous detail):

org.eclipse.jdt.core/ToolFactory
```
public static ICodeFormatter createCodeFormatter(){
  Plugin jdtCorePlugin = JavaCore.getPlugin();
  IExtensionPoint extension =
     jdtCorePlugin.getDescriptor().getExtensionPoint(
       JavaModelManager.FORMATTER_EXTPOINT_ID);
  IExtension[] extensions =  extension.getExtensions();
  for(int i = 0; i < extensions.length; i++){
    IConfigurationElement [] configElements =
      extensions[i].getConfigurationElements();
    for(int j = 0; j < configElements.length; j++){
      try {
        Object execExt= configElements[j].
          createExecutableExtension("class");
        if (execExt instanceof ICodeFormatter){
          return (ICodeFormatter)execExt;
        }
      } catch(CoreException e){
      }
    }
  }
}
```

The code shown above only loads the first extension, violating the Diversity Rule. We want to load all extensions.

The process of loading extensions is as follows:

1. Get the extension point from the platform. (Remember that the platform reads all the manifest files on start-up, so our extension point will be there.)

2. Get the registered extensions (IExtension). These are also created by reading the manifest files, looking for:

   ```
   <extension point=
     "org.eclipse.contribution.junit.listeners">.
   ```

3. For each extension, get the XML elements inside it (`IConfiguration-Element`):

```
<listener class=
  "org.eclipse.contribute.junit.TestRunAction$Listener"/>.
```

4. For each configuration element, create an object whose class will be based on the contents of the `class` attribute. Validate that the defined attributes are complete.

5. Save the newly created extensions in a collection (instead of just returning the first one as in the `ToolFactory` example).

The plug-in registry (the root of the shadow world described above) gives us descriptions of all the extensions of our extension point discovered at load time. Starting there, we will get the extensions and the elements inside the extensions, and create our listeners.

org.eclipse.contribution.junit/JUnitPlugin
```
private static final String listenerId=
  "org.eclipse.contribution.junit.listeners";

private List computeListeners() {
  IPluginRegistry registry= Platform.getPluginRegistry();
  IExtensionPoint extensionPoint=
    registry.getExtensionPoint(listenerId);
  IExtension[] extensions= extensionPoint.getExtensions();
  ArrayList results= new ArrayList();
  for (int i= 0; i < extensions.length; i++) {
    IConfigurationElement[] elements=
      extensions[i].getConfigurationElements();
    for (int j= 0; j < elements.length; j++) {
      try {
        Object listener=
          elements[j].createExecutableExtension("class");
        if (listener instanceof ITestRunListener)
          results.add(listener);
      } catch (CoreException e) {
        e.printStackTrace();
      }
    }
  }
  return results;
}
```

After we create the listener, we explicitly check to make sure it conforms to our expected interface (Conformance Rule). We are also careful to protect the creation of our listeners. We call the listener class's constructor, which could have problems (Safe Platform Rule) inside a try-catch block.

If we eliminate the dynamic listener and declare the same listener class as an extension, we get the same dialog. Now we are playing fair. We are using

Extension Instantiation

Frameworks have to solve the problem of how to create client objects. By definition, you don't know what objects you'll be creating when you write the framework. `ConfigurationElement.createExecutableExtension()` is a flavor of Factory Method. The important difference is that Factory Method creates a static dependency on the extension class. Here, we use Java's class-loading facility to load and instantiate the extension class, without having any static dependency between the extension creator and the extension.

For the curious, here is what is going inside `createExecutableExtension()`. From the configuration element `createExecutableExtension()` retrieves the name of the class to be instantiated and the declaring plug-in. The declaring plug-in is then requested to instantiate the class. It forwards the request to its plug-in class loader (see "How Eclipse Finds Your Classes at Runtime" on page 54). If the declaring plug-in isn't activated yet, the request to load and create an instance of the class activates the plug-in as a side effect.

the same mechanism for behavior inside the plug-in as we intend to publish for external use.

We haven't yet looked at the Eclipse way to invoke extensions. Once we've done that, the functionality for Circle One is complete. We have a simple UI for running tests. Before doing so, we'll review:

- We decided to open up our plug-in for further contribution and to use the same mechanism ourselves instead of cheating.

- We declared an extension point, `listeners`, that would allow multiple objects to listen to test progress.

- We loaded the extensions lazily, creating an `ITestRunListener` for each element in the extensions.

8.1 Forward Pointers

- *Defining an extension point schema file (.exsd)*—PDE offers a guided way to define an extension in the manifest editor. This requires us to tell PDE more about our extension and its structure. This information is captured in an XML schema file with the suffix *.exsd*.

- `IExecutableExtension`—If you need additional arguments for the extensions created by the factory, define them in the XML and declare your extension to implement `IExecutableExtension`, and the parameters will be passed to your newly created object with a call to `setInitializationData()`.

❍ *Activating a plug-in early*—There are some rare situations when a plug-in needs to be loaded early (when Eclipse starts). Consider a plug-in that starts a server to which external clients need to connect. When a plug-in hosting such a server is loaded lazily, clients will never be able to connect to the server, because it isn't running. For these rare situations, Eclipse can activate a plug-in as soon as the workbench is up and running. To force early plug-in activation, use the `org.eclipse.ui.startup` extension point. Because this is an extension point with a potential for abuse, Eclipse lets users disable the early start-up of a plug-in with the preferences: **Preferences > Workbench > Startup.**

CHAPTER 9

Notifying Extensions

When we notify an extension, we don't have any control over what happens next. The contract we would like to maintain is that we notify all extenders regardless of failures. Consider a malicious listener:

```
public static class BadListener implements ITestRunListener {
  ...
  public void testsStarted(int testCount) {
    throw new NullPointerException();
  }
}
```

If we wrote a simple loop to notify all extensions, when we got to our BadListener an exception would be thrown, terminating the loop prematurely. So, here's another Eclipse rule:

> **GOOD FENCES RULE**   When passing control outside your code, protect yourself.

Applying this rule, when we notify our extensions, we need to do so safely. Because this is a common idiom in Eclipse, ISafeRunnable wraps potentially dangerous code. You can look at implementors of ISafeRunnable for lots of good examples. Our usage of it will be simple:

org.eclipse.contribution.junit/JUnitPlugin
```
public void fireTestsStarted(final int testCount) {
  for (Iterator all= getListeners().iterator(); all.hasNext();) {
    final ITestRunListener each= (ITestRunListener) all.next();
    ISafeRunnable runnable= new ISafeRunnable() {
```

```
      public void handleException(Throwable exception) {
      }
      public void run() throws Exception {
        each.testsStarted(testCount);
      }
    };
    Platform.run(runnable);
  }
}
```

ISafeRunnable defines the hook methods run() and handleException(), which are invoked by the Platform. If anything goes wrong, the Platform takes care of the exception handling.

What if you have an extension that once it has gone crazy will continue throwing exceptions? A refinement of the idiom above is to remove an extension once it has thrown an exception. Applied to the situation above, we would insert the following line into the code above:

org.eclipse.contribution.junit/JUnitPlugin.fireTestsStarted()
```
public void handleException(Throwable exception) {
  all.remove();
}
```

We use Iterator.remove() to avoid the problem of modifying a collection while iterating over it. You would only want to remove extensions if you were certain that their problems weren't transient.

We need to implement analogous methods fireTestsFinished(), fireTestStarted(String klass, String method), and fireTestFailed(String klass, String method, String stacktrace).

The functionality for Circle One is done. We have a small but complete plug-in. Before we leave the circle, we will prepare what we've done so far for use by others. Reviewing this chapter, we:

○ Designed an extension point that could be extended multiple times

○ Loaded the extensions only when they were about to be used

○ Safely notified extensions using ISafeRunnable and Platform.run()

CHAPTER 10

Publishing

We've extended Eclipse. So far, though, only we can use our plug-in, and we only can use it in a run-time workspace. The next stage on the Contribution Circle is to move from Extender to Publisher by making our plug-in available to others. Then we will have contributed to the Eclipse community. We will have closed the circle.

In this chapter we will

○ Package the plug-in for use on our machine

○ Package the plug-in for installation by others (a feature)

○ Package the feature for downloading and installation (an update site)

10.1 Package the Plug-In

When running the plug-in in the run-time workspace, we just run the class files. The advantage of this is we can quickly make and test a change. To run in the host workspace the classes need to be packaged in the library defined in the manifest. Here is how `org.eclipse.jdt.ui` defines its library:

org.eclipse.jdt.ui/plugin.xml
```
<runtime>
  <library name="jdt.jar">
    <export name = "*"/>
  </library>
</runtime>
```

Not only do we have to define the JAR file for the plug-in, we have to explicitly say which classes will be visible outside of the plug-in. The Eclipse practice is to export all classes. We err on the side of assuming extenders will act responsibly. Therefore we export all classes:

org.eclipse.contribution.junit/plugin.xml
```
<runtime>
  <library name="contribjunit.jar">
    <export name = "*"/>
  </library>
</runtime>
```

Now we want to build the library. The *plugin.xml* manifest file defines the name of our library, but not how it is built. We therefore have to provide PDE with additional information about how to build the plug-in. This is done in the *build.properties* file. The PDE project wizard creates the *build.properties* file when it creates the project (see Figure 10.1).

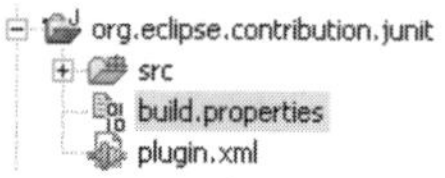

Figure 10.1

The *build.properites* file is a standard Java properties file that defines a set of key value pairs. The key to defining where the source for a library lives is `source.<libraryname>`, in our case `source.contribjunit.jar`. PDE by default puts the source in a folder *src*, and it also defines the corresponding key-value pair in the *build.properties* file:

org.eclipse.contribution.junit/build.properties
```
source.contribjunit.jar = src/
```

This tells the build process that the source for `contribjunit.jar` is in the folder *src*. With this information PDE can build the library. The other piece of information we have to provide is which files in our project should be included when we bundle or deploy the plug-in for other users. This is done with the `bin.includes` variable. PDE fills in the following value by default:

org.eclipse.contribution.junit/build.properties
```
bin.includes = plugin.xml,\
               *.jar,\
               contribjunit.jar
```

The deployed plug-in should include the library `contribjunit.jar` and the *plugin.xml*. In addition, PDE includes any other JAR files contained in the project. When your project includes additional resources like icons that need to be included in the deployed plug-in, then you have to add them to this comma-separated list. You can use the standard Ant patterns to define the value of a variable. For example here is the value of `bin.includes` for `org.eclipse.jdt.ui`:

org.eclipse.jdt.ui/build.properties
```
bin.includes = plugin.xml,\
               about.html,\
               icons/,\
               plugin.properties,\
               *.jar
```

PDE provides a custom editor for editing the *build.properties* file. Changes in the **Runtime** tab of the manifest editor require updating the *build.properties* file. PDE protects you from concurrent changes by making the `build.properties` editor read-only when the manifest editor is open.

Before we build the library file, now is a good time to review the plug-in prerequisites (see Figure 10.2). In the heat of development, it is easy to temporarily use another plug-in and forget to remove it. Too-large dependency lists slow down the class lookup. More important, thinking about dependencies gives you a chance to take a global look at your design.

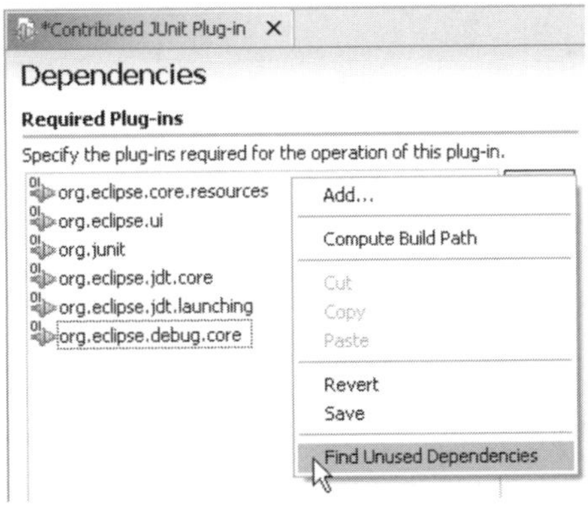

Figure 10.2

The **Dependencies** tab in the manifest editor helps you find and delete any plug-in dependencies you no longer use. For each required plug-in, PDE searches for referenced types from that plug-in. If it doesn't find any, it gives you the choice of removing the dependency.

We are now ready to deploy our plug-in. The simplest way to do so is with the PDE plug-in exporter: **File > Export... > Deployable plug-ins and fragments**. Select the plug-in project to be exported and define the location of the generated zip file, as shown in Figure 10.3.

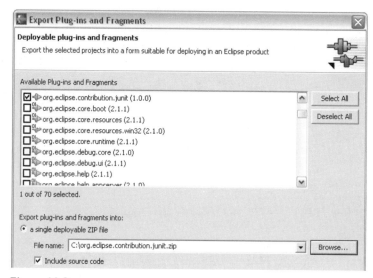

Figure 10.3

This will create a zip file containing a deployable version of your plug-in that is ready to be installed. Let's verify the contents by opening the zip file (see Figure 10.4).

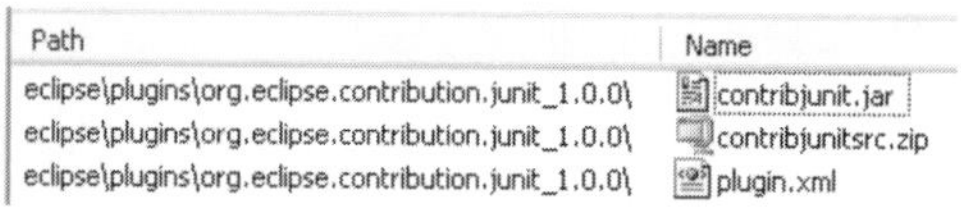

Path	Name
eclipse\plugins\org.eclipse.contribution.junit_1.0.0\	contribjunit.jar
eclipse\plugins\org.eclipse.contribution.junit_1.0.0\	contribjunitsrc.zip
eclipse\plugins\org.eclipse.contribution.junit_1.0.0\	plugin.xml

Figure 10.4

Because we have checked **Include source code** in the **Export Plug-ins and Fragments** dialog, we see a zip file containing the source. When a file is missing, start by checking the value of `bin.includes` in the *build.properties*.

If we want to use our plug-in in the host workspace, we unzip *org.eclipse. contribution.junit.zip* in the Eclipse installation directory.

10.2 Bundling the Plug-In into a Feature

Now we have a plug-in ready to be installed. Before we can let others install it, we have to introduce another concept—the *feature*. First, the simple way of bundling a plug-in—zipping up the plug-in and making it available on the Web for others to download and unzip—still works. However, there is a better way. Given a large number of tools, installing them should be straightforward. In particular, given the modularity of Eclipse where everything is a plug-in, it is critical that the set of plug-ins is still manageable. Otherwise an Eclipse installation ends up as plug-in soup. The implementation of a tool can range from a single plug-in to dozens of plug-ins. To simplify plug-in download, installation, and management, Eclipse has features. Features are the unit of download and installation.

Plug-ins are too simple to install as standalones because they are missing important information like license terms. Features bundle together a set of plug-ins and this extra installation-oriented information.

You can see all the currently installed features in **Help > About Eclipse Platform > Feature Details** (see Figure 10.5).

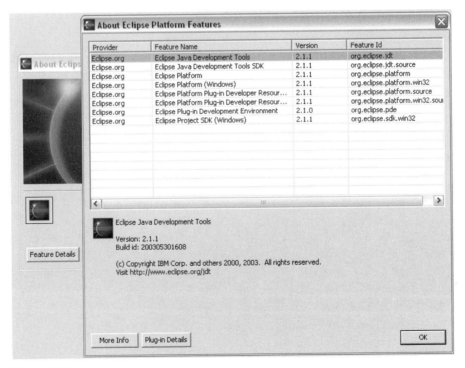

Figure 10.5

The Eclipse Feature Structure

Eclipse contains three large features which correspond to the three layers of Eclipse (see Figure 1.3):

- **Platform**—The Eclipse language-neutral base
- **JDT**—The Java development tooling
- **PDE**—The plug-in development tooling

Eclipse is packaged this way so you can build applications using only the platform and ignoring all the Java tools.

The source is bundled as separate features. Again, this allows you to distribute Eclipse with or without source.

We can import an existing feature into a project to examine its structure by choosing **File > Import... > External Features > org.eclipse.jdt** (see Figure 10.6).

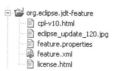

Figure 10.6

Like plug-ins, features are represented as a directory in a *features* folder. The files are:

- *cpl*—(incidental) The common public license definition, version 1.0. It is referenced by the license file.
- *Eclipse_update_120.jpg*—(optional) The picture displayed with the feature.
- *Feature.properties*—(optional) The internationalized strings.
- *Feature.xml*—The feature manifest.
- *License.html*—(incidental) The details of the license, referred to from *feature.xml*.

Now we need to write the *feature.xml* for our JUnit feature bundling our plug-in. *Feature.xml* has a single element:

org.eclipse.contribution.junit-feature/feature.xml

```
<feature
```

```
    id="org.eclipse.contribution.junitfeature"
    label="org.eclipse.contribution.junit-feature"
    version="1.0.0"
    provider-name="">
</feature>
```

The feature `id` is a globally unique `id`, similar to what you've seen already in plug-in manifests. The label is used to present the feature in the **About** dialog shown above. The `version` identifies the version of the feature. The goal of features is safe installation. Therefore, installation must be fully version-aware.

Another aspect of safe installation is the presence of all prerequisite plug-ins. We can compute our prerequisite plug-ins as the union of the prerequisites of all of the plug-ins in this feature:

org.eclipse.contribution.junit-feature/feature.xml
```
<requires>
  <import plugin="org.eclipse.core.resources"/>
  <import plugin="org.eclipse.ui"/>
  <import plugin="org.eclipse.jdt.launching"/>
  <import plugin="org.eclipse.jdt.core"/>
  <import plugin="org.eclipse.debug.core"/>
  <import plugin="org.junit"/>
</requires>
```

Eclipse will not allow you to load a feature unless license text is specified, a consequence of the License Rule:

LICENSE RULE Always supply a license with every contribution.

We add the following element to the feature manifest to specify the license:

org.eclipse.contribution.junit-feature/feature.xml
```
<license>
License text goes here.
</license>
```

This defines the "click-through" license that is presented to the user in a simple dialog with the options to accept or reject. There is an optional `url` attribute that allows you to define a link to the full license text as HTML. Finally, the feature has to specify the IDs and versions of the plug-ins bundled into this feature:

org.eclipse.contribution.junit-feature/feature.xml
```
<plugin
  id="org.eclipse.contribution.junit"
  version="1.0.0"/>
```

The good news is this feature manifest can be generated by a PDE wizard: **New Project > Plug-in Development > Feature Project.** You name the feature and select the plug-ins to be bundled. It is simple, but as mentioned above, do not forget to specify the license text in the **Information** tab.

Our feature is ready to be made available for installation.

10.3   Contributing

Just as a feature bundles a set of plug-ins, an *update site* makes a set of features available at a URL. This can be on the web or in a file system. Eclipse users can visit your update site and download and install one or more features. Users can bookmark an update site and query it on a regular basis for new versions of installed features.

A site is represented by a directory, as shown in Figure 10.7.

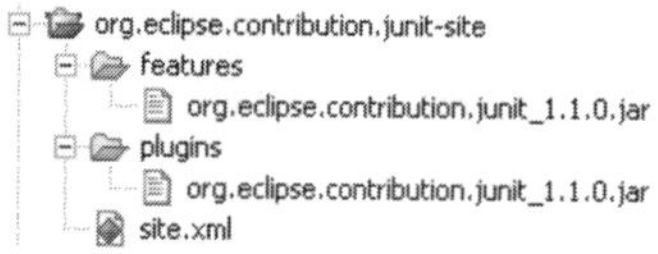

```
□ ☐ org.eclipse.contribution.junit-site
    □ ☐ features
              ☐ org.eclipse.contribution.junit_1.1.0.jar
    □ ☐ plugins
              ☐ org.eclipse.contribution.junit_1.1.0.jar
         ☐ site.xml
```

Figure 10.7

The *features* directory contains the Java-archived form of the features with the version numbers encoded in the file names. You can have several versions of a feature simultaneously available on a site. The *plugins* directory similarly contains the archived form of the plug-ins referenced by the features, again, with the version numbers encoded in the file names. Finally, *site.xml* is the site manifest, containing a description of the contents of the site.

org.eclipse.contribution.junit-site/site.xml
```
<site>
  <feature
    id="org.eclipse.contribution.junitfeature"
    url="features/org.eclipse.contribution.junitfeature_1.0.0.jar"
    version="1.0.0"/>
</site>
```

The `id` of the feature is the name of the feature's directory, suitably sanitized. The URL is the relative location of the archived form of the feature.

The simplest way to create an update site is to use PDE's site creation wizard. The site creation wizard creates a project for your update site. You need to add the features to the site. Be sure to the check the features to make them publicly available. The manifest editor for *site.xml* will build the site's directory structure when you click **Build Now** on the **Build** tab.

To test your new site, go to the Install/Update perspective (**Help > Software Updates > Update Manager**). In the **Feature Updates** view, navigate to your Eclipse workspace directory under **My Computer.** You should see the site as an update site `org.eclipse.contribution.junit-site` instead of a generic folder (see Figure 10.8).

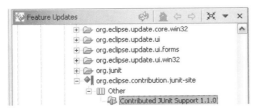

Figure 10.8

If the site appears to be empty, check that you have saved the *site.xml*. We can now test the update site by installing the feature into our host Eclipse installation. Up to now the feature is only stored in the our development workspace. To test the update site, select the *org.eclipse.contribution.junit-feature;* its summary shows up in the **Preview** view, shown in Figure 10.9.

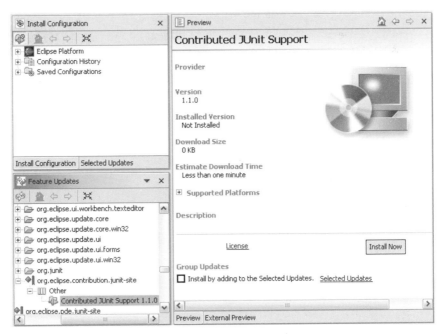

Figure 10.9

Because we followed the License Rule, the **Install Now** button is shown and we can install the contributed JUnit feature. Once you have stepped through the installer you are asked if you want to restart Eclipse. After Eclipse restarts you have the contributed JUnit functionality available in your host workbench.

Now the update site is ready to be pushed to a web site. You can do so manually via file transfer protocol (FTP) or WebDav. Eclipse also has plug-ins to incrementally deploy features and sites using either of these protocols.

10.4 Forward Pointers

○ FTP and WebDav plug-ins are available from the Eclipse update site: *http://download.eclipse.org/updates*.

○ *Making a new version*—Increment the plug-in version numbers. Increment the feature version number. Build the site. Upload the new contents. Increment the version numbers so install/update discovers the new version.

○ *Information about a feature*—You can define additional information for a feature in a *feature plug-in*. A feature plug-in is a plug-in referenced by a feature with the same name as the feature. In its *about.ini* file, you can define additional attributes like whether the feature has a welcome page, its image, initial perspective, and a link to tips and tricks for using the feature. For an example, refer to the `org.eclipse.jdt` plug-in; it is the feature plug-in for the JDT feature.

○ *Primary feature*—One of the installed features can be tagged as the primary feature. The primary feature defines the "branding" of an Eclipse product. This includes attributes like the splash screen, the initial welcome page, and the **About** dialog.

CHAPTER 11

Closing Circle One

Before we move onto the next circle, where we will add enough functionality to our plug-in to fully integrate testing into programming and touch all of the activities necessary to build production-quality plug-ins, let's review what we've seen so far.

Much of the architecture of Eclipse is driven from the desire to build the whole environment out of plug-ins but to maintain fast startup. Startup time should be constant, not proportional to the number of installed plug-ins. In particular, you don't want to pay for plug-ins that are installed but not used. If I have a C++ environment installed but I don't use it, it should have no impact at all on my computing experience. Resolving the conflict between building the system out of lots of little pieces and being able to start up quickly drives the Eclipse architecture.

We laid out a design for our contributed JUnit plug-in as a core test runner with various presentations of tests and results. Our goal in Circle One was to take the core test runner through the entire Contribution Circle.

PDE extends the basic Eclipse Java development functionality with support for editing the declarative plug-in description (the manifest, stored in *plugin.xml*). PDE lets us run our new plug-in in a separate workspace.

Rather than clump all of our functionality together monolithically, we divided our system into the core test-running functionality and an extension point that would allow presentations to be notified of testing progress. Extensions were only loaded the first time a test was run, keeping startup time to a minimum.

We packaged our plug-in for automated installation and discovery. The plug-in was put into a feature and the feature was placed on an update site. The plug-in is ready to be extended.

CHAPTER 12

Interlude: Test-Driven Plug-In Development

When we began writing the code for this book, we did it in a classic explor-atory style. We thought of some functionality we'd like to add. We browsed in Eclipse to get some ideas about how to implement it. We put some code together. We looked at the result of the new code in the run-time workspace. We repeated as necessary.

As we made progress, we quickly learned developing only in the explor-atory style we were not able to write code without errors. Say we had added some functionality. Were we sure we hadn't broken something? We aggres-sively refactored our code to improve its structure. Were we sure we hadn't broken something? We wanted a way to regain confidence in our code.

The benefits we were looking for from our development strategy were:

○ Confidence—We wanted to be able to add and restructure functionality without worrying about breaking something.

○ Learning—We wanted to be able to quickly and confidently learn about new areas in Eclipse.

○ Design—We wanted encouragement to think appropriately about design, especially the external interface of our code, before thinking about implementation.

One way we develop is with Test-Driven Development (TDD). The TDD cycle looks like this:

1. Write a test for the next bit of functionality you have in mind. The test should succeed only when the functionality has been implemented correctly.

2. Make the test compile by creating stubs for all the missing classes and methods referenced by the test.

3. Run the test. It should fail.

4. Implement just enough functionality to get the test to succeed.

5. Clean up the implementation as much as possible, typically by removing duplication.

Running the tests thrown off by TDD provides us with confidence, especially in high-stress situations. The tests can also provide objective feedback about whether we have learned a concept. For us, writing the tests is as much an exercise in design as it is in testing. But how do we apply the TDD cycle to plug-in development?

In this interlude we describe how to do test-driven plug-in development. The resulting picture will be complex. The fact that our example is about a plug-in for running tests makes it even more challenging to describe. We therefore present the plug-in testing picture in three steps:

1. We start with PDE JUnit. It is an extension to JUnit for running plug-in tests.

2. Next we introduce a test setup for running plug-in tests.

3. Finally, we write a plug-in test for our contributed plug-in.

From now on we have to deal with different JUnit test runners and we therefore need to be more precise when talking about them. These are the test runners and how we refer to them:

○ **Eclipse JUnit**—the JUnit support that is integrated in Eclipse.

○ **PDE JUnit**—JUnit support for plug-in tests.

○ **Contributed JUnit**—the JUnit support we implement in our example. It has similar functionality to Eclipse JUnit. It doesn't provide any plug-in testing support as offered by PDE JUnit.

12.1   PDE JUnit

Eclipse JUnit allows you to run tests for normal Java applications. When you run a plug-in test with Eclipse JUnit the test fails since it doesn't run inside an Eclipse workspace.

Therefore, to run plug-in tests you needed an extended version of JUnit that takes care of initializing Eclipse and that runs the tests inside an Eclipse workspace. This is the purpose of PDE JUnit.

Installing PDE JUnit

Since Milestone 3 of the Eclipse 3.0 development stream, PDE JUnit comes with Eclipse, so no additional installation steps are required. When using earlier versions you have to install PDE JUnit yourselves. You can download a zipped version of the PDE JUnit plug-in from *www.dev.eclipse.org*. To install the zipped version of PDE JUnit you

1. Go to *www.dev.eclipse.org/viewcvs/index.cgi/~checkout~/jdt-ui-home/ plugins/org.eclipse.jdt.junit/index.html*.

2. Click on the latest release of PDE JUnit. It will download and unzip.

3. Extract to your *ECLIPSE_HOME/plugins* directory.

4. Restart Eclipse.

There is also an update site from which you can install PDE JUnit using the Eclipse update manager. The URL to the update site is *www.dev.eclipse.org/ viewcvs/index.cgi/~checkout~/jdt-ui-home/plugins/org.eclipse.jdt.junit/PDE-JUnit-Site*.

After you have installed PDE JUnit the **Run As** menu has an additional item for starting a PDE JUnit test, as shown in Figure 12.1.

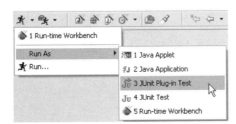

Figure 12.1

To understand how launching with PDE JUnit works, let's first take a closer look at some of the other launching options. Each of these launching options defines a different setup for running a particular target.

We start with the simplest one: **Run As > Java Application.** It starts a main class from a project in the workspace in a separate VM, as shown in Figure 12.2.

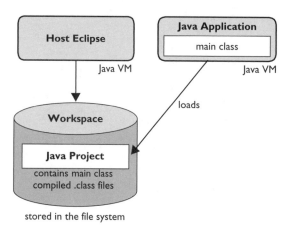

Figure 12.2   A Java Application Is Launched in a Separate VM

Next let's consider the setup when launching a JUnit test with **Run As > JUnit Test**. This launching option starts a JUnit test runner executing tests in the workspace in a separate VM, as shown in Figure 12.3.

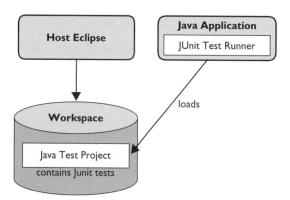

Figure 12.3   The JUnit Test Runner Runs Tests in a Separate VM

Run As > Run-Time Workbench is a PDE-contributed launching option. It launches a run-time Eclipse with the plug-in projects contained in your workspace.[1] Starting a second Eclipse will also create a run-time workspace that is initially empty (see Figure 12.4).

---

1. PDE supports different ways to set up and launch a run-time Eclipse workbench, but this is the one we use for plug-in development.

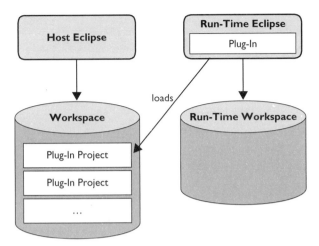

Figure 12.4   PDE Launches a Run-Time Eclipse from the Workspace

Now on to the next step: running plug-in tests. Before we can run them we have to write some tests. In Eclipse everything is a plug-in, including the tests. When launching with **Run As > JUnit Plug-in Test** we get the setup shown in Figure 12.5.

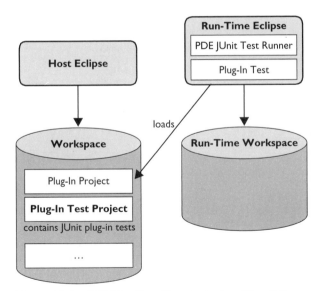

Figure 12.5   PDE JUnit Runs Tests in the Run-Time Eclipse

In this setup the following steps are executed:

1. The run-time Eclipse is started from the workspace.
2. Control is passed to a JUnit test runner that runs the tests.
3. The JUnit test runner runs all tests inside the same workspace.
4. When all tests are finished Eclipse is shut-down.

Now we are ready to implement the simplest plug-in test. Create a new plug-in project, as in the Hello, World example (Chapter 3). To write a test, we have to refer to the JUnit types like `junit.framework.TestCase`. To do so we need to have access to the JUnit library. Because everything in Eclipse is a plug-in, the JUnit library is also packaged in a separate plug-in called `org.junit`.

---

org.junit—A Library Plug-In

How can you make an existing library available to Eclipse? The only way to add code to Eclipse is in the form of a plug-in. This means we have to package an existing library as a plug-in. The Eclipse developers have already done this for JUnit and created a plug-in `org.junit`. The `org.junit` plug-in doesn't contribute to any extension point. It contains the *junit.jar* and defines it as the plug-in's run-time library in the plug-in manifest as shown below:

```
<plugin
  name="JUnit Testing Framework"
  id="org.junit"
  version="3.8.1"
  provider-name="org.junit">

  <runtime>
    <library name="junit.jar">
      <export name="*"/>
    </library>
  </runtime>
</plugin>
```

The `org.junit` plug-in doesn't contribute to any extension point so it is also referred to as a *library plug-in*. You can create library plug-ins for libraries you want to use with Eclipse plug-ins.

The `org.junit` plug-in illustrates a good practice for integrating an existing tool:

○ Create a library plug-in for the existing code (`org.junit`).

○ Create a separate plug-in that integrates the tool into Eclipse (`org.eclipse.jdt.junit`).

The default dependencies of a new plug-in are `org.eclipse.core.resources` and `org.eclipse.ui`. To get access to `org.junit` at runtime, we need to add it to the `requires` element of the plug-in manifest:

```
<requires>
  <import plugin="org.eclipse.core.resources"/>
  <import plugin="org.eclipse.ui"/>
  <import plugin="org.junit"/>
</requires>
```

To get access to the JUnit class at buildtime we add `org.junit` to the build class path. Let PDE take care of this by executing **Compute Build Path** on the **Dependencies** tab of the manifest editor. Here's the world's simplest JUnit test:

```
public class ExampleTest extends TestCase {
  public void testNothing() {
  }
}
```

When you run the ExampleTest with **Run As > JUnit Plug-in Test,** you get the familiar JUnit feedback, but you'll see a new workbench created before the tests are run. When the tests are finished, the workbench will disappear (see Figure 12.6).

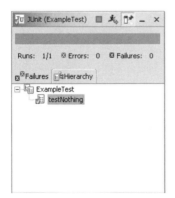

Figure 12.6

Test Plug-Ins

Should the tests live in the plug-in we are creating? It's tempting to put them together and avoid a proliferation of plug-ins. However, aesthetics and practicality both argue for putting tests in a separate plug-in. The aesthetic argument is based on plug-in dependencies: You'd like each plug-in to have the minimal set of prerequisite plug-ins. If you have tests in a plug-in, you'll need to depend on `org.junit`, or you'll need to carry around a copy of the JUnit JAR file. This extra dependency is not necessary for proper functioning of your plug-in, so it should be avoided, if possible. The practical argument stems from our desire to test-drive all aspects of our plug-in. We need to create the test plug-in first, then make it depend on our new plug-in in order to completely drive the creation of our new plug-in from tests.

12.2   A Test Project Fixture

PDE JUnit starts a test run in a fresh and empty workspace. Most serious plug-in tests don't run in an empty workspace. They need a workspace containing some data. For example, JDT tests operate on Java projects containing Java source code. Tests for our Contributed JUnit test runner operate on a Java project containing JUnit test cases. To simplify the creation of such test projects in the run-time workspace we implemented the `TestProject` class. It helps us create the *fixture* for a test, a predictable initial state so the test can run consistently. `TestProject` allows us to create a project, create a package inside the project, and create a class inside the package. It goes through all the Eclipse details necessary to create a project and its contents.

How do you use `TestProject` to create a fixture? First we have to remember that PDE JUnit runs all tests inside the same workspace. This avoids having to start Eclipse for each test and speeds up test runs. However, tests should leave the world exactly as they found it. Therefore, you should create the fixture project inside the `setUp()` method of a test case and you should dispose the fixture project in `tearDown()` as shown below:

```
public class SomePluginTest extends TestCase {
  private TestProject testProject;

  protected void setUp() throws Exception {
    testProject= new TestProject();
  }
```

```
protected void tearDown() throws Exception {
  testProject.dispose();
  }
}
```

When you forget to implement `tearDown()` and dispose the fixture project you will get test failures. The next test will not be able to create a fresh test project fixture since the test project already exists.

For a particular test you populate the test project using methods provided by `TestProject`. The `testSomeTest()` illustrates how to create a Java project with the contents shown in Figure 12.7.

```
Project-1
  src
    pack1
      AClass.java
        AClass
          m()
  JRE System Library [jdk1.4.1]
```

Figure 12.7

```
public void testSomeTest() throws CoreException {
  IPackageFragment package= testProject.createPackage("pack1");
  IType type= testProject.createType(package, "AClass.java",
      "public class AClass {public void m(){}}");
  }
}
```

`TestProject` provides the following methods:

- ❍ `TestProject()`—Creates a Java project named *Project-1* with a folder *bin* and assigns it the Java nature. This configures the Java builder for the project. The project's build class path is set up to include the system libraries (*rt.jar*, etc.). The project's output folder is set to the *bin* folder.

- ❍ `IPackageFragment createPackage(String name)`—Returns a package with the given name in the project's source folder, *src*. A source folder is created if it doesn't exist yet and it is added to the project's build class path.

- ❍ `IType createType(IPackageFragment p, String compilation-Unit, String source)`—Creates a compilation unit in the given package and returns the top-level type. The argument source defines the contents of the compilation unit.

- ❍ `addJar(String plugin, String jar)`—Adds a JAR file from a plug-in contained in your Eclipse installation to the build class path.

- ❍ `dispose()`—Deletes the project from the workspace.

Most of these methods throw exceptions. To simplify your tests, you should add `throws` declarations to your test methods instead of catching them yourself. There is no need to catch them yourself since JUnit does it for you.

The full source of the `TestProject` fixture is included in Appendix B. It is a good example of how to create and initialize projects programmatically. To complete our test set-up picture we can now add a `TestProject` fixture to the run-time workspace, as shown in Figure 12.8.

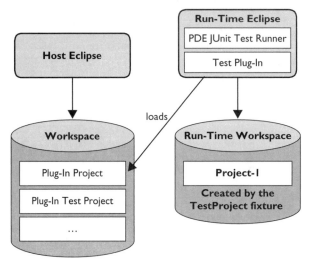

Figure 12.8   The TestProject Fixture Creates a Project in the Run-Time Workspace

12.3   Testing the Contributed JUnit Plug-In

The techniques so far are useful for plug-in testing in general. Now, let's use these techniques to implement a test case for our Contributed JUnit plug-in. The test is presented here after you've seen the code of the Contributed JUnit plug-in, but we actually wrote it before we wrote the code. The test we show verifies that a test failure properly notifies the `ITestRunListener`. Here are our initial steps:

1. Create a plug-in project `org.eclipse.contribution.junit.test`.

2. Add the following imports in the plug-in's manifest file:

```
<import plugin="org.junit"/>
<import plugin="org.eclipse.contribution.junit"/>
<import plugin="org.eclipse.jdt.core"/>
<import plugin="org.eclipse.core.resources"/>
<import plugin="org.eclipse.jdt.launching"/>
```

We need to import `org.junit` since we are writing JUnit tests. We import `org.eclipse.contribution.junit` since these are the classes we are testing. The other imports are required by the `TestProject` class.

3. Create a package `org.eclipse.contribution.junit.test` in the project's source folder *src*.

4. Copy the `TestProject` into this package.

5. Create a JUnit test case called `ListenerTest` in `org.eclipse.contribution.junit.test`.

Now let's start with the `ListenerTest`'s test setup.

org.eclipse.contribution.junit.test.ListenerTest
```
public class ListenerTest extends TestCase {
  private TestProject project;

  protected void setUp() throws Exception {
    project= new TestProject();
  }

  protected void tearDown() throws Exception {
    project.dispose();
  }
}
```

Our Contributed JUnit plug-in runs tests. We therefore need to set up a Java project containing test cases. With the help of `TestProject` we implement a `testFailure()` method and create a project with a single package *pack1* containing a class `FailedTest` with a failing test method `testFailure()`:

org.eclipse.contribution.junit.test/ListenerTest
```
public void testFailure() throws Exception {
    IPackageFragment pack= project.createPackage("pack1");
    IType type= project.createType(pack, "FailTest.java",
      "public class FailTest extends junit.framework.TestCase {"+
      "public void testFailure() {fail();}}"
    );
    project.addJar("org.junit", "junit.jar");
}
```

Since our code refers to JUnit classes the project has to include the JUnit JAR file on its build class path. We can use the JUnit JAR file that is contained in the library plug-in `org.junit`.

To run the failing test with the Contributed JUnit plug-in we call `JUnitPlugin.getPlugin().run(type)`.

This will run the test contained in the project created by the `TestProject` fixture using the Contributed JUnit test runner. However, until now we haven't tested anything. We have to verify that the `ITestRunListener`'s testFailure() method is called properly. How can we test such a call back? These are the steps:

1. Implement a listener inside ListenerTest.

2. Record the fact that the listener was called in the listener implementation.

3. Register the listener with the Contributed JUnit plug-in and run the failing test. We will register the listener as a dynamic listener, since it should only be registered during the test run.

4. Verify with an assert that the recorded value is the expected one.

We implement the test listener as a static inner class of ListenerTest. We only implement the testFailure() method; all the other listener methods are implemented to do nothing:

org.eclipse.contribution.junit.test.ListenerTest$Listener
```
public static class Listener implements ITestRunListener {
  String testFailed;
  public void testFailed(String klass,String method,String trace) {
    testFailed=method + " " + klass;
  public void testsStarted(int testCount) {
  }
  public void testsFinished() {
  }
  public void testStarted(String klass, String method) {
  }
}
```

In testFailed() we capture the failed test information in a string that we can easily verify with an assertion.[2] We can now complete the testFailure() test:

org.eclipse.contribution.junit.test.ListenerTest
```
public void testFailure() throws Exception {
  pack= project.createPackage("pack1");
  IType type= project.createType(pack, "FailTest.java",
    "public class FailTest extends junit.framework.TestCase {"+
    "public void testFailure() {fail();}}"
  );
  project.addJar("org.junit", "junit.jar");
  Listener listener= new Listener();
  JUnitPlugin.getPlugin().addTestListener(listener);
  JUnitPlugin.getPlugin().run(type);
  assertEquals("testFailure pack1.FailTest", listener.testFailed);
}
```

We tested other listener behavior in a single test called testRunning().

---

2. This technique, Log String, was described in *Test-Driven Development: By Example*.

Now that we have tests, we run them with PDE JUnit by executing **Run > Run As > JUnit Plug-in Test**. The dialog with test results will pop up. This dialog comes from the contributed test-run listener. We will implement a better UI for test results in the next chapter and since this dialog gets annoying let's remove this contributed listener. We remove both its declaration in the manifest file and its implementation in the `RunTestAction`.

org.eclipse.contribution.junit/plugin.xml
```
<extension
  point="org.eclipse.contribution.junit.listeners">
  <listener
    class="org.eclipse.contribute.junit.RunTestAction$Listener">
  </listener>
</extension>
```

We will add more test classes as we go. When we want to run all tests, then we let PDE JUnit find all the tests inside the `org.eclipse.contribution.junit.test` package for us. To do so we select the package and execute **Run > Run As > JUnit Plug-in Test**. This will run all our tests without having to manually maintain a JUnit `TestSuite`.

Those who have studied the details of the Contributed JUnit test runner know that the call `JUnitPlugin.getPlugin().run(type)` creates a separate VM to run tests. Now we have three VMs. Figure 12.9 shows the setup when running tests verifying the proper behavior of the Contributed JUnit plug-in.

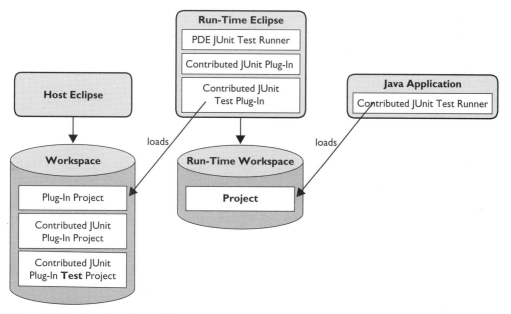

Figure 12.9   Our Contributed Test Runner Runs in a Third VM

12.4   And Now...

With test-driven development and the beginnings of our new Contributed JUnit plug-in, we're ready to make progress on new functionality. Circle Two will introduce new features to our test runner, forcing us (just coincidentally) to show you new areas in Eclipse. From time to time, we'll extend our discussion to include tests for the functionality we write about (see Figure 12.10). In addition to illustrating how to write plug-in tests, this also allows us to touch on various aspects of the Eclipse APIs.

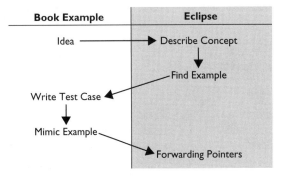

Figure 12.10   Chapter Flow with a Test Case

PART III

Circle Two:
The Rest of the Plug-In

Circle One has left us with the basics of a plug-in. We have some functionality running, we can deploy it for easy installation, and, with the testing techniques just introduced, we can extend it.

By the end of Circle Two we will integrate our test runner more deeply into Eclipse, touching along the way most of the areas that you will encounter as you write your own contributions. In addition, we will surround our plug-in with all the trappings of a full-fledged product.

In this circle, we'll encounter the following topics:

○ A view built out of existing widgets (Chapter 13)

○ A context menu that accepts contributions (Chapter 14)

○ A new kind of marker (Chapter 15 and Chapter 16)

○ Searching a Java project programmatically (Chapter 17)

○ A custom nature and builder (Chapter 18)

○ A new project property page (Chapter 19)

○ Exception handling and error logging (Chapter 20)

○ Tracing (Chapter 21)

○ Long-running operations supporting **Cancel** (Chapter 22)

○ A tabular display (Chapter 23)

○ A simple editor (Chapter 24)

○ Observing changes to the Java model (Chapter 25)

○ Perspectives (Chapter 26)

○ General contributions to help and context-sensitive help (Chapter 27)

○ Internationalization (Chapter 28)

○ Publishing an interface for other programmers (Chapter 29)

If you are feeling confused about where in Eclipse you are as you work through this circle, you may want to skim Circle Three for the corresponding information. Circle Three gives you more detail about the Eclipse architecture, so you can place what you are doing in the tutorial in the context of Eclipse as a whole.

CHAPTER 13

Viewing Results

A dialog is too intrusive to use as an interface for displaying test results. Over time we'd like to integrate the tests more thoroughly into the flow of programming, much as the compiler has gone from being a separate tool to becoming air—something vital that's always around. A step in the right direction is to display test results in a view. If we run a test successfully, the view should turn green. If a test fails, the view should turn red.

In this chapter we'll see

○ How to add a view extension

○ How to put a widget in a view

○ How to change the widget's color based on the updates it receives

13.1 Contributing a View

We want to add a view that will change colors based on the results of running tests. The views in Eclipse live in pages of the workbench window, as shown in Figure 13.1.

This picture shows that the workbench window has several pages, only one of which is active at a time. Each page contains views. Shown here are some of the views in the Java perspective. We'll need to get our view installed in this list.

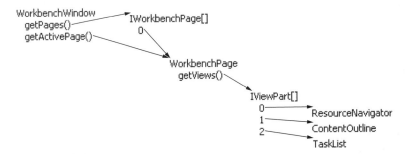

Figure 13.1   Views Live in Pages

Views are extensions of `org.eclipse.ui.views`. We can look at `Content-Outline`, for example:

org.eclipse.ui/plugin.xml
```
<extension
  point="org.eclipse.ui.views">
  ...
  <view
    name="%Views.ContentOutline"
    icon="icons/full/cview16/outline_co.gif"
    category="org.eclipse.ui"
    class="org.eclipse.ui.views.contentoutline.ContentOutline"
    id="org.eclipse.ui.views.ContentOutline">
  </view>
  ...
</extension>
```

In a pattern that is becoming familiar, the `view` extension point has a collection of elements, each of which declares a view class to use when creating the view. The `icon` and `category` are used to present the view in **Windows > Show View**. We won't bother with this for our example.

Since we are test-driving our code when possible, the next thing we have to do is figure out how to test our new view. To start we create a new test case `ViewTest` in our test plug-in `org.eclipse.contribution.junit.test`. Since we reference classes from `org.eclipse.ui` we add an import of this plug-in to the test plug-in's manifest and also update the project's build class path.

For the moment, it will be a step forward just to make the view appear. We can test this by asking the active page to display a view whose `id` is `org.eclipse.contribution.junit.resultsView`. First we need a utility method which will return the current active page:

org.eclipse.contribution.junit.test/ViewTest
```
private IWorkbenchPage getPage() {
  IWorkbench workbench= PlatformUI.getWorkbench();
```

```
IWorkbenchWindow window= workbench.getActiveWorkbenchWindow();
return window.getActivePage();
}
```

`PlatformUI` is a Façade[1] for accessing the Eclipse user interface. We use it to get at the workbench.

Using this, we can write our test. Tests should leave the world in exactly the state they found it. We're careful to close the view before leaving the test:

org.eclipse.contribution.junit.test/ViewTest
```
public void testShowHide() throws PartInitException {
  IViewPart view= getPage().showView(
    "org.eclipse.contribution.junit.resultView"
  );
  getPage().hideView(view);
}
```

This is an odd kind of test, containing no assertions. We often start with such tests when we're taking baby steps. They always grow some assertions. Even without assertions, running the test gives us feedback—Eclipse can't create the view (probably because we haven't implemented it). We use the common JUnit practice of just propagating exceptions—in this case, the `PartInitException`.

```
org.eclipse.ui.PartInitException: Could not create view: org.
eclipse.contribution.junit.testView
```

Copying the structure of our example, we next declare our view as an extension:

org.eclipse.contribution.junit/plugin.xml
```
<extension
  point="org.eclipse.ui.views">
  <view
    id="org.eclipse.contribution.junit.resultView"
    name="Contributed Result View"
    class="org.eclipse.contribution.junit.ResultView">
  </view>
</extension>
```

Running the test we get a new error message:

```
org.eclipse.ui.PartInitException[0]: org.eclipse.core.runtime.
CoreException[2]: java.lang.ClassNotFoundException: org.eclipse.
contribution.junit.ResultView
```

---

1. See E. Gamma, R. Helm, R. Johnson, and J. Vlissides. *Design Patterns: Elements of Reusable Object-Oriented Software.* Addison-Wesley, Reading, MA, 1995.

Looking for extenders of `org.eclipse.ui.views`, we find, for example, `ContentOutline`. `ContentOutline` is a subclass of `ViewPart`, as are most implementors of `IViewPart` (check this with **Navigate > Open Type In Hierarchy...**). We will subclass `ResultView` from `ViewPart` also.

Interface/Implementation Pair

`IViewPart`/`ViewPart` is an example of the Interface/Implementation Pair pattern that you will find in several places in the Eclipse API. `IViewPart` defines the protocol for how clients interact with the view part. Method signatures referring to a view in the Eclipse API therefore reference `IViewPart`. `ViewPart` is an abstract base intended for implementors of a view. It provides additional default behavior and simplifies implementing a view part.

The class creation wizard is good enough to provide stubs for the abstract superclass methods:

org.eclipse.contribution.junit/ResultView
```
public class ResultView extends ViewPart {
  public void createPartControl(Composite parent) {
  }

  public void setFocus() {
  }
}
```

And our test passes. By running a run-time workbench, we can see our view. Figure 13.2 shows how to display our new view.

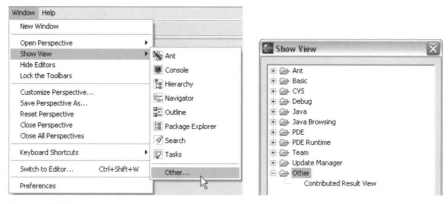

Figure 13.2

The result (Figure 13.3) is a view with no contents.

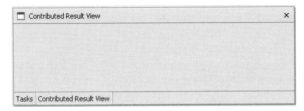

Figure 13.3

13.2   **Listening to Testing Progress**

Now we want the view to turn colors when tests run. If all tests run successfully, the view should turn green. If a test fails, it should turn red. We can divide the work to get this functionality running into two parts:

1. Setting up an `ITestRunListener`

2. Responding to the test callbacks by changing the color

How do we want to set up a listener? One way would be to extend the test listener extension point we declared towards the end of Circle One. However, this would mean that our view would have to handle test callbacks whether it was open or not. Using a dynamic listener better matches the life cycle of the view because the view can be opened and closed.

We first tested for this by checking to make sure a listener with a certain class was on the list of listeners. This seemed to us a bit too tied to the implementation. A simpler testing strategy is to just count the listeners. When the view opens there should be one more listener than before, and after the view is closed there should be the same number as at the start. First we introduce a couple of helper methods to make the tests read better and we also store the view in an instance variable:

org.eclipse.contribution.junit.test/ViewTest

```
private ResultView view;

public void showView() throws PartInitException {
  view= (ResultView) getPage().showView(
       "org.eclipse.contribution.junit.resultView"
  );
}
public void hideView() {
  getPage().hideView(view);
}
```

This in place, we can count listeners:

org.eclipse.contribution.junit.test/ViewTest
```
public void testViewListener() throws PartInitException {
  int count= JUnitPlugin.getPlugin().getListeners().size();
  showView();
  try {
    assertEquals(count + 1,
      JUnitPlugin.getPlugin().getListeners().size());
  } finally {
    hideView();
  }
  assertEquals(count,
    JUnitPlugin.getPlugin().getListeners().size());
}
```

Now we need to make the test work. First, we need a stub listener inner class. It can be private, because no one else needs to use it:

org.eclipse.contribution.junit/ResultView$Listener
```
private class Listener implements ITestRunListener {
  public void testsStarted(int testCount) {
  }
  public void testsFinished() {
  }
  public void testStarted(String klass, String method) {
  }
  public void testFailed(String klass,String method,String trace) {
  }
}
```

We've already seen `createPartControl()`, the life-cycle method used to open a view. We don't have to create any widgets yet, but we do need to hook up a listener:

org.eclipse.contribution.junit/ResultView
```
private ITestRunListener listener;
public void createPartControl(Composite parent) {
  listener= new Listener();
  JUnitPlugin.getPlugin().addTestListener(listener);
}
```

We'll need to override a life-cycle method we haven't seen before, `dispose()`, to unhook the listener when the view is hidden. We need to be careful unhooking the listener, because it's possible for `dispose()` to be called without `create-PartControl()` being called first. `CreatePartControl()` is called as lazily as possible. It is only called *when* the view actually has become visible. However, `dispose` is always called independent of the view's visibility status. This is an asymmetry in the API life cycle (there is no `disposePartControl()`). This asymmetry in the API can easily result in `NullPointerExceptions`. Because we are using the presence of an object in the field `listener` as a flag, we need to make sure we clear the field after we've unhooked the listener.

org.eclipse.contribution.junit/ResultView
```
public void dispose() {
  if (listener != null)
    JUnitPlugin.getPlugin().removeTestListener(listener);
  listener= null;
}
```

The test passes. We now have a view that registers and unregisters a test listener. Next we need to respond to the test callbacks.

13.3 Changing Colors

We need to change the color of the view based on the results of running tests. First, how are we going to test? The form of these tests will be to open a view, run a test, and close the view. Since we don't need to do anything else when we are opening or closing the test, we can copy our previous test class to a new test class, `ViewColorTest` and we delete the existing test methods. We can then use JUnit's `setUp()` and `tearDown()` methods to guarantee that we close the view once it's been opened:

org.eclipse.contribution.junit.test/ViewColorTest
```
public void setUp() throws PartInitException {
  view= (ResultView) getPage().showView(
      "org.eclipse.contribution.junit.resultView"
  );
}

public void tearDown() {
  getPage().hideView(view);
}
```

It may seem a bit strange to devote a whole new testing class to this small change. We find that if we have the slightest difference in setup, it's worth it to have a new test class.

We'll work backwards to our first test, the one that makes sure that if the tests pass the view turns green. To test the color, we need access to the view's control. `Org.eclipse.swt.widgets.Control` represents an atomic widget on the screen. It is the abstract class in which the method `getBackground()` is defined.

Abstract-Class-Based APIs vs. Interface-Based APIs

Eclipse contains two styles of API definitions. We've seen the interface-based API before. In it, almost all the published APIs are in terms of interfaces. For example, we've seen `IType` already. We have no idea what concrete class will be used to represent any given type. In the other example we have seen `IViewPart` with its implementation pair `ViewPart`. Notice that when Eclipse uses an interface-based API this doesn't mean you are allowed to implement every interface. You should always check the API specification before implementing. Don't implement interfaces with comments like, "This interface is not intended to be implemented by clients."

SWT uses a different style of API definition. In it you will see real classes, like `Control` above. As a client, if you want to maintain maximum flexibility, it is your responsibility to use the most abstract class possible.

The assertion will compare the actual color of our control to the expected color:

org.eclipse.contribution.junit.test/ViewColorTest
```
public void testResultViewGreen() throws PartInitException {
  // Run tests
  Display display= view.getControl().getDisplay();
  Color green= display.getSystemColor(SWT.COLOR_GREEN);
  assertEquals(green, view.getControl().getBackground());
}
```

Programming by Intention

When writing code test-first we often invoke methods that we wish existed. For example, in the test above we call the not-yet-existing method `getControl()`. Quick Fix (Ctrl + 1) helps us to fix errors. One proposed fix for a not-yet-existing method is to create a stub for it:

```
             Color green= view.getControl().getDisplay().getSystemColor(SWT.COLOR
...
return listener;                              ● Create method 'getControl()' in ResultView.java

public Object getControl() {
// TODO Auto-generated method stub
return null;
}
}

        assertEquals(red, view.getControl().getBackground());
```

We want to create the effect of having successfully run a test inside test-
ResultViewGreen() without actually running a test, which would require
more setup. We can simulate the broadcast messages we expect to be generated by a correctly running test—starting and ending the tests. We simulate
test running by calling the ITestRunListener methods directly:

org.eclipse.contribution.junit.test/ViewColorTest
```
public void testResultViewGreen() throws PartInitException {
  view.getListener().testsStarted(0);
  view.getListener().testsFinished();
  Display display= view.getControl().getDisplay();
  Color green= display.getSystemColor(SWT.COLOR_GREEN);
  assertEquals(green, view.getControl().getBackground());
}
```

To make the test compile, we need to provide access to both a control and the
listeners of the ResultView. We use **Source > Generate Getters and Setters...**
to create the getters.

org.eclipse.contribution.junit/ResultView
```
private ITestRunListener listener;
private Control control;

public Control getControl() {
  return control;
}
public ITestRunListener getListener() {
  return listener;
}
```

The simplest control is a Label. We can initialize it in createPart-
Control():

org.eclipse.contribution.junit/ResultView
```
public void createPartControl(Composite parent) {
  listener= new Listener();
  JUnitPlugin.getPlugin().addTestListener(listener);
  control= new Label(parent, SWT.NONE);
}
```

For now, it suffices to set the background color of the control to green when
the tests finished. (We'll test for red on failure in a moment.) We get access to
a resource representing green exactly the same way we did in the test. It's common for work done writing the test to come in handy when the time comes to
make the test pass.

org.eclipse.contribution.junit/ResultView
```
public void testsFinished() {
  Display display= view.getControl().getDisplay();
```

```
Color green= display.getSystemColor(SWT.COLOR_GREEN);
control.setBackground(green);
}
```

The test for red is similar to the test for green. We simulate the failure of a test, then check to make sure the view is red. After the tests finish, the view should still be red. Since the actual class and method of the failing test don't matter at the moment, we can just fill in bogus values.

org.eclipse.contribution.junit.test/ViewColorTest
```
public void testResultViewRed() throws PartInitException {
  view.getListener().testsStarted(0);
  view.getListener().testFailed("class", "method", "trace");
  Display display= view.getControl().getDisplay();
  Color red= display.getSystemColor(SWT.COLOR_RED);
  assertEquals(red, view.getControl().getBackground());
  view.getListener().testsFinished();
  assertEquals(red, view.getControl().getBackground());
}
```

To make this work, we need to set a flag in the listener when the tests start running. If a test ever fails, the view's color is set to red. When the tests finish, the view is only set to green if all the tests succeeded:

org.eclipse.contribution.junit/ResultView$Listener
```
private boolean success;

public void testsStarted(int testCount) {
  success= true;
}

public void testsFinished() {
  if (success) {
    Display display= control.getDisplay();
    Color green= display.getSystemColor(SWT.COLOR_GREEN);
    control.setBackground(green);
  }
}

public void testFailed(String klass, String method, String trace) {
  Color red= control.getDisplay().getSystemColor(SWT.COLOR_RED);
  control.setBackground(red);
  success= false;
}
```

And the tests, both red and green, succeed. Now we have a view that turns green and red depending on the results of running a test. You may want to take a moment to start up a run-time workbench, show the view, and run a couple of tests to verify that the colors are correct. Over time we'd like our test suite to demonstrate satisfaction—if the tests all run we're perfectly satisfied with the behavior of our current functionality. The tests will never be perfect predictors, but over time we can hope to make them good enough that we can act like they are, with only occasional unpleasant surprises.

We'll clean-up one item before we move on. It is easy to forget even though Eclipse generates a To Do reminder for us. The class creation wizard created setFocus() as follows:

org.eclipse.contribution.junit/ResultView
```
public void setFocus() {
  //TODO Auto-generated method stub
}
```

Let's check the API specification for this method. When setFocus() is selected, we can select the method name and with **Open Super Implementation** from the context menu we can see the definition in IWorkbenchPart.

org.eclipse.ui/IWorkbenchPart
```
/**
 * Asks this part to take focus within the workbench.
 * <p>
 * Clients should not call this method (the workbench
 * calls this method at appropriate times).
 * </p>
 */
```

Our ResultView doesn't take focus yet. To fix this we just tell the Label created in createPartControl() to take the focus:

org.eclipse.contribution.junit/ResultView
```
public void setFocus() {
  control.setFocus();
}
```

It is good Eclipse practice to always check the API contract of methods you implement. This leads us to the Program to the API Contract rule:

> **PROGRAM TO API CONTRACT RULE**   Check and program to the Eclipse API contract.

The next feature we'll add to our user interface is a menu in the view. Before starting on that, we'll review. In this chapter we

○ Extended the org.eclipse.ui.views extension point

○ Wrote a test to show and hide the view

○ Implemented a new `IViewPart`

○ Tested and implemented a test listener tied to the life-cycle methods of our view

○ Tested and implemented changing the view's color in response to test runner broadcast messages

CHAPTER 14

Menu Contributions

In this chapter, we'll see how to create a context menu that accepts contributions.

Here's the scenario. We've written and run a test. It fails. We change code in various files to try to make the test pass. We'd like to rerun the failing tests without having to navigate back to our test class.

The view is still sitting there on the screen, balefully glaring red. We could add a pop-up menu to the view containing (at the moment) a single menu item to rerun the failing test. There are several other possible user interfaces, but this is one that will allow us to demonstrate implementing a contribution-enabled menu, so we'll go with this one at the moment. In any case, the UI is about to take a dramatic right-angle turn, so even if the current interface design isn't perfect, it won't be a problem for long.

14.1 Creating Context Menus

The Invitation Rule says that where possible, we should invite others to contribute to our contributions. Context menus are an excellent example. The contents of context-sensitive menus can be extremely complex:

○ Different combinations of items based on the selection or combination of selections

○ Complex enable/disable logic

Trying to express all the combinations in the manifest would result in either hideously complicated XML, or in menus having far too many items. Therefore a view's context menu is typically constructed in code in the view part. However, it is defined in a way that others can contribute to it. A context menu can only be shown when the view is visible, so creating a menu in code doesn't affect lazy loading.

To enable others to contribute, we have to tell Eclipse about our menu so it can still act as an extension point. Where will we find an example to copy? The workbench provides a set of standard views like the **Task, Navigator,** or **Bookmarks** views. These are all good examples to mimic. To find their implementation classes we do either of the following:

○ Perform a plug-in search and look for all declarations of the `org.eclipse.ui.views` extension point. Because the workbench follows the Fair Play Rule we will find its contributed views. The name space of the workbench is `org.eclipse.ui`.

○ Use the **Spider Navigator** to find the implementors.

Using the "Spider Click" to Find Objects of Interest

The Spider allows us to explore an object structure. The **Spider Navigator** shows top-level objects from the running Eclipse that are of interest for an object exploration. Another way to get at the object of interest is by using the magnifier in the toolbar of the **Spider Navigator** view. After clicking the toolbar item you can click at any visible object to start the exploration from there.

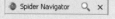 The clicked-on object is opened in the Spider canvas.

Let's take the **Task** view as the base for mimicking our implementation. In its source we find the following code related to creating a menu:

org.eclipse.ui.views.tasklist/TaskList
```
MenuManager menuManager = new MenuManager("#PopupMenu");
menuManager.setRemoveAllWhenShown(true);
menuManager.addMenuListener(new IMenuListener() {
  public void menuAboutToShow(IMenuManager manager) {
    TaskList.this.fillContextMenu(manager);
  }
});
Menu menu = menuManager.createContextMenu(table);
table.setMenu(menu);
getSite().registerContextMenu(menuManager, viewer);
```

To fill a context menu before it pops-up you register an `IMenuListener` with the menu manager. The listener is notified before the menu is shown so that you can fill its contents. The call to `setRemoveAllWhenShown(true)` makes sure that the menu is emptied before the listener is called to populate the menu. Finally, `registerContextMenu()` makes the menu known to Eclipse so that others can contribute to it.

How do menus fit in with views? Here is a picture showing the **Task List** and how it connects to its menu. The menu itself is associated with a `Widget`. Inside the menu is a list of items, as shown in Figure 14.1.

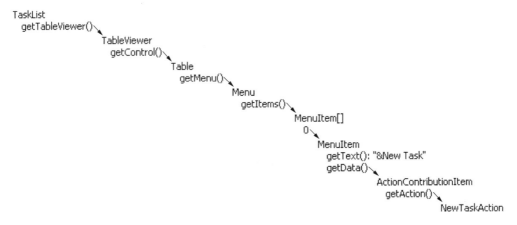

Figure 14.1   A Task List's Menu Contains Actions

Where is our test for all this? We couldn't write one. Eclipse doesn't provide public API to programatically force the creation of the contributed menu items. This is the first case where Eclipse's obsession with lazy loading made our testing job impossible. We had to rely on manual verification to make sure the menu item appeared as expected.

When we start up a run-time workbench and try to pop up a menu, nothing happens. The other examples of context menus we saw were all initialized in `createPartControl()`, so we'll do the good monkey thing and copy that structure:

org.eclipse.contribution.junit/ResultView
```
public void createPartControl(Composite parent) {
  listener= new Listener();
  JUnitPlugin.getPlugin().addTestListener(listener);
  control= new Label(parent, SWT.NONE);
  createContextMenu();
}

private void createContextMenu() {
  MenuManager menuManager = new MenuManager();
```

```
menuManager.setRemoveAllWhenShown(true);
menuManager.addMenuListener(new IMenuListener() {
  public void menuAboutToShow(IMenuManager manager) {
    fillContextMenu(manager);
  }
});
Menu menu= menuManager.createContextMenu(control);
control.setMenu(menu);
}
```

We register a menu listener so that we can populate the menu before it pops up. To get the correct menu items we look at how this is done in the task list. It populates its menus in `fillContextMenu()`:

org.eclipse.ui.views.tasklist/TaskList
```
void fillContextMenu(IMenuManager menu) {
  menu.add(newTaskAction);
  menu.add(gotoTaskAction);
  menu.add(new Separator());
  menu.add(new Separator(IWorkbenchActionConstants.MB_ADDITIONS));
  menu.add(new Separator(IWorkbenchActionConstants.MB_ADDITIONS+
    "-end"));
  menu.add(propertiesAction);
}
```

Here we see the pattern:

1. Add some items.

2. Add a separator.

3. Add more items.

4. Add two separators with well-known names meaning "put contributed menu items here."

Eclipse will only show separators as needed, so the adjacent separators aren't a problem. The name of the well-known separator is defined in the MB_ADDITIONS constant provided by the workbench and is defined as "additions." The convention is to contribute both an MB_ADDITIONS and an MB_ADDITIONS"-end" separator. This gives contributors the choice of making their contributions appear either at the top or at the bottom of the contributed items section.

Most of the context menus in views are built by explicitly adding menu items by calling IMenuManager.add(IAction). The advantage of explicitly adding actions is that you can control the order of presentation of menu items. You can group contributed items, but you can't precisely order them. Another advantage with explicitly built menus is it is easier to eliminate inappropriate items using logic in code, shortening view context menus (Relevance Rule).

This is an example where the Fair Play Rule is violated. A view's context menu is not using the same mechanisms as its clients. In practice, your context menus are likely to be a combination—first a set of items precisely placed by hand followed by a section for contributed items.

Following this pattern, we manually add a not yet implemented rerun action and add the special separators. The other thing we must do to prepare for contributions is to tell the workbench that this menu accepts contributions. In `TaskList`, the method we saw used was `registerContextMenu()`. We can try it, too:

org.eclipse.contribution.junit/ResultView
```
private void createContextMenu() {
  MenuManager menuManager = new MenuManager();
  menuManager.setRemoveAllWhenShown(true);
  menuManager.addMenuListener(new IMenuListener() {
    public void menuAboutToShow(IMenuManager manager) {
      fillContextMenu(manager);
    }
  });
  Menu menu= menuManager.createContextMenu(control);
  control.setMenu(menu);
  getSite().registerContextMenu(menuManager,
      getSite().getSelectionProvider());
}
```

> ### Site
>
> All workbench parts have a site. The site is a Façade, giving you access to the world outside the part—the ID of the workbench part, the ID of the plug-in, the shell, and the workbench window. Whenever possible, use the site to get at this information instead of trying to navigate to it through other objects.
>
> The workbench part hierarchy is mirrored in the workbench site hierarchy. Views and editors are kinds of parts. View sites and editor sites are kinds of sites.

We don't want to recreate our actions each time the context menu is popped up. We store an action in an field of the `ResultView`. We mimic the task list and create the action in `createPartControl()`. We don't want to create it sooner in the constructor. We defer action creation in order to create the action as lazily as possible.

org.eclipse.contribution.junit/ResultView
```
private Action rerunAction;
public void createPartControl(Composite parent) {
  listener= new Listener();
  JUnitPlugin.getPlugin().addTestListener(listener);
```

```
control= new Label(parent, SWT.NONE);
createContextMenu();
rerunAction= new RerunTestAction();
}
```

We implement `fillContextMenu()` to populate the menu called from the `IMenuListener`:

org.eclipse.contribution.junit/ResultView
```
void fillContextMenu(IMenuManager menu) {
  menu.add(rerunAction);
  menu.add(new Separator(IWorkbenchActionConstants.
    MB_ADDITIONS));
  menu.add(new Separator(IWorkbenchActionConstants.
    MB_ADDITIONS+"-end"));
}
```

We implement the `RerunTestAction` as an inner class of `ResultView`.

org.eclipse.contribution.junit.ResultView$RerunTestAction
```
private class RerunTestAction extends Action {
  private RerunTestAction() {
    setText("Re-run");
  }

  public void run(){
    rerunTest();
  }
}
```

The `run()` method called when the menu item is selected forwards the request to a `rerunTest()` method. We skip the implementation of the `rerunTest()` method, because it will not provide us with further insight into Eclipse. At this point the menu item will appear as expected (see Figure 14.2).

Figure 14.2

14.2   Contributing Menu Items

Now that the context menu is ready for contributions let's extend it. We extend `org.eclipse.ui.popupMenus` with a viewer contribution.

Object Contributions vs. Viewer Contributions

When contributing actions to a context menu you have the choice between an object contribution and a viewer contribution. An object contribution shows up whenever an object of a particular type is selected. A viewer contribution is targeted at a particular UI part (view or editor). When the action isn't selection sensitive, you must use a viewer contribution. An object contribution makes your action available in all views whenever an object of the particular type is selected.

Search all files called *plugin.xml* for `viewerContribution` with a file search (**Search > File...**). We'll use the viewer contributions in `org.eclipse.debug.ui` as a model:

org.eclipse.debug.ui/plugin.xml
```
<extension point = "org.eclipse.ui.popupMenus">
  <viewerContribution
    id="org.eclipse.debug.ui.debugview.popupMenu"
    targetID="org.eclipse.debug.ui.DebugView">
    <action
      id="org.eclipse.debug.ui.debugview.popupMenu.
        copyToClipboard"
      menubarPath="editGroup"
      class="org.eclipse.debug.internal.ui.actions.
        CopyToClipboardActionDelegate"
      label="%CopyToClipboardAction.label">
    </action>
  </viewerContribution>
</extension>
```

We need to extend `popupMenus` with an element called `viewerContribution`. The `targetID` specifies the unique identifier of the context menu you want to extend. The `targetID` is defined when a menu is registered with its site by calling `registerContextMenu()` as we just did.

We will copy the structure of the above extension point definition:

org.eclipse.contribution.junit/plugin.xml
```
<extension point="org.eclipse.ui.popupMenus">
  <viewerContribution
    id="org.eclipse.contribution.junit.popupMenu"
    targetID="org.eclipse.contribution.junit.resultView"/>
</extension>
```

Targeting Context Menus

The convention is to register a context menu under the same identifier as its part, or when a part has more than one context menu to use the part identifier as the prefix. For historical reasons there are some exceptions. The context menus of the text editors are identified differently. The target identifiers for some popular editors are:

- ○ `#CompilationUnitEditorContext`—The context menu in the Java editor.

- ○ `#CompilationUnitRulerContext`—The context menu in the Java editor's ruler.

- ○ `#ClassFileEditorContext`—The context menu in the Java class file editor.

- ○ `#ClassFileRulerContext`—The context menu in the class file editor's ruler.

Each viewer contribution contains several actions, each of which will translate into a menu item. Copying the structure above, we reach:

org.eclipse.contribution.junit/plugin.xml
```
<viewerContribution
  id="org.eclipse.contribution.junit.popupMenu"
  targetID="org.eclipse.contribution.junit.resultView">
  <action
    id = "org.eclipse.contribution.junit.popupMenu.item"
    label="Contributed Item"
    menubarPath="additions">
  </action>
</viewerContribution>
```

The menubar path must be set or the item won't appear. We contribute our action to the "additions" slot, which we added to the menu when we created it as the place holder for contributions. Running in a run-time workbench, the menu item appears (see Figure 14.3).

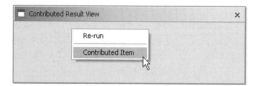

Figure 14.3

Where Can You Contribute Actions?

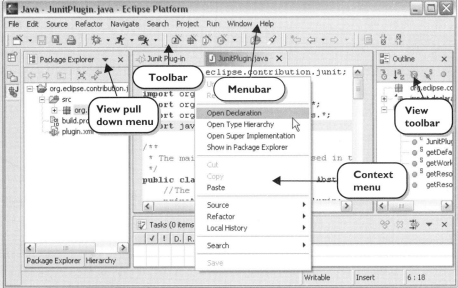

Plug-ins can contribute actions in many places:

○ *The main menubar and toolbar*—The extension point id is `org.eclipse.ui.`
`actionSets`. The action must conform to `org.eclipse.ui.IWorkbench-`
`WindowActionDelegate`.

○ *The view toolbar and pulldown menu*—The extension point id is `org.eclipse.ui.`
`viewActions`. The action must conform to `org.eclipse.ui.IViewAction-`
`Delegate`.

○ *The editor toolbar and menu*—The extension point is `org.eclipse.ui.editor-`
`Actions`. These actions will only be shown while the associated editor is active. The
action must conform to `org.eclipse.ui.IEditorActionDelegate`.

○ *The view and editor context menus*—The extension point id is `org.eclipse.ui.`
`popupMenus`. To contribute to a selected object, use the `objectContribution`
element. In this case, the action must conform to `org.eclipse.ui.IObject-`
`ActionDelegate`. To contribute to a specific menu independent of the selection,
use the `viewerContribution` element. In this case, the action must conform to
`org.eclipse.ui.IViewActionDelegate` when contributing to a view menu, and
`org.eclipse.ui.IEditorActionDelegate` when contributing to an edit menu.

The screen shot above illustrates the opportunities for extensions.

When we select the menu item, we get an error message because there is no class attached to the item. Since we contributed the class as a viewer contribution to a view, it has to conform to the `IViewActionDelegate`.

Next we want to leave the UI extensions for a while and look into some extensions at the Eclipse core (non-UI) level. First, we'll review what we did in this chapter. We

❍ Created a context menu

❍ Registered it to receive contributions

❍ Contributed a menu item to a view's context menu

14.3   Forward Pointers

❍ *Action filters*—For some object contributions the class of the selected object defined with the attribute `objectClass` isn't specific enough to conform to the Relevance Rule. A *filter element* describes an attribute of the selected object using name-value pairs. For example, to only contribute an action when the selected file is read-only you add the following filter element to the definition of an object contribution:

```
<extension point="org.eclipse.ui.popupMenus">
  <objectContribution
    id="…"
    objectClass="org.eclipse.core.resources.IFile">
    <filter name="readOnly" value="true"/>
    <action … />
  </objectContribution>
</extension>
```

You can define additional filters for your objects using the `IAction-Filter` interface.

❍ *Selection providers*—To enable the workbench to track the current selection, you have to register an `ISelectionProvider` with the site. The selection provider reveals a part's current selection and notifies its listeners about changes. The result view introduced in this chapter doesn't have a selection at all. In this particular case, we could also have created the context menu statically. (See Chapter 23 for a more complex view part example.)

CHAPTER 15

Failed Tests Are Compile Errors

Now we come to what passes for a dramatic plot twist in the story of a software project. We thought of ten or twenty features we could add to our JUnit view: progress bars, hierarchical test suite browsers, and on and on. However, something was missing—rhythm. Intimately interleaving testing and programming has a whole different rhythm than programming for a while, then testing for a while. The difference is much the same as the difference between an incremental compiler that runs all the time and a batch compiler that takes long enough to drink a café macchiato.

Bing, the light bulb lit. What if failed tests were treated just like compile errors? Every time we make a change to the source, the tests will be run. Any failing test will result in a marker just like the markers the compiler creates when it detects a syntax error. We'll use the same mechanisms to navigate semantic errors (failing tests) that we use to navigate compile errors.

We've seen this pattern repeated in Eclipse. At first a tool comes into Eclipse as a separate thing—view, editor, or even a separate perspective. With experience, though, you begin to see how the new functionality is really a variant of the existing functionality in Eclipse. By looking at your idea using the existing metaphors in Eclipse, you can make the user's experience of your tool less like a new thing to learn and more like a better Eclipse.

When you let a drop of blue paint fall into water, it is clear at first where the paint is and where the water is. Over time, though, the paint disperses and the boundary blurs. Wait long enough and you just have water that's now a little blue. It is so with contributions.

INTEGRATION RULE   Integrate, don't separate.

Markers and Resources

Resources are the Eclipse-internal representation of resources like files and folders. *Projects* are also resources, a folder with additional attributes that allow the contents to be built.

Markers are general-purpose annotations on resources. Any resource can have markers attached. Markers also have an open-ended set of attributes. By convention, sets of *attributes* are used to describe common markers like compile errors. Attributes are also used to indicate the marker location inside of, for instance, a text file. The `type` attribute and the marker extension point are used to group markers in a lattice. By making your marker a sub-type of an existing marker, your marker should work anywhere the existing marker works.

Markers are also used to note tasks to do, breakpoints, bookmarks, and search results. Markers appear in the task list, in special purpose views like the bookmarks view, and the margins of text editors. Markers are useful any time you want to provide feedback in the context of a particular resource.

Scalability comes into play with the Integration Rule. Imagine we have thousands of contributions. If each of them comes with their own pet mechanism, you have thousands of mechanisms and a big mess. By reusing the existing metaphors and extension points, you increase the value of your contribution. Blurring the boundaries between contributions gives the user the experience of a single tool.

We will implement our new "failed tests are compile errors" metaphor in steps:

1. Each time tests are run, we will turn failed tests into markers.

2. We will attach a property to a project to decide whether tests should run automatically.

3. We will install the test-run builder when the property is set.

4. We will automatically find the tests in a project.

CHAPTER 16

Test Failures as Markers

In this chapter, we want to transform test failures into markers, just like the markers used to indicate compile errors. In this chapter, we will

- ○ Explore the structure of markers
- ○ Attach markers to resources
- ○ Define a new marker type as an variation of an existing type
- ○ Delete markers from resources

16.1   Test for a Marker

Our first test will

- ○ Write a failing test
- ○ Run it
- ○ Ensure a marker was created

As good little monkeys, our first task is to see what a compile error looks like as a marker (see Figure 16.1).

Markers have types, represented by a field.[1] Other than `type`, each marker type stores different state.[2] Marker attributes are stored in a compact map

---

1. See "Common State" in K. Beck, *Smalltalk Best Practice Patterns*. Prentice Hall PTR, Upper Saddle River, NJ, 1997.

2. Ibid.

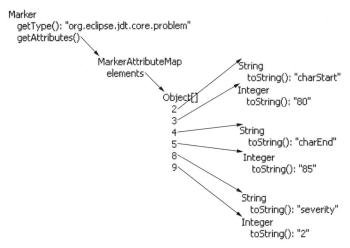

Figure 16.1   Marker Attributes Stored in a Compact Map

represented by an array with alternating keys and values. The values are constrained to be one of a small number of primitive types, because markers persist and Eclipse needs to support compatibility between releases of marker
definitions.

    Let's find an example of marker creation. Searching for users of `Resource.`
`createMarker()`, we find `TextSearchResultCollector.accept()`:

org.eclipse.search.internal.ui.text/TextSearchResultCollector.accept()
```
IResource resource= proxy.requestResource();
IMarker marker= resource.createMarker(SearchUI.SEARCH_MARKER);
HashMap attributes= new HashMap(4);
attributes.put(SearchUI.LINE, line);
attributes.put(IMarker.CHAR_START, new Integer(start));
attributes.put(IMarker.CHAR_END, new Integer(start + length));
attributes.put(IMarker.LINE_NUMBER, new Integer(lineNumber));
marker.setAttributes(attributes);
```

So we need a resource, then we need to create a marker, then we need to set
its attributes. We could use API for setting the attributes one at a time. If we
did that, though, all resource listeners would be notified each time an attribute
changed. Resource notifications are always expensive, because all participants
will react and try to update.

How are we going to test for the expected behavior? First, we need a failing test to run:

org.eclipse.contribution.junit.test/MarkerTest
```
public class MarkerTest extends TestCase {
  private TestProject testProject;
  private IPackageFragment pack;
```

```
private IType type;
protected void setUp() throws Exception {
  testProject= new TestProject();
  testProject.addJar("org.junit", "junit.jar");
  pack= testProject.createPackage("pack1");
  type= testProject.createType(pack, "FailTest.java",
    "public class FailTest extends junit.framework.TestCase {"+
      "public void testFailure() {fail();}}");
  }
}
```

When the test is finished, we need to delete our test project, something we do for all test cases involving `TestProject`:

org.eclipse.contribution.junit.test/MarkerTest
```
protected void tearDown() throws Exception {
  testProject.dispose();
}
```

We need a utility method to fetch all the markers representing test failures. Each marker type has a unique `id`. We'll use `org.eclipse.contribution.junit.failure` as the `id` for markers representing test failures:

org.eclipse.contribution.junit.test/MarkerTest
```
private IMarker[] getFailureMarkers() throws CoreException {
  IWorkspaceRoot root= ResourcesPlugin.getWorkspace().getRoot();
  return root.findMarkers(
    "org.eclipse.contribution.junit.failure",
    false,
    IResource.DEPTH_INFINITE);
}
```

We search starting at the workspace root, which is the parent of all resources. This ensures we'll get all markers. The additional parameters to `findMarkers()` are:

○ A boolean stating whether to search for subtypes. Remember that marker types form a lattice. In this case, we only want markers we've generated ourselves, not any possible future refinements. We can imagine in the future having a subtype for failures (violated assertions) and another for errors (unexpected exceptions).

○ An enumeration for how far down the resource tree to search. The values are just this resource, this resource and its immediate children, and all resources.

Now we're ready to write our test.

Ju   **org.eclipse.contribution.junit.test/MarkerTest**

```
public void testErrorMarker() throws Exception {
  JUnitPlugin.getPlugin().run(type);
  IMarker marker= getFailureMarkers()[0];
  IMethod method= type.getMethods()[0];
  int start= method.getSourceRange().getOffset();
  assertEquals(start, marker.getAttribute(IMarker.CHAR_START, 0));
  int end= start + method.getSourceRange().getLength();
  assertEquals(end, marker.getAttribute(IMarker.CHAR_END, 0));
  assertTrue(marker.isSubtypeOf(
    IJavaModelMarker.JAVA_MODEL_PROBLEM_MARKER));
  assertEquals(IMarker.SEVERITY_ERROR,
    marker.getAttribute(IMarker.SEVERITY, -1));
}
```

We use the Java model API to find the source range of the failing test method. We just created the test class with a single method, so we feel justified in fetching the first method. We check the marker attributes that position the marker in the source text. Selecting the marker should select the whole failing test.

Another attribute we care about is the type of the marker. The type should be a kind of Java model problem. This ensures that all the other Eclipse behaviors, like annotating icons in the package explorer with error ticks, will work correctly. The final attribute is the severity, which needs to be SEVERITY_ ERROR to get the correct error indication.

This seems to us like a lot to test for in one test. We took a few iterations before we discovered exactly which attributes were important to make the failure markers behave like compile errors. We added the assertions one at a time until the marker behaved as expected.

16.2   Passing the Project

The test fails. How are we going to implement it?

First, we need a refactoring. We need to know the project within which tests are running. Imagine we had ten different projects and tests were running simultaneously for all of them. When we started the tests for the tenth project, we would want to delete the markers, for just that project, in much the same way the compiler deletes the markers for a compilation unit when it begins to compile. We need to extend the API of test running in JUnitPlugin to take the project into account.

In JUnitPlugin.run(IType), since there is only one test class being run, the project is not ambiguous:

org.eclipse.contribution.junit/JUnitPlugin

```
public void run(IType type) throws CoreException {
  new TestRunner().run(new IType[] {type}, type.getJavaProject());
}
```

The `TestRunner` will save the project within which tests are running and pass it as a parameter when it wants to broadcast progress to the test listeners.

org.eclipse.contribution.junit/TestRunner
```
public class TestRunner {
  private IJavaProject project;
  public TestRunner(IJavaProject project) {
    this.project= project;
  }
}
```

We need to pass the project along to the various `fire*` methods in `JUnit-Plugin`. Use **Change Method Signature** to add a parameter to each of these methods (see Figure 16.2).

Figure 16.2

We set the default value of the parameter to `FIXME` so the compiler reminds us with errors in the **Task** view which calls we have to revisit to fill in the value of the new argument.

org.eclipse.contribution.junit/TestRunner
```
private void parseMessage(String line) {
  ...
  JUnitPlugin.getPlugin().fireTestsFinished(project);
  ...
}
```

Finally, use **Change Method Signature** to add a parameter to each of the
`ITestRunListener` methods.

org.eclipse.contribution.junit/ITestRunListener
```
public interface ITestRunListener {
  void testsStarted(IJavaProject project, int testCount);
  void testsFinished(IJavaProject project);
  void testStarted(IJavaProject project, String klass,
    String methodName);
  void testFailed(IJavaProject project, String klass,
    String method, String trace);
}
```

Now we can move on to `MarkerCreator`.

16.3   Creating Markers

Which object should be responsible for creating the markers? None of the
existing objects make much sense. `JUnitPlugin` is already busy broadcasting
test progress. The `TestRunner` is handling socket communications. We need
a `MarkerCreator` for a given project, an object that listens for test progress
and creates markers:

org.eclipse.contribution.junit/JUnitPlugin
```
public void run(IType[] classes, IJavaProject project)
    throws CoreException {
  ITestRunListener listener= new MarkerCreator(project);
  addTestListener(listener);
  try {
    new TestRunner(project).run(classes);
  } finally {
    removeTestListener(listener);
  }
}
```

`MarkerCreator` needs to implement `ITestRunListener`. It keeps its project
in a field:

org.eclipse.contribution.junit/MarkerCreator
```
public class MarkerCreator implements ITestRunListener {
  private IJavaProject project;
  public MarkerCreator(IJavaProject project) {
    this.project= project;
  }
}
```

The first `ITestRunListener` method we need to implement is `testFailed()`,
where we will create a marker:

org.eclipse.contribution.junit/MarkerCreator
```
public void testFailed(IJavaProject testProject, String klass,
      String method, String trace) {
  if (! project.equals(testProject))
    return;
  IType type= null;
  try {
    type= project.findType(klass);
  } catch (JavaModelException e) { // Fall through
  }
  if (type == null) return; //TODO: Log later
  try {
    IResource resource= type.getUnderlyingResource();
    IMarker marker= resource.createMarker(
        "org.eclipse.contribution.junit.failure");
    IMethod testMethod= type.getMethod(method, new String[0]);
    setMarkerAttributes(marker, testMethod, trace);
  } catch (CoreException e) {
    // TODO Log later
  }
}
```

We'll explain the utility method `setMarkerAttributes()` in a moment. We defined the `ITestRunListener` API in terms of `Strings`, not `JavaElements`. For remote communication, `Strings` make sense. Inside Eclipse, however, we'd like to communicate Java elements. The question is, where do we do the mapping from `Strings` to Java elements? As long as the only purpose we had for the broadcast information was to display it in the user interface, there was no cost to using strings. Now that we want to further process the test progress information inside of Eclipse, though, it's starting to seem like the `ITestRunListener` should communicate `JavaElements` instead of `Strings`.

The flow of this test is to map from the string representation of the class back to the `IType`. From the type we can fetch the `Resource` (a file) to which we attach a marker of the appropriate type. `JavaElements` give you a Java-specific view of the resources. You can navigate to the underlying resource by calling `getUnderlyingResource()`. Now we have all the information we need to set the attributes of the marker.

Our test relied on a helper method. We mimic the marker attribute setting code from our original example:

org.eclipse.contribution.junit/MarkerCreator
```
private void setMarkerAttributes(IMarker marker,
    IMethod testMethod, String trace)
    throws JavaModelException, CoreException {
  ISourceRange range= testMethod.getSourceRange();
  Map map= new HashMap(4);
  map.put(IMarker.CHAR_START, new Integer(range.getOffset()));
  map.put(IMarker.CHAR_END, new Integer(range.getOffset() +
    range.getLength()));
```

```
map.put(IMarker.SEVERITY,
  new Integer(IMarker.SEVERITY_ERROR));
map.put(IMarker.MESSAGE, extractMessage(trace));
map.put("trace", trace);
marker.setAttributes(map);
}
```

Instead of having the source range of the marker passed explicitly, we derive the source range from the range of the test method. We introduce a helper `extractMessage()` to shorten the failure trace to a one line message. For completeness here is the code:

org.eclipse.contribution.junit/MarkerCreator
```
private String extractMessage(String trace) {
  String filteredTrace= BaseTestRunner.getFilteredTrace(trace);
  BufferedReader br= new BufferedReader(
    new StringReader(filteredTrace));
  String line, message= trace;
  try {
    if ((line= br.readLine()) != null)  {
      message= line;
      if ((line= br.readLine()) != null)
      message+= " - "+line;
    }
    return message.replace('\t', ' ');
  } catch (Exception IOException) {
  }
  return message;
}
```

The `IMarker.MESSAGE` attribute is used to show the marker in the task list and when hovering over an error in the editor. In addition, we store the full trace in a separate "trace" attribute of the marker so that we do not loose this information.

The test still fails the assertion about our marker being a subtype of `org.eclipse.jdt.core.problem`. Notice how the test declares the intent of our marker:

```
assertTrue(marker.isSubtypeOf(
  IJavaModelMarker.JAVA_MODEL_PROBLEM_MARKER));
```

Passing this assertion requires that we declare our marker type in the manifest. `Org.eclipse.core.resources.markers` is the extension point for declaring marker types and their attributes:

org.eclipse.contribution.junit/plugin.xml
```
<extension
  point="org.eclipse.core.resources.markers"
```

```
      id="failure"
      name="Test Failure">
      <super type="org.eclipse.jdt.core.problem"/>
      <persistent value="true"/>
</extension>
```

The test passes. Notice that the marker `id` is plug-in relative. Markers can persist across sessions or not. This is enabled by the `persistent` attribute. A failed test remains a failed test even if you restart the workbench, so we enable persistence.

Our marker is shown in Figure 16.3.

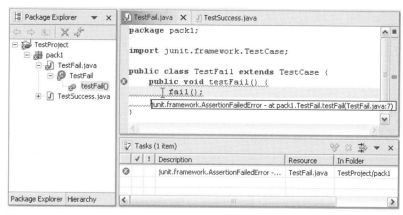

Figure 16.3

The task filter now shows our marker type as part of the Java problem marker hierarchy, as shown in Figure 16.4.

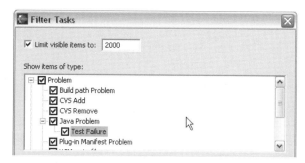

Figure 16.4

16.4   Deleting Markers

There's one more problem. If we run tests twice, we will get a marker for each time the tests fail. Here is a test for this:

Ju   **org.eclipse.contribution.junit.test/MarkerTest**
```
public void testMarkerClearing() throws CoreException, IOException {
  JUnitPlugin.getPlugin().run(type);
  JUnitPlugin.getPlugin().run(type);
  IMarker[] markers= getFailureMarkers();
  assertEquals(1, markers.length);
}
```

To make this test run, we need to clear the markers for a project when a new test suite is run.

org.eclipse.contribution.junit/MarkerCreator
```
public void testsStarted(IJavaProject project, int testCount) {
  try {
    project.getProject().deleteMarkers(
      "org.eclipse.contribution.junit.failure",
      false,
      IResource.DEPTH_INFINITE);
  } catch (CoreException e) {
    // TODO Log later
  }
}
```

Notice that we have to navigate from the `IJavaProject` to the underlying `IProject` resource before we can delete the markers. `IJavaProjects` wrap `IProjects`, giving a Java-oriented view of the underlying resources.

Be careful when modifying resources, because resource change notifications are expensive. With our current implementation we are still triggering two notifications:

org.eclipse.contribution.junit/MarkerCreator.testFailed()
```
IResource resource= type.getUnderlyingResource();
IMarker marker= resource.createMarker(
    "org.eclipse.contribution.junit.failure");
IMethod testMethod= type.getMethod(method, new String[0]);
setMarkerAttributes(marker, testMethod, trace);
```

We trigger a first notification when the marker is created and a second change notification when its attributes are set. To reduce the change notification overhead, Eclipse supports the batching of notifications. To do so we can execute workspace modifications with an `IWorkspaceRunnable`. The runnable is passed to the workspace for execution. During the execution of the runnable the workspace accumulates changes and fires them at the end. Since change

notifications are always expensive, we should adapt our code to use an
`IWorkspaceRunnable`:

org.eclipse.contribution.junit/MarkerCreator
```
public void testFailed(IJavaProject testProject, String klass,
    final String method, final String trace) {
  if (! project.equals(testProject))
    return;
  Type type= null;
  try {
    type= project.findType(klass);
  } catch (JavaModelException e) { // Fall through
  }
  if (type == null)
    return; //TODO: Log later
  final IType finalType= type;
  try {
    final IResource resource= type.getUnderlyingResource();
    IWorkspaceRunnable runnable= new IWorkspaceRunnable() {
      public void run(IProgressMonitor monitor)
        throws CoreException {
        IMarker marker= resource.createMarker(
          "org.eclipse.contribution.junit.failure");
        IMethod testMethod= finalType.getMethod(method,
          new String[0]);
        setMarkerAttributes(marker, testMethod, trace);
      }
    };
    resource.getWorkspace().run(runnable, null);
  } catch (CoreException e) {
    // TODO Log later
  }
}
```

16.5   Marker Images

To finish this chapter we'll polish a little and illustrate more Eclipse extension
options. First we want to distinguish a test failure from a compile error in the
editor's vertical ruler. Currently both markers use the same image. Let's do a
 plug-in search for marker related extension points (see Figure 16.5).

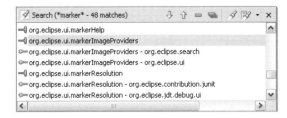

Figure 16.5

The extension point `markerImageProvider` looks like a good candidate. When opening its description (using **Show Description** from the context menu) we can verify this. Following the example in the description, we define an association between our failure marker type and an image that we have copied to the icons folder of our plug-in:

org.eclipse.contribution.junit/plugin.xml
```
<extension
  point="org.eclipse.ui.markerImageProviders">
  <imageprovider
    markertype="org.eclipse.contribution.junit.failure"
    icon="icons/testerr.gif"
    id="org.contribution.junit">
  </imageprovider>
</extension>
```

After making this contribution we can now distinguish test failures from compiler problems in the vertical ruler, as shown in Figure 16.6.

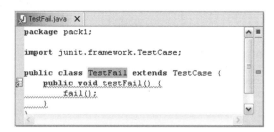

Figure 16.6

16.6   Marker Resolution

As the final polish we want to simplify rerunning a failed test by integrating it with the Java development tool's **Quick Fix**. Up to now you could use **Quick Fix** to correct compile errors like missing imports, missing methods and so on. You fix a problem by clicking an error annotation or by pressing **Ctrl+1** while the cursor is inside an error. We want to support fixing a failed test.

We don't expect to fix tests automatically, but it would be nice to offer a quick-fix action that helps us to rerun a failed test after we think we've fixed the failed code so that the marker disappears. The `markerResolution` extension point we have found in the above plug-in search fills our bill. It allows us to associate an `IMarkerResolutionGenerator` with a marker and some of its attribute values. The resolution generator is responsible for creating an array of `IMarkerResolutions`. We associate a marker resolution generator

I*2 Interfaces to Preserve API Compatibility

When browsing for the `IMarkerResolutionGenerator` you will also find an interface `IMarkerResolutionGenerator2`. The `IMarkerResolution-Generator2` extends the `IMarkerResolutionGenerator` interface and adds a new method `hasResolutions()`. The need for this additional method was discovered over time, since some marker resolutions are expensive to compute. Instead of computing a resolution it is more efficient to just determine whether there are any resolutions. This is a nice example of preserving API compatibility. Adding the method to the existing `IMarkerResolutionGenerator` interface would be a breaking API change. When you add a new method to an existing interface you break all implementors of this interface. All existing implementors of the existing interface would have to change, and as unsynchronized as the Eclipse community is, it would be simply impossible to do this all at once. Instead, the I*2 interface was created and the new method was added in a separate interface. Clients of the `IMarkerResolutionGenerator` interface now have to use an `instanceof` test to determine whether a contributor provides the old or the new interface:

```
if(generator instanceof IMarkerResolutionGenerator2) {
  if(((IMarkerResolutionGenerator2)generator).
    hasResolutions(marker))
    return true;
} else {
  IMarkerResolution[] resolutions=generator.
    getResolutions(marker);
  if (resolutions.length > 0)
    return true;
}
```

This is a little ugly, but it is better than trying to get the entire world-wide Eclipse community to march in lock step. If you use the **Open Type** dialog and search for "`I*2`" or "`I*Extension`", you will find several examples of API preserving interface extensions.

with the failure marker type. The resolver is not contributed to a particular marker attribute value and is available for any failure marker:

org.eclipse.contribution.junit/plugin.xml
```
<extension point="org.eclipse.ui.markerResolution">
  <markerResolutionGenerator
    markerType="org.eclipse.contribution.junit.failure"
```

```
    class="org.eclipse.contribution.junit.
       RerunMarkerResolutionGenerator">
  </markerResolutionGenerator>
</extension>
```

Finally, we implement the `IMarkerResolutionGenerator` interface and return a resolution that reruns a test. A resolution has a label and a run method. The intent of the run method is to eliminate the need for the marker. In our case, we rerun the current test method in the hope that it is fixed and the marker disappears.

org.eclipse.contribution.junit/RerunMarkerResolutionGenerator

```
public class RerunMarkerResolutionGenerator
     implements IMarkerResolutionGenerator {
  public RerunMarkerResolutionGenerator() {
  }

  public IMarkerResolution [] getResolutions(IMarker marker)  {
    IMarkerResolution resolution= new IMarkerResolution() {
      public String getLabel() {
        return "Re-run test";
      }
      public void run(IMarker marker) {
        // TODO implement re-run
      }
    };
    return new IMarkerResolution[] {resolution};
  }
}
```

We will implement rerunning a failed test in Chapter 18. With this code in place, a rerun test action is offered when we press **Ctrl+1** in a failed test method, as shown in Figure 16.7.

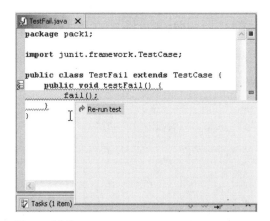

Figure 16.7

The rerun-test quick fix is also available in the task list when a failure marker is selected. In this case, the available quick fixes are shown in a dialog, as shown in Figure 16.8.

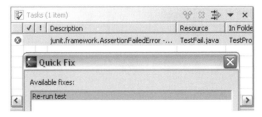

Figure 16.8

Our next task on the road to test failures as compile errors is to find all the test classes in a given project. Before we do that, let's review. In this chapter we

- ❍ Set the correct attributes of our marker so it would let the user navigate directly to the broken test
- ❍ Attached the marker to a resource using `IResource.createMarker()`
- ❍ Created our `failure` marker type as a subtype of `org.eclipse.jdt.core.problem`, the type used for compile errors
- ❍ Deleted all markers attached to an `IProject`
- ❍ Defined a custom image for our marker
- ❍ Contributed marker resolution generator to rerun a failed test

CHAPTER 17

Finding Tests

Now we get feedback in the form of markers when a test fails. Which tests should we run? There is a strong tendency to be miserly running tests. This seems to be a legacy from the days of limited computing cycles. Our philosophy is to always run all the available tests. When performance makes this totally impossible, we find a way to write more granular tests that provide nearly the same feedback with far fewer CPU cycles. In theory we always run all tests, but we pragmatically allow reality to diverge from this theory on occasion.

Following this theory, we should run all the tests in a project whenever the project changes. How do we find all the tests in a project? In this chapter, we'll learn how to

- ○ Create type hierarchies
- ○ Query Java element attributes
- ○ Prepare our code for politely running long operations

This search functionality doesn't seem to fit nicely with any of our existing classes, so we'll create a new object, the `TestSearcher`:

org.eclipse.contribution.junit/TestSearcher
```
public class TestSearcher {
}
```

The external API for the searcher is to pass it a project and receive in return an array of `IType`s, representing the test classes in the project. We are ignoring test suites and other implementors of the `Test` interface for the moment.

The test for the searcher, `SearchTest`, relies on a `TestProject` being created in `setUp()` and disposed in `tearDown()`:

org.eclipse.contribution.junit.test/SearchTest
```
private TestProject testProject;
private IPackageFragment pack;
protected void setUp() throws Exception {
  testProject= new TestProject();
  testProject.addJar("org.junit", "junit.jar");
  pack= testProject.createPackage("pack1");
}
protected void tearDown() throws Exception {
  testProject.dispose();
}
```

The test adds three types to the project:

- An abstract subclass of `TestCase`, which shouldn't be found
- A subclass of `Object`, which shouldn't be found
- A `TestCase` subclass ready to be run

org.eclipse.contribution.junit.test/SearchTest
```
public void testSearch() throws Exception {
  testProject.createType(pack, "AbstractTest.java",
    "public abstract class AbstractTest " +
    " extends junit.framework.TestCase { }");
  testProject.createType(pack, "NotATest.java",
    "public class NotATest { }");
  IType type= testProject.createType(pack, "ATest.java",
    "public class ATest extends junit.framework.TestCase { }");
  TestSearcher searcher= new TestSearcher();
  IType[] tests=searcher.findAll(testProject.getJavaProject(),
    null);
  assertEquals(1, tests.length);
  assertEquals(type, tests[0]);
}
```

Notice that we've added a parameter to `TestSearcher.findAll()`. For operations that are likely to run for a long time, Eclipse adds a Collecting Parameter,[1] `IProgressMonitor`. We'll be calling methods that invite participation in reporting progress, so we want to give our clients the same opportunity. For testing purposes, we just pass in a null. We could also pass in an instance of `NullProgressMonitor`.[2]

---

1. See K. Beck, *Smalltalk Best Practice Patterns*. Prentice Hall PTR, Upper Saddle River, NJ, 1997, p. 75.

2. This is an instance of the Special Case pattern. See M. Fowler, *Patterns of Enterprise Application Architecture*, Addison-Wesley, Boston, 2003, p. 496.

org.eclipse.contribution.junit/TestSearcher
```
public IType[] findAll(IJavaProject project, IProgressMonitor pm)
    throws JavaModelException {
  IType[] candidates= getAllTestCaseSubclasses(project, pm);
  return collectTestsInProject(candidates, project);
}
```

We'll use a couple of helper methods to first get all visible subclasses of test case, then filter out the ones that don't actually live in this project. Notice that the API is written to return a typed array and not a `List`. It's easier for a client to deal with a typed array than a generic list, particularly if the array is only accessed and not modified. Typed arrays also eliminate the possibility of `ClassCastExceptions`.

We fetch all the subclasses of `TestCase` by first finding the `IType` representing the base type. If it doesn't exist in this project, there can be no test cases, so we return an empty array. From the type, we create its hierarchy. From the hierarchy, we fetch an array of all the subclasses.

org.eclipse.contribution.junit/TestSearcher
```
private IType[] getAllTestCaseSubclasses(IJavaProject project,
    IProgressMonitor pm) throws JavaModelException {
  IType testCase= project.findType("junit.framework.TestCase");
  if (testCase == null)
    return new IType[0];
  ITypeHierarchy hierarchy= testCase.newTypeHierarchy(project, pm);
  return hierarchy.getAllSubtypes(testCase);
}
```

Why do we have to go through the intermediate `ITypeHierarchy`? Why can't we get all subclasses from the `IType`? Type hierarchy computation is expensive, particularly finding all subtypes. You have to know the entire state of the world to compute the subtypes correctly. Most users of `IType` don't need this information. By separating the `ITypeHierarchy`, most users of `IType` don't have to pay the performance penalty. Notice that `IType.newTypeHierarchy()` takes an `IProgressMonitor` as a parameter, a hint that it can take a long time. If you only need the supertypes, use `newSupertypeHierarchy()`, don't create the whole hierarchy.

Now we have candidate types, but some of the test case classes may live in other projects or external libraries. We need to filter these out before returning the results.

org.eclipse.contribution.junit/TestSearcher
```
private IType[] collectTestsInProject(IType[] candidates,
    IJavaProject project) {
  List result= new ArrayList();
  for (int i= 0; i < candidates.length; i++) {
```

```
  try {
    if (isTestInProject(candidates[i], project))
      result.add(candidates[i]);
  } catch (JavaModelException e) {
    // Fall through
  }
}
return (IType[]) result.toArray(new IType[result.size()]);
}
```

If we encounter a problem while evaluating a particular type, we'll just ignore that type and move on to the next one.

How do we decide if an `IType` is in a given project? First, we exclude all types that are external, contained in an external JAR and therefore have no underlying resource. We also exclude types whose "home" project is different than the project we're searching. Finally, we exclude abstract classes.

org.eclipse.contribution.junit/TestSearcher
```
private boolean isTestInProject(IType type, IJavaProject project)
    throws JavaModelException {
  IResource resource= type.getUnderlyingResource();
  if (resource == null)
    return false;
  if (! resource.getProject().equals(project.getProject()))
    return false;
  return ! Flags.isAbstract(type.getFlags());
}
```

Notice that you don't query an `IType` directly for its modifiers, `type.isAbstract()`. Instead, you ask for its flags and you call a helper class to decode the flags for you. This is consistent with the style introduced in the Java reflection API.

Next we'll see how to participate in the build process, so we can invoke the tests we've found. Summarizing this chapter, we

○ Created an `ITypeHierarchy` to get all subtypes

○ Used `Flags` to query the Java element attributes

○ Passed along an `IProgressMonitor` to the potentially long-running operation of calculating a full type hierarchy

CHAPTER 18

Builders and Natures

We want to extend the process of building a Java project to include running tests. If there was only one way to build a project, building would simply be represented by a method on IProject. However, the build process is complex and differs from project-to-project. In this chapter, we'll see how to contribute to the build process. In particular, we will see how to

- ❍ Use natures to configure builders
- ❍ Use builders to participate in the build process
- ❍ Declare natures and builders

Each project has associated with it a set of builders. Each builder is informed any time Eclipse decides to build a project. A builder can transform resources to bring them up to date or it can validate that the resources are in a consistent state. Projects can be built explicitly, by choosing **Project > Rebuild Project,** or by enabling auto-build. You can turn the auto-build behavior on or off by choosing **Preferences > Workbench > Perform build automatically on resource modification.**

A complicated builder like the one that runs the Java compiler carefully examines the details of the changes to minimize the amount of recompilation. We don't need to be nearly that clever yet. We will just run all the tests after any change.

18.1   Resource Listeners Versus Builders

You can register an `IResourceChangeListener` with the workspace. Your
listener will be informed whenever a resource changes (files added and
deleted, file contents changed, marker changes). The changes are communicated in the form of a *resource delta*, a tree describing the difference between
the state at the previous notification and the current state.

A builder is attached to a project. When the project is built, the builder is
notified, also with a resource delta, but builders receive a delta only describing
changes since the last build.

There are several distinctions between resource listeners and builders:

○ *Heartbeat*—Resource change listeners are run every time a resource
   changes. Builders are only run when the project builds. If auto-build is
   turned on, a listener and a builder will see a similar stream of deltas.

○ *Builder order dependency*—Resource listeners are invoked in an unspec-
   ified order. Builders are explicitly ordered.

○ *Project order dependency*—When building the workspace, projects are
   built based on their prerequisite relationships. You can see the dependencies on the **Project References** page of the project properties. Dependent
   projects are guaranteed to be built after their referenced projects. This
   order can be modified by the **Build Order** global preference page.

○ *Granularity*—With resource listeners, there is no notion of "change all
   the resources in the system" like there is with **Build All,** which will
   invoke all builders for all projects.

○ *Independence*—Resource change listeners should not depend on each
   other. Builders, because they are called in a defined order, can depend on
   each other. For example, you might generate HTML with one builder
   and check link consistency with another.

○ *Sharing*—Resource listeners are dynamically created. Builders are permanently attached to projects, stored in the repository, and shared by
   everyone using the project (builders are stored in the *.project* file, the
   serialized form of the `ProjectDescription`).

○ *Scope*—Resource listeners are notified by changes anywhere in the workspace. A builder is only notified about changes to resources within its
   project.

You can see the registered builders by looking at the **External Tools Builders**
property page. On this page you can add additional builders that should be
run. The builders registered programmatically are shown on this page as well.
Figure 18.1 shows the builders for a plug-in project, as seen in Eclipse.

Because this is a PDE plug-in project, it has additional builders for validating plug-in manifests. The plug-in manifest builder is an example of a builder that has validation as its primary purpose (see Figure 18.1).

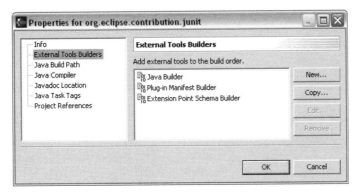

Figure 18.1

The same builders are represented in Eclipse as an array of builder `ids` contained in the project's `ProjectDescription`. A `ProjectDescription` stores the metadata for a project, as shown in Figure 18.2.

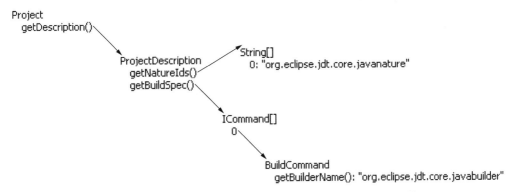

Figure 18.2   ProjectDescription

Here are the levels involved in describing a project's builders:

○ `Project`—Represents an Eclipse project internally

○ `ProjectDescription`—Stores information about the project, like how the project is built and how this project depends on other projects

○ `ICommand`/`BuildCommand`—A record that describes build arguments

A nature configures the capabilities of a project. A common use of natures is to install and uninstall builders. Eclipse takes care of managing natures during the life cycle of a project.

The natures are just represented by strings in the description. Note that a project can have multiple natures as well as multiple builders. For instance, plug-in projects have the Java nature and the plug-in nature. The Java nature installs the Java builder and the plug-in nature installs the plug-in manifest builder and the schema builder.

18.2   Using Natures to Configure Builders

From Figure 18.2 we can infer that when the Java nature was configured, it installed the Java builder. We will want to create an auto-test nature that will install an auto-test builder. The test looks like this. We have our usual setup and teardown using a `TestProject`:

org.eclipse.contribution.junit.test/BuilderTest
```
private TestProject testProject;
protected void setUp() throws Exception {
  testProject= new TestProject();
  testProject.addJar("org.junit", "junit.jar");
}
protected void tearDown() throws Exception {
  testProject.dispose();
}
```

We need a home for the logic required to install a nature. It doesn't seem to fit smoothly into any of the existing classes. In cases like this, where we know we need a well-known entry point, the plug-in class provides a convenient location. How can we write a test that will specify the behavior of this method before we try to implement it?

org.eclipse.contribution.junit.test/BuilderTest
```
public void testNatureAddAndRemove() throws CoreException {
  IProject project= testProject.getProject();
  JUnitPlugin.getPlugin().addAutoBuildNature(project);
  assertTrue(project.hasNature(JUnitPlugin.AUTO_TEST_NATURE));
  ICommand[] commands= project().getDescription().getBuildSpec();
  boolean found= false;
  for (int i = 0; i < commands.length; ++i)
    if (commands[i].getBuilderName().equals(
        JUnitPlugin.AUTO_TEST_BUILDER))
      found= true;
  assertTrue(found);
  JUnitPlugin.getPlugin().removeAutoBuildNature(project);
  assertFalse(project.hasNature(JUnitPlugin.AUTO_TEST_NATURE));
}
```

We use methods provided by the JUnitPlugin to add and remove our new
nature. Notice that we pass the IProject and not the IJavaProject, because
natures are associated with all projects. The assertions state that as a result of
adding and configuring an auto-test nature, we should install a new builder.

org.eclipse.contribution.junit/JUnitPlugin
```
public void addAutoBuildNature(IProject project)
    throws CoreException {
 if (project.hasNature(AUTO_TEST_NATURE))
  return;

 IProjectDescription description = project.getDescription();
 String[] ids= description.getNatureIds();
 String[] newIds= new String[ids.length + 1];
 System.arraycopy(ids, 0, newIds, 0, ids.length);
 newIds[ids.length]= AUTO_TEST_NATURE;
 description.setNatureIds(newIds);
 project.setDescription(description, null);
}
public void removeAutoBuildNature(IProject project)
    throws CoreException {
 IProjectDescription description = project.getDescription();
 String[] ids = description.getNatureIds();
 for (int i = 0; i < ids.length; ++i) {
   if (ids[i].equals(AUTO_TEST_NATURE)) {
     String[] newIds = new String[ids.length - 1];
     System.arraycopy(ids, 0, newIds, 0, i);
     System.arraycopy(ids, i + 1, newIds, i, ids.length - i - 1);
     description.setNatureIds(newIds);
     project.setDescription(description, null);
     return;
   }
 }
}
```

Here we see the disadvantage of communicating via typed arrays instead of
lists. We want to insert our nature on the end of the list of natures. With a
List, we could just say add(). With an array, we need to allocate a larger
array, copy the contents of the old array, and assign the new value.

Before we can successfully install a new nature, we need to declare it as an
extension.

org.eclipse.contribution.junit/plugin.xml
```
<extension point="org.eclipse.core.resources.natures"
  id="autoTestNature"
  name="Auto Test">
  <runtime>
    <run class="org.eclipse.contribution.junit.AutoTestNature"/>
  </runtime>
  <requires-nature id="org.eclipse.jdt.core.javanature"/>
  <builder id="org.eclipse.contribution.junit.autoTestBuilder"/>
</extension>
```

The nature `id` is plug-in relative. The nature `id` used in the program text must match the qualified `id`. We introduce constants for both the nature `id` and the builder `id` matching the values in the manifest.

org.eclipse.contribution.junit/JUnitPlugin
```
public static final String AUTO_TEST_NATURE=
    "org.eclipse.contribution.junit.autoTestNature";
public static final String AUTO_TEST_BUILDER=
    "org.eclipse.contribution.junit.autoTestBuilder";
```

When a nature with this `id` is installed, an instance of `AutoTestNature` will be created. The `requires-nature` element declares the constraint that we can't install our nature unless the Java nature is already present. In addition, this declaration tells Eclipse to configure our nature after the Java nature. The final line tells Eclipse not to run the auto-test builder unless the auto-test nature is present.

The `AutoTestNature` implements `IProjectNature`, which declares four methods. The first two initialize the project for a nature:

org.eclipse.contribution.junit/AutoTestNature
```
public class AutoTestNature implements IProjectNature {
  IProject project;
  public AutoTestNature() {
  }
  public IProject getProject()  {
    return project;
  }
  public void setProject(IProject project)  {
    this.project= project;
  }
}
```

The main effort is contained in the life-cycle methods `configure()` and `deconfigure()`, which in our case will install and uninstall the auto-test builder.

org.eclipse.contribution.junit/AutoTestNature
```
public void configure() throws CoreException {
  IProjectDescription description= getProject().getDescription();
  ICommand[] commands= description.getBuildSpec();
  for (int i = 0; i < commands.length; ++i)
    if (commands[i].getBuilderName().equals(
        JUnitPlugin.AUTO_TEST_BUILDER))
      return;

  ICommand command= description.newCommand();
  command.setBuilderName(JUnitPlugin.AUTO_TEST_BUILDER);
  ICommand[] newCommands= new ICommand[commands.length + 1];
  System.arraycopy(commands, 0, newCommands, 0, commands.length);
```

```
newCommands[newCommands.length-1]= command;
description.setBuildSpec(newCommands);
getProject().setDescription(description, null);
}
```

We use the same trick to install the builder that we did to install the nature. If the builder is already present, we stop. Then we copy the current list of builders into a new array and add our new builder (an instance of `ICommand`). We are careful here to install our builder as the last, so the programs will have been compiled before we try to run them. The method `deconfigure()` is similar, removing the builder from the list of build commands.

Once again, before we can successfully install the builder, we must declare it as an extension. The declaration looks a lot like the nature declaration:

org.eclipse.contribution.junit/plugin.xml
```
<extension point="org.eclipse.core.resources.builders"
  id="autoTestBuilder"
  name="Auto Test Builder">
  <builder>
    <run class="org.eclipse.contribution.junit.AutoTestBuilder"/>
  </builder>
</extension>
```

The test case will now pass. Now we're ready for the real end-to-end test case—save a failing test and watch it fail immediately, invoked by the builder.

org.eclipse.contribution.junit.test/BuilderTest
```
public void testAutoTesting() throws Exception {
  IWorkspaceRunnable runnable= new IWorkspaceRunnable() {
    public void run(IProgressMonitor monitor)
        throws CoreException {
      IProject project= testProject.getProject();
      JUnitPlugin.getPlugin().addAutoBuildNature(project);
      IPackageFragment pack= testProject.createPackage("pack1");
      IType type= testProject.createType(pack, "FailTest.java",
        "public class FailTest extends junit.framework.TestCase{"+
        "public void testFailure() {fail();}}");
    }
  };
  ResourcesPlugin.getWorkspace().run(runnable, null);
  IMarker[] markers= getFailureMarkers();
  assertEquals(1, markers.length);
}
```

We wrapped the project creation in a `IWorkspaceRunnable` to reduce the number of change notifications. We call the helper `getFailureMarkers()` to determine the number of markers. We just copied this method from `MarkerTest`. The insights we gain by eliminating duplication in test code are seldom worth the effort, unlike the insights gained from refactoring model code.

Now we need our builder to run the tests. We start by extending `Incremental-ProjectBuilder`, as specified in the extension point documentation:

org.eclipse.contribution.junit/AutoTestBuilder
```
public class AutoTestBuilder extends IncrementalProjectBuilder {
  public AutoTestBuilder() {
  }
}
```

The API is `build()`, which takes

- An enumeration representing the type of build—full, incremental, or automatic

- A map containing builder arguments you find in the manifest (we didn't declare any above)

- An `IProgressMonitor`, because a build is potentially a long-running operation

Our implementation of build first checks to see whether there were any build errors:

org.eclipse.contribution.junit/AutoTestBuilder
```
public boolean hasBuildErrors() throws CoreException {
  IMarker[] markers= getProject().findMarkers(
    IJavaModelMarker.JAVA_MODEL_PROBLEM_MARKER, false,
    IResource.DEPTH_INFINITE);
  for (int i= 0; i < markers.length; i++) {
    IMarker marker= markers[i];
    if (marker.getAttribute(IMarker.SEVERITY, 0) ==
        IMarker.SEVERITY_ERROR)
      return true;
  }
  return false;
}
```

It makes no sense to run the tests if the code didn't compile. Also, because builders are potentially invoked often, you should stop building quickly in as many cases as possible.

org.eclipse.contribution.junit/AutoTestBuilder
```
protected IProject[] build(int kind, Map args, IProgressMonitor pm)
    throws CoreException {
  if (hasBuildErrors())
    return null;
  IJavaProject javaProject= JavaCore.create(getProject());
  IType[] types= new TestSearcher().findAll(javaProject, pm);
  JUnitPlugin.getPlugin().run(types, javaProject);
  return null;
}
```

The body of the build method uses our handy search object to find the test types, then invokes them through `JUnitPlugin` methods. The builder contains the `IProject` on which it is working. However, our search and test run methods take an `IJavaProject`. We translate by asking `JavaCore` to get a project for us. Going the other way is a simple accessor, `IJavaProject.get-Project()`.

Our test runs. Before we can see the behavior in action, we have to provide a user interface for adding and removing the auto-test nature. Reviewing this chapter:

○ We declared an `AutoTestNature` and an `AutoTestBuilder`.

○ We added the `AutoTestNature` to a project by adding its identifier to a list of nature identifiers. When it was added, the nature got the chance to also add the `AutoTestBuilder` to the same project.

○ When the `AutoTestBuilder` was told to `build()`, we ran the tests in the project.

18.3 Forward Pointers

○ *Passing arguments to a builder*—The build specification defined with `ICommand` allows you to register additional arguments in the form of key-value pairs. One builder class can be used a little differently in different places.

○ *Incremental build*—The `AutoTestBuilder` is not incremental. Builders can access the list of changes since the last build (`IncrementalProject-Builder.getDelta()`) to limit the work they do. The changes are stored in a resource delta. For instance, the resource delta could be used to reduce the amount of searching for tests or to run only a the subset of the tests that possibly could have changed.

○ *Nature image*—Natures can be presented to the user as adornments to project icons. Java Project

○ For additional background information on natures and builders refer to the article at *www.eclipse.org/articles/Article-Builders/builders.html.*

CHAPTER 19

Auto-Test Property

We don't want auto-testing for all projects. We would like to switch it off and on for individual projects. In this chapter we will

○ Create a project property page with a checkbox for auto testing so that the user can turn on and off the auto-test builder

○ Call the methods that add or remove a nature

First, we need to get the property page to appear when we bring up the properties of a Java project. Eclipse can attach properties to any object. As a developer, you can allow a user to edit the properties of anything. To do so you provide property pages though an extension point. In the property page, you decide how to store and retrieve the property values. For example, Eclipse already supports attaching persistent properties to a resource.

We can copy the declaration from one of the other project property pages (see Figure 19.1).

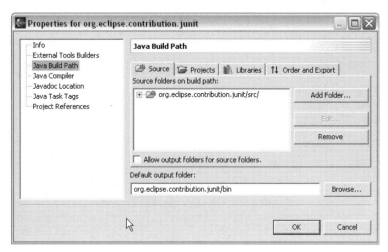

Figure 19.1

 To find the property page extension point, we can use the plug-in search to find the declaration of an extension point called `*property*`, as shown in Figure 19.2.

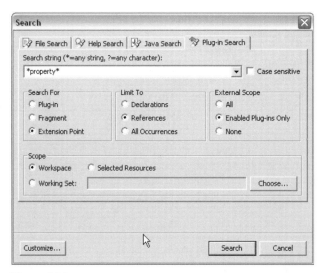

Figure 19.2

Clicking on `org.eclipse.jdt.ui`, we see many property pages. Here's one:

 org.eclipse.jdt.ui/plugin.xml
```
<extension point="org.eclipse.ui.propertyPages">
```

```
<page
  name="%buildPathPageName"
  id="org.eclipse.jdt.ui.propertyPages.BuildPathsPropertyPage"
  objectClass="org.eclipse.core.resources.IProject"
  class="org.eclipse.jdt.internal.ui.preferences.
    BuildPathsPropertyPage">
  <filter name="nature" value="org.eclipse.jdt.core.
    javanature"/>
</page>
</extension>
```

The Relevance Rule is in action in this declaration. The filter element has a predefined set of possible keys: nature and persistent property. The declaration above says only projects having the Java nature will show this property page. Copying this into our manifest, we get:

org.eclipse.contribution.junit/plugin.xml

```
<extension point="org.eclipse.ui.propertyPages">
  <page
    id="org.eclipse.contribution.junit.autotestproperty"
    name="Auto-test"
    objectClass="org.eclipse.jdt.core.IJavaProject"
    class="org.eclipse.contribution.junit.ui.
      AutoTestPropertyPage">
    <filter name="nature" value="org.eclipse.jdt.core.
      javanature"/>
  </page>
</extension>
```

In the run-time workbench, we can create a Java project. When we look at the project's properties, we see the name of the property page, as shown in Figure 19.3, but when we select it, we get an error because the class hasn't been implemented yet.

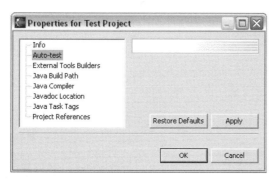

Figure 19.3

If we show the project in the **Navigator** (instead of the **Package Explorer** in the Java perspective), the property page doesn't appear. Why not? The object class specified in the declaration is checked against the type of the currently selected element. In the **Package Explorer,** the elements are IJava-Projects. The Navigator shows IProjects. How can we make our property page appear in both places?

One solution used occasionally in Eclipse is to declare the property page twice, once for an IProject and once for an IJavaProject. This is not an elegant solution. A better solution, also used in Eclipse, is to enable the resource adapter for the contribution (Chapter 31). Applying the resource adapter to an IJavaProject will reveal its IProject.

org.eclipse.contribution.junit/plugin.xml
```
<extension point="org.eclipse.ui.propertyPages">
  <page
    id="org.eclipse.contribution.junit.autotestproperty"
    name="Auto-test"
    objectClass="org.eclipse.core.resources.IProject"
    adaptable="true"
    class="org.eclipse.contribution.junit.ui.
      AutoTestPropertyPage">
    <filter name="nature" value="org.eclipse.jdt.core.
      javanature"/>
  </page>
</extension>
```

At runtime, Eclipse will look at the selection. If it's an IProject, no problem. The property page sticks. If the selection is anything else, Eclipse will ask to see if the selection can be adapted to an IProject (for more on adapters, see Chapter 31). IJavaProjects are adaptable to IProjects, so the page sticks. Other elements are not adaptable to IProjects, so the page will not stick to, for example, compilation units.

To implement the property page, we can look at an example. BuildPaths-PropertyPage extends PropertyPage, so we will, too:

org.eclipse.contribution.junit/AutoTestPropertyPage
```
public class AutoTestPropertyPage extends PropertyPage {
  public AutoTestPropertyPage() {
  }
  protected Control createContents(Composite parent) {
    return null;
  }
}
```

Notice that, as usual, we have to implement the default constructor. Because AutoTestPropertyPage is an extension class it will be created via reflection.

Now when we select the auto-test property page, we get a page with no contents, as shown in Figure 19.4.

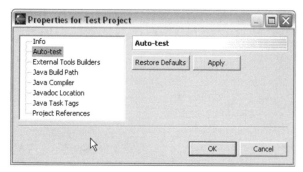

Figure 19.4

Just as we did with the JUnit view, we need to add controls to the page. In our case, we want to add a checkbox with the label **Auto-test**. Looking at all the other implementors of `createContents()` (there are more than 100 of them), it looks like we only need to add a `Button` and return it as the value of the method:

org.eclipse.contribution.junit/AutoTestPropertyPage
```
Button autoTest;
protected Control createContents(Composite parent) {
  Button autoTest= new Button(parent, SWT.CHECK);
  autoTest.setText("Auto-test");
  return autoTest;
}
```

Figure 19.5 shows the new page.

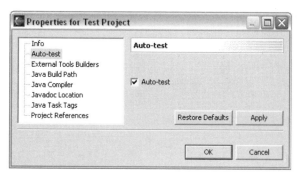

Figure 19.5

We would like a more attractive layout than this and we need to connect our
property page to the `JUnitPlugin` methods for adding and removing the
auto-test nature.

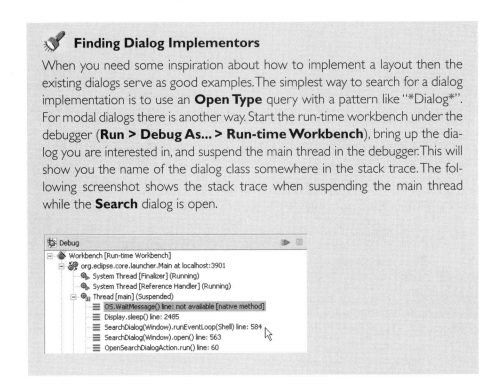

To improve the appearance, we'll first extract a method to create the widgets:

org.eclipse.contribution.junit/AutoTestPropertyPage
```
protected Control createContents(Composite parent) {
  noDefaultAndApplyButton();
  Control composite= addControl(parent);
  try {
    boolean hasNature= getProject().hasNature(
      JUnitPlugin.AUTO_TEST_NATURE);
    autoTest.setSelection(hasNature);
  } catch (CoreException e) {
    // TODO Error dialog
  }
  return composite;
}
```

Notice that we've hidden the **Restore Defaults** and **Apply** buttons. These only
make sense for complicated property pages where you want to preview the

effects of your choices. The method `getProject()` retrieves the input to the property page, which is an `IProject`:

org.eclipse.contribution.junit/AutoTestPropertyPage
```
private IProject getProject() {
  return (IProject) getElement();
}
```

We would like to have a short description of the auto-test property above the checkbox. `GridLayout` provides a way to arrange widgets in a grid.

org.eclipse.contribution.junit/AutoTestPropertyPage
```
private Control addControl(Composite parent) {
  Composite composite= new Composite(parent, SWT.NULL);
  GridLayout layout= new GridLayout();
  layout.numColumns= 1;
  composite.setLayout(layout);
  GridData data= new GridData();
  data.verticalAlignment= GridData.FILL;
  data.horizontalAlignment= GridData.FILL;
  composite.setLayoutData(data);

  Font font= parent.getFont();
  Label label= new Label(composite, SWT.NONE);
  label.setText("When auto-testing, after every build all "+
    "tests in this project will be run.");
  label.setFont(font);
  autoTest= new Button(composite, SWT.CHECK);
  autoTest.setText("Auto-test");
  autoTest.setFont(font);
  return composite;
}
```

Because we want to add several controls, we need to put them together in a `Composite`, for which we define a `GridLayout`. The new page is shown in Figure 19.6.

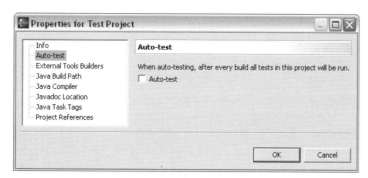

Figure 19.6

Notice that we must separately set the parent's font for each control. Without this, our controls would not appear in the user's preferred dialog font.

Hot Code Replace

When you run your target on a JDK version later than 1.4.1, you can reload changed classes without having to restart the target program. This is particularly handy when experimenting with different layout settings. Start the run-time workbench under the debugger. When you don't see the expected layout in a dialog, property page, or preference page; close it, tweak the code, rebuild, and reopen the dialog. This will immediately show you the effect of your changes without having to restart the run-time Eclipse after each change.

All that's left is to install (or uninstall) the auto-test nature when the user clicks **OK.** We override the hook method `performOk()` to do this:

org.eclipse.contribution.junit/AutoTestPropertyPage
```
public boolean performOk() {
  try {
    JUnitPlugin plugin= JUnitPlugin.getPlugin();
    if (autoTest.getSelection())
      plugin.addAutoBuildNature(getProject());
    else
      plugin.removeAutoBuildNature(getProject());
  } catch (CoreException e) {
    // TODO Error dialog
  }
  return true;
}
```

We return true because we don't ever want to veto the acceptance of the changes. We can run a run-time workspace to see the auto-test feature in action. Once we've selected auto-test and clicked **OK,** the auto-test builder appears in our project's properties, as shown in Figure 19.7.

To further confirm that we are getting the expected results, we can start a run-time workbench. There we can create a project, set the auto-test property, look at the contents of the *.project* file, and see the auto-test nature and builder attached to our project.

```
<projectDescription>
  <name>Java Project</name>
  <comment></comment>
```

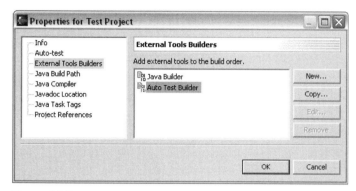

Figure 19.7

```
<projects>
</projects>
<buildSpec>
  <buildCommand>
    <name>org.eclipse.jdt.core.javabuilder</name>
    <arguments>
    </arguments>
  </buildCommand>
  <buildCommand>
    <name>org.eclipse.contribution.junit.autoTestBuilder</name>
    <arguments>
    </arguments>
  </buildCommand>
</buildSpec>
<natures>
  <nature>org.eclipse.jdt.core.javanature</nature>
  <nature>org.eclipse.contribution.junit.autoTestNature</nature>
</natures>
</projectDescription>
```

The main development of the auto-test feature is complete. However, we still have a lot of polishing to do, starting with handling errors gracefully, whether we notify the user or just log the problem. Reviewing this chapter, we

○ Declared `AutoTestPropertiesPage` in the manifest. We made sure it appeared in the **Navigator** and the **Package Explorer** by attaching it to `IProjects` and making it adaptable. We made sure it only attached to Java projects by specifying a filter requiring the presence of the Java nature.

○ Implemented the `AutoTestPropertiesPage`, including using a `GridLayout` to enhance the appearance of the controls.

○ Implemented `performOk()` to install or uninstall the auto-test nature.

19.1   Forward Pointers

○ *Preference pages*—the implementation of a preference page is very similar to the implementation of a property page. In fact, the class `PropertyPage` extends `PreferencePage` and adds the notion of an input. When implementing a preference page you can also use field editors. A field editor helps you manage and validate preference settings. See *www.eclipse.org/articles/Article-Field-Editors/field_editors.html* for more details.

CHAPTER 20

Exception Handling

Let's say you create a marvelously successful plug-in. You have thousands—no millions—of satisfied customers. What a disaster!

Why a disaster? Even with test-driven plug-in development some percentage of users will have problems. The more users, the more problems. Pretty soon, support costs will eat you out of house and home.

In this chapter we'll talk about Eclipse features that collectively reduce support costs:

○ Handling Eclipse exceptions

○ Presenting exceptions to the user using an error dialog

○ Logging errors to the Eclipse log

An important rule to improve the serviceability of your plug-ins is a bit of a paradox:

RESPONSIBILITY RULE   Clearly identify your plug-in as the source of problems.

How can telling the user a mistake is yours reduce your cost of service?

○ If you have an open source plug-in, the community will collectively provide first level service. If you provide the necessary information in log entries and error dialogs, most problems will be solved before you ever see them.

○ If you know problems can be traced directly to your plug-in, you will be careful to write robust code. The test-driven techniques introduced in the Interlude can go far towards eliminating problems at the source if applied carefully.

20.1 IStatus, CoreException

To address the Responsibility Rule, exceptions thrown by plug-ins have to carry an `IStatus` object. The `IStatus` object identifies the plug-in and contains a severity, a status code, a message, and optionally, an exception. The contained exception typically comes from a lower layer that should not be exposed to clients. `CoreException` is the root of the Eclipse exception hierarchy and carries an `IStatus`.

When an exception occurs, you want to inform the user that it happened. If you cannot show the exception to the user, then you want to at least log it to help you service problem reports. For example, it is always safe to inform the user of an exception when it happens in your action code. Then you know the context the user is in, that is, they just invoked the action. The situation is less clear when you don't know the calling context. You have to decide whether you want to propagate the exception, inform the user, or to just log the exception.

Searching for references to `CoreException` is a good way to learn more about the Eclipse exception-handling conventions. Of the many examples, we'll look at the code for opening a file in the workspace as implemented in the `OpenWorkspaceFileAction`:

org.eclipse.ui.internal.actions/OpenWorkspaceFileAction
```
public void run(IAction action) {
  //...
  try {
    IWorkbenchPage page = workbenchWindow.getActivePage();
    if (page != null)
      page.openEditor(file);
  } catch (CoreException x) {
    String title = "Open File"
    String message = "An Exception occurred while "+
      "opening the resource";
    WorkbenchPlugin.log(title, x.getStatus());
    ErrorDialog.openError(workbenchWindow.getShell(), title,
      message, x.getStatus());
  }
}
```

When a `CoreException` happens, your first decision is whether you want to inform the user with a dialog or whether you want to just log the problem. If you are in a context where you can show a dialog, then you should always do so. If this is not possible, you should log the problem. If you have informed the user of the problem with a dialog, there is no need to also log the problem unless you feel it will help you service problem reports later. Never just swallow an exception. In the snippet above, the developer has decided to both inform the user and to log the problem.

The `Plugin` class provides access to the log. It is common to provide a static helper method returning the log. The helper takes an `IStatus` object and passes it on to the log as shown below:

org.eclipse.ui.internal/WorkbenchPlugin
```
public static void log(String message, IStatus status) {
  //...
  getDefault().getLog().log(status);
}
```

20.2 Presenting Exceptions in an Error Dialog

To inform the user about a problem Eclipse provides an `ErrorDialog` that can present the `IStatus` to the user. It is used in the snippet above.

Here are some other error situations and hints for how to do the error reporting:

- *You don't have a `CoreException` or an exception carrying an `IStatus`—* Inform the user with the `MessageDialog` (`MessageDialog.openError()`). To log the exception create an `IStatus` object and log it.

- *A single conceptual operation can have multiple errors and you do want to proceed despite a single error—*In this case, collect all of the `IStatus`' in a `MultiStatus` and pass the `MuliStatus` to the `ErrorDialog` or the log.

Let's apply what we have learned to our example. A good place to use an error dialog in our code is the `AutoTestPropertyPage`. When the user clicks **OK**, our method `performOk()` is called. The methods we call, like `JUnitPlugin.addAutoTestNature()`, can throw a `CoreException`. Opening an error dialog makes perfect sense, since we're in the middle of a user interface operation:

org.eclipse.contribution.junit/AutoTestPropertyPage
```
public boolean performOk() {
  try {
    JUnitPlugin plugin= JUnitPlugin.getPlugin();
    if (autoTest.getSelection())
      plugin.addAutoBuildNature(getProject());
```

```
    else
      plugin.removeAutoBuildNature(getProject());
  } catch (CoreException e) {
    ErrorDialog.openError(getShell(), "Error",
      "Cannot set auto-test property", e.getStatus());
  }
  return true;
}
```

We can force this dialog to appear by throwing an exception in the body of the `try` block.

org.eclipse.contribution.junit/AutoTestPropertyPage
```
public boolean performOk() {
  try {
    JUnitPlugin plugin= JUnitPlugin.getPlugin();
    Exception exception= null;
    String id= plugin.getDescriptor().getUniqueIdentifier();
    int code= 42;
    IStatus status= new Status(IStatus.ERROR, id, code,
      "Status message", exception);
    throw new CoreException(status);
  } catch (CoreException e) {
    ErrorDialog.openError(getShell(), "Error",
      "Cannot set auto-test property", e.getStatus());
  }
  return true;
}
```

Then we see the error dialog shown in Figure 20.1.

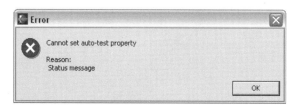

Figure 20.1

This code also serves to show you how to throw a `CoreException`. As described above, each `CoreException` has associated with it an `IStatus`, an object that bundles information about an operation. We're using it to report a problem (`IStatus.ERROR`). The status also carries a human-readable error message (you can see it in the dialog above), an error code, and the original exception, if any.

We left several TODO comments about places in the code where we wanted to do a more thorough job of error handling. We'll fill in one of those places here.

20.3   Logging Errors

In `MarkerCreator`, we had to clear the test failure markers any time a project's tests restarted. Removing the markers potentially throws a `Core-Exception`. In this case, we cannot make any assumption about the calling context of this method, so we cannot simply show an `ErrorDialog`. Therefore we just log the problem:

org.eclipse.contribution.junit/MarkerCreator$Listener
```
public void testsStarted(IJavaProject project, int testCount) {
  try {
    IResource resource= project.getUnderlyingResource();
    resource.deleteMarkers(
      "org.eclipse.contribution.junit.failure", false,
      IResource.DEPTH_INFINITE);
  } catch (CoreException e) {
    JUnitPlugin plugin= JUnitPlugin.getPlugin();
    IStatus status= new Status(IStatus.ERROR,
      plugin.getDescriptor().getUniqueIdentifier(), 0,
      "Problem deleting markers", e);
    plugin.getLog().log(status);
  }
}
```

Now when we force the problem to occur:

org.eclipse.contribution.junit/MarkerCreator$Listener
```
public void testsStarted(IJavaProject project, int testCount) {
  JUnitPlugin plugin= JUnitPlugin.getPlugin();
  try {
    IStatus status= new Status(IStatus.ERROR,
      plugin().getDescriptor().getUniqueIdentifier(), 42,
      "Status message", null);
    throw new CoreException(status);
  } catch (CoreException e) {
    IStatus status= new Status(IStatus.ERROR,
      plugin.getDescriptor().getUniqueIdentifier(), 0,
      "Problem deleting markers", e);
    plugin.getLog().log(status);
  }
}
```

We get the error log entry shown in Figure 20.2. To see the entry we first open the **Error Log** view, shown in Figure 20.3.

Figure 20.2

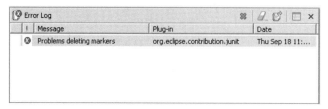

Figure 20.3

Bringing up the properties of the entry, we see the stack trace including our error messages, shown in Figure 20.4.

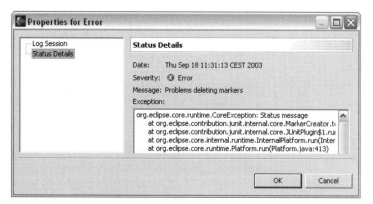

Figure 20.4

In addition to browsing the log with the **Error Log** view, you can always access the log file directly. It is located in the target workspace's *.metadata* folder with the name *.log*.

Another aspect of reducing the cost of servicing your plug-ins is instrumenting your plug-in with code that can be optionally enabled. We'll cover that in the next chapter. Reviewing this chapter, we

○ Opened an error dialog when we received a `CoreException` during a user interface operation

○ Wrote a message to the log file when we received a `CoreException` in a context where we didn't want to show a dialog

CHAPTER 21

Tracing—Instrumenting a Plug-In

Good exception handling and error reporting are critical for the serviceability of your plug-in. In addition, you might also want to instrument your plug-in with optional debugging code that can help you localize plug-in problems in the field. You will want to selectively turn on or off this debugging code. Therefore, in this chapter we will instrument our plug-in using the Eclipse trace facility.

Auto-testing is tightly integrated into the builder and is almost fully transparent to the user. How do we react to a customer problem report indicating that not all of their tests are automatically run? We would like to be able to ask the user for more information. To prepare our code for such a question, we instrument the `AutoTestBuilder` with debugging code that prints to the console the list of test cases found.

We will use the `org.eclipse.jdt.core` plug-in as our example, as it is heavily traced. The tracing options and their values are defined in a *.options* file that is located in the plug-in folder (see Figure 21.1).

Figure 21.1

Inside the *.options* file the options values are defined using a "plug-in id/ option path" syntax:

org.eclipse.jdt.core/.options
```
# Reports incremental builder activity
org.eclipse.jdt.core/debug/builder=false
# Reports compiler activity
org.eclipse.jdt.core/debug/compiler=false
```

You can enable or disable these option in the *.options* file. The debug options provided by a plug-in are presented on the **PDE target run-time** tab (see Figure 21.2).

In your plug-in code you can query an option setting by calling `Platform.getDebugOption()` with your option path.

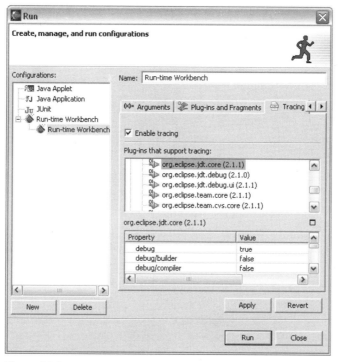

Figure 21.2

To instrument the test-finding code, we mimic the *.options* file from `org.eclipse.jdt.core` and add a similar *.options* file to the `org.eclipse.contribution.junit` plug-in project. We support only a single option to trace the test classes found:

org.eclipse.contribution.junit/.options
```
# Reports the found tests when in auto test mode
org.eclipse.contribution.junit/trace/testfinding=false
```

In the `AutoTestBuilder` class we want to test whether this option is set and, depending on its value, write the tests found to the console. An option's value cannot be changed at runtime. Therefore we only look up its value once. The option values are surfaced by the `Platform` Façade. We use a static initializer to perform the test once and store the result in a static trace variable:

org.eclipse.contribution.junit/AutoTestBuilder
```
private static boolean trace= false;
static {
  String value= Platform.getDebugOption(
    "org.eclipse.contribution.junit/trace/testfinding");
  if (value != null && value.equalsIgnoreCase("true"))
    AutoTestBuilder.trace= true;
}
```

Next, we instrument the build method as follows:

org.eclipse.contribution.junit/AutoTestBuilder
```
protected IProject[] build(int kind, Map args, IProgressMonitor pm)
    throws CoreException {
  if (hasBuildErrors())
    return null;
  IJavaProject javaProject= JavaCore.create(getProject());
  IType[] types= new TestSearcher().findAll(javaProject, pm);
  if (AutoTestBuilder.trace)
    printTestTypes(types);
  JUnitPlugin.getPlugin().run(types, javaProject);
  return null;
}
```

Finally, `printTestTypes()` prints the fully qualified type names to `System.out`.

org.eclipse.contribution.junit/AutoTestBuilder
```
private static void printTestTypes(IType[] tests) {
  System.out.println("Auto Test: ");
  for (int i= 0; i < tests.length; i++) {
    System.out.println("\t"+tests[i].getFullyQualifiedName());
  }
}
```

With this in place we can enable tracing in the launch configuration dialog, as shown in Figure 21.3.

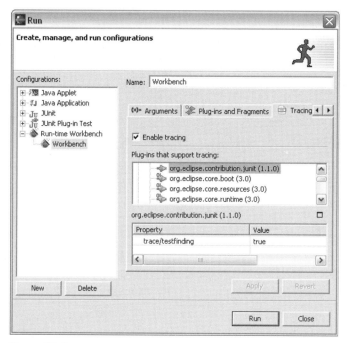

Figure 21.3

With the option set to **true** we get the test-finding trace output in the console:

```
Auto Test:
  junit.samples.money.MoneyTest
  pack1.FailTest
```

During development you can use PDE to enable and disable tracing options as shown above. To enable tracing options for Eclipse in the field, use the `-debug` command line option followed by the location of the *.options* file. For example:

```
eclipse.exe -debug c:/eclipse/plugins/org.eclipse.contribution.
junit/.options
```

Now if a user has trouble with tests not being found, we can ask them to rerun Eclipse with the tracing options set and we have a chance to understand the problem. Next we'll make our test-failure error markers more powerful by letting the user rerun failed tests from a marker. In this chapter we

- ❍ Defined a tracing option in the plug-in's *.options* file

- ❍ Retrieved the option value at runtime and emitted additional trace information

21.1   **Forward Pointers**

○ Eclipse comes with a rich set of tracing options. Experimenting with tracing options can provide insights into Eclipse.

○ *Timing operations*—Another good use of tracing options is to time performance critical operations.

CHAPTER 22

Marker Resolution—Invoking a Long-Running Operation

We have a left over TODO from Chapter 16. We still need to implement the Rerun Marker Resolution:

org.eclipse.contribution.junit/RerunMarkerResolutionGenerator
```
public IMarkerResolution [] getResolutions(IMarker marker)  {
    IMarkerResolution resolution= new IMarkerResolution() {
      public String getLabel() {
        return "Re-run test";
      }
      public void run(IMarker marker) {
        // TODO implement this
        System.out.println("not implemented yet");
      }
    };
    return new IMarkerResolution[]  {resolution};
}
```

The purpose of the marker resolution is to give the user a quick way to fix, or at least investigate, the problem represented by the marker. We would like to quickly rerun a failed test, perhaps after setting a breakpoint. In this chapter we implement rerunning a test from a marker. While we do so you will see

❍ How to invoke a build operation programmatically

❍ How to invoke a long-running operation with progress and cancellation support

Before we can rerun the test we have to make sure that

❍ The changes the user did to fix the failure are saved.

○ The workspace is built before we run the test so that the test runs on the
latest compiled code.

22.1   Testing Marker Resolution

Let's start by specifying the expected behavior with a test. We use MarkerTest
as our template:

org.eclipse.contribution.junit.test/MarkerResolutionTest
```
public void testMarkerResolution() throws Exception {
  JUnitPlugin.getPlugin().run(type);
  IMarker[] markers= getFailureMarkers();
  assertEquals(1, markers.length);

  fixProblem();

  RerunMarkerResolutionGenerator generator=
    new RerunMarkerResolutionGenerator();
  IMarkerResolution[] resolutions=
    generator.getResolutions(markers[0]);
  resolutions[0].run(markers[0]);
  markers= getFailureMarkers();
  assertEquals(0, getFailureMarkers().length);
}
```

We run a test in the failure-test setup we have used in the previous chapters.

22.2   Build and Rerun

After running the tests we expect one test failure marker. After we fix the problem we invoke the MarkerResolution and assert that there are no more failure
markers. We fix the problem in a crude way by just deleting the failing test:

org.eclipse.contribution.junit/RerunMarkerResolutionGenerator
```
private void fixProblem() throws JavaModelException {
  IMethod testMethod= type.getMethod("testFailure", new String[0]);
  testMethod.delete(true, null);
}
```

Run() is implemented as follows:

org.eclipse.contribution.junit/RerunMarkerResolutionGenerator
```
public void run(final IMarker m) {
  if (!save())
    return;
  if (!build())
    return;
```

```
    IType type= findTest(m);
    JUnitPlugin.getPlugin().run(type);
}
```

We

1. Save the editor's contents

2. Invoke a build

3. Rerun the test

If either the save or the build fails, we return early. We first have to save the editors. Editors are contained in the WorkbenchWindow (see Figure 22.1).

Figure 22.1   WorkbenchWindow Contains Editors

To save the editors, we tell the workbench window to save all editors:

org.eclipse.contribution.junit/RerunMarkerResolutionGenerator
```
private boolean save() {
  IWorkbench workbench= PlatformUI.getWorkbench();
  return workbench.saveAllEditors(false);
}
```

We retrieve the workbench from the PlatformUI Façade, the central place for accessing the Eclipse UI through static methods.

Next we have to invoke a build operation so that our tests are rerun with the latest compiled code. We could just build the project under consideration, but this project might depend on code changes in another project. Therefore we incrementally build the entire workspace. Given the rule that an incremental builder should return quickly when there is nothing to do, the overhead of building a project that hasn't changed can be ignored. The method to build the entire workspace in IWorkspace is:

org.eclipse.core.resources/IWorkspace
```
public void build(int kind, IProgressMonitor pm)
    throws CoreException;
```

The kind parameter is an enumeration with the options to do either a full or an incremental build. We will call build() with IncrementalProject-Builder.INCREMENTAL_BUILD.

22.3   Showing Progress

The fact that `build` takes a progress monitor indicates that `build()` is a long-running operation. For operations that take a while to complete it is good UI practice to

○ Show the user how the operation is progressing

○ Offer the user a way to cancel the operation

Before taking care of showing progress, let's look at `IProgressMonitor`. The `IProgressMonitor` argument is a collecting parameter. An operation calls it to inform the user about progress. Here is the `IProgressMonitor` interface:

org.eclipse.core.runtime/IProgressMonitor
```
public interface IProgressMonitor {
  public void beginTask(String name, int totalWork);
  public void worked(int work);
  public void done();
  public boolean isCanceled();
}
```

With `beginTask()` the operation gives its name and the total number of expected units of work. An operation calls `worked()` when some amount of work is completed. Calling `done()` indicates that the operation is complete.

To find out whether a user has requested a cancellation, the operation should call `isCanceled()` frequently. If the user requests a cancellation, the operation should be terminated by throwing an exception. The exception can be either an `InterruptedException` or an `OperationCanceledException`. We prefer `InterruptedException` because wherever possible you want to reuse existing exception types rather than introduce your own. (`Operation-CanceledException` is still supported for backwards compatibility.) This is the snippet you will find in many Eclipse operations:

```
if (monitor.isCanceled())
  throw new InterruptedException();
```

Now that we know how progress is reported by an operation we can look into presenting this progress information. The consumer of the progress information is an `IRunnableContext`. Whereas `IProgressMonitor` is from the headless (UI-independent) core layer, `IRunnableContext` is defined in the UI layer. It has a single method to run an operation. The `IRunnableContext` is responsible for showing a progress indicator and a cancel button. Browsing the type hierarchy for `IRunnableContext` shows us that there is more than one implementation, as shown in Figure 22.2.

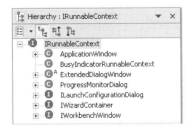

Figure 22.2

For example, wizards show the progress embedded in the wizard dialog, ProgressMonitorDialog shows a separate dialog, and Application-Window shows the progress in the status bar of a window. For our purpose, we choose ProgressMonitorDialog. It is the simplest, but it is also the most obtrusive way to show progress, because it pops up a modal dialog. So we are ready to write the build() method:

org.eclipse.contribution.junit/RerunMarkerResolutionGenerator
```
protected boolean build() {
  ProgressMonitorDialog dialog= new ProgressMonitorDialog(
    getShell());
  try {
    dialog.run(true, true, new IRunnableWithProgress() {
      public void run(IProgressMonitor monitor)
        throws InvocationTargetException {
        // invoke build
      }
    });
  } catch (InterruptedException e) {
    return false;
  } catch (InvocationTargetException e) {
    Throwable target= e.getTargetException();
    // TODO inform about target exception
    return false;
  }
  return true;
}
```

First we create a ProgressMonitorDialog and pass a shell as its parent so that it is properly layered in the UI. Since we have no access to an IWorkbench-Site, we fetch the shell from the currently active workbench window. The active workbench window can be null, but we can return null from getShell() because the ProgressMonitorDialog safely handles null as a shell. We can't get to a site, which always returns a workbench window. Access the work-bench window through PlatformUI only as a last resort, as in this case.

org.eclipse.contribution.junit/RerunMarkerResolutionGenerator
```
private Shell getShell() {
  IWorkbench workbench= PlatformUI.getWorkbench();
```

```
IWorkbenchWindow window= workbench.getActiveWorkbenchWindow();
if (window == null)
  return null;
return window.getShell();
}
```

After we have created the dialog, we call the `run()` method implemented from the `IRunnableContext`. The first two flags define whether the operation can be cancelled and whether it should run in a separate thread. Both flags are true in our case. The next argument is an `IRunnableWithProgress`, which allows us to define the code that should run with a progress monitor. From this runnable we will invoke build.

The `run()` method can throw either an `InterruptedException` or an `InvocationTargetException`. The `InterruptedException` indicates that the user canceled the operation and we just return **false** to propagate this fact. An `InvocationTargetException` is used to transport an exception from the operation to the caller. It wraps the exception that occurred during the operation. Therefore, to get at its wrapped exception we have to call `getTarget-Exception()` and process this exception.

Finally, let's fill in the body of the run method. We call an incremental build on the workspace, which we retrieve from the resources plug-in:

org.eclipse.contribution.junit/RerunMarkerResolutionGenerator.build()
```
...
try {
  ResourcesPlugin.getWorkspace().build(
    IncrementalProjectBuilder.INCREMENTAL_BUILD, monitor);
} catch (CoreException e) {
  throw new InvocationTargetException(e);
}
```

`Build()` throws a `CoreException` that we have to wrap in an `Invocation-TargetException` so that it can be transported back from the `run()` method and handled there. There is one small twist. When auto-test is **on,** then the build will also trigger a full test run of all the tests inside the project. However, we want to run just the failed test. To address this problem, we add a flag to the `AutoTestBuilder` so that we can temporarily disable it:

org.eclipse.contribution.junit/AutoTestBuilder
```
public class AutoTestBuilder extends IncrementalProjectBuilder {
  private static boolean enabled= true;
  public static void setEnabled(boolean isEnabled) {
    AutoTestBuilder.enabled= isEnabled;
  }
  protected IProject[] build(int kind, Map args, pm monitor)
    throws CoreException {
```

```
if (hasBuildErrors() || !AutoTestBuilder.enabled)
  return null;
```

org.eclipse.contribution.junit/RerunMarkerResolutionGenerator.build()
```
...
try {
  AutoTestBuilder.setEnabled(false);
  ResourcesPlugin.getWorkspace().build(
    IncrementalProjectBuilder.INCREMENTAL_BUILD, monitor);
} catch (CoreException e) {
  throw new InvocationTargetException(e);
} finally {
  AutoTestBuilder.setEnabled(true);
}
```

The alternative to all this code is to have a UI with no progress, no cancellation support, and windows that do not redraw during an operation.

22.4   Rerunning the Test

How do we rerun the failed tests? We'll simplify the functionality to run all the tests in the same class as the failed test.

org.eclipse.contribution.junit/RerunMarkerResolutionGenerator.run()
```
...
IType type= findTest(m);
JUnitPlugin.getPlugin().run(type);
```

Marker resolutions fix a problem by inspecting the values of the marker they are intended to fix. In our case, all we need is the resource corresponding to the marker. From there we use the Java model to find the top-level type:

org.eclipse.contribution.junit/RerunMarkerResolutionGenerator
```
protected IType findTest(IMarker m) {
  IResource resource= m.getResource();
  ICompilationUnit cu= (ICompilationUnit)JavaCore.create(resource);
  return cu.findPrimaryType();
}
```

To navigate from the resource to the corresponding compilation unit, we ask `JavaCore` to create an `ICompilationUnit` for us. Finally, `findPrimaryType()` returns us the top-level type. Since test cases always have to be in a top-level, type this is good enough for us.

Done. The test is indeed green. To finish, we wrap the call to run the tests inside a `WorkspaceRunnable`, as shown below:

org.eclipse.contribution.junit/RerunMarkerResolutionGenerator

```
public void run(final IMarker m) {
  if (!save())
    return;
  if (!build())
    return;
  IWorkspaceRunnable runnable= new IWorkspaceRunnable() {
    public void run(IProgressMonitor monitor)throws CoreException {
      IType type= findTest(m);
      JUnitPlugin.getPlugin().run(type);
    }
  };
  try {
    ResourcesPlugin.getWorkspace().run(runnable, null);
  } catch (CoreException e) {
    // TODO error handling
  }
}
```

In the next chapter we'll write another view that provides us more information about a test run. Reviewing this chapter, we

○ Saved all editors with `PlatformUI.getWorkbench().saveAllEditors(false)`

○ Invoked an `IncrementalProjectBuilder` build all projects

○ Wrapped building in an `IWorkspaceRunnable` to improve error handling and reporting

22.5   Forward Pointers

○ `SubProgressMonitors`—Sometimes operations are composed of multiple operations. To show accurate progress in such a situation, use a `SubProgressMonitor`. The top-level operation divides the operation into suboperations and gives each suboperation its own progress monitor.

CHAPTER 23

Test Report View— Using JFace

In this chapter we'll see how to

- ○ Create a view using the JFace viewer framework
- ○ Configure a viewer using a label provider and a content provider
- ○ Use PDE to define a new extension
- ○ Open a Java element in a Java editor

In Chapter 13 we implemented a simple view using only SWT widgets. In this chapter we will contribute a more complex view using the JFace viewer framework. This illustrates that to contribute a view you can use a framework, but you don't have to. Frameworks have a particular scope. It's hard to program when your problem doesn't fit into a framework but you still have to use it. Eclipse works hard to offer frameworks without imposing them.

Our example JUnit plug-in allows us to see failures as markers. Markers display the most important information we need about failing tests. Sometimes you want additional information about a whole test run. For example, you may want to know which tests actually were executed and how long an individual test took. In this chapter we'll implement a view displaying such information, as shown in Figure 23.1.

The first column shows the test name and its status and the second column shows how long a test run took.

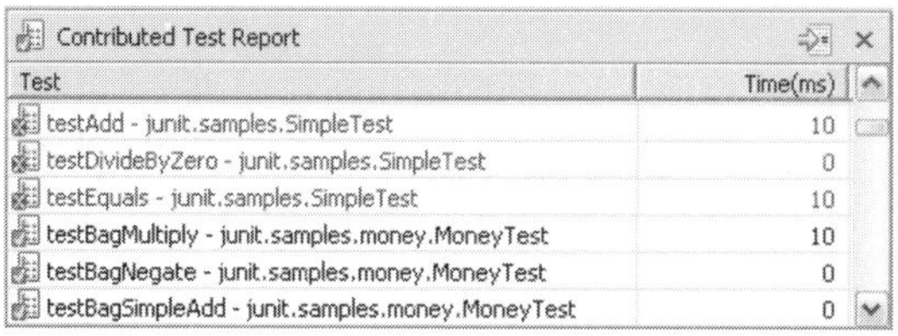

Figure 23.1

To implement this view, we will cover the following topics:

❍ Using a JFace viewer to implement a view

❍ Using JFace content and label providers

❍ Dynamically updating a viewer

JFace

JFace sits on top of the SWT widget toolkit and provides a set of frameworks that help with common application-development tasks. JFace helps you manage images and fonts, supports the creation of wizards and preference pages, and provides the basic action support that we have already encountered.

The most interesting JFace component is the *viewer*. A viewer is attached to a SWT widget and helps you present objects from your domain model. A viewer populates an SWT widget with objects from your domain and helps you keep the widget in sync when the domain changes. JFace provides standard viewers for lists, tables, and trees. A viewer is configured with a content provider and a label provider. The content provider knows how to access objects from your domain. The label provider knows how to present domain objects with an icon and a label.

The Eclipse **Bookmarks** view looks very similar to our view. We can take it as an example. When exploring the **Bookmarks** view with the Spider, we create the diagram shown in Figure 23.2.

From the Spider diagram we can derive the following to-do list:

❍ Create a `TableViewer`

❍ Create a `Table` widget with columns

❍ Implement a content provider

❍ Implement a label provider

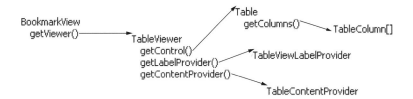

Figure 23.2   TableViewer with Parts

Before we can address these JFace-related work items, we have to define the model representing a test run.

23.1   **TestResult**

We represent a test run as a list of test results, where a test result captures the name of a test, its project, class, and status (0 = OK, 1 = failure), and the start and end time.

org.eclipse.contribution.junit/TestResult
```
public class TestResult {
  public final static int OK= 0;
  public final static int FAILED= 1;
  public IJavaProject project;
  public String klass;
  public String method;
  public int status;
  public long startTime;
  public long endTime;
}
```

`TestResult` provides methods to be used for reporting:

org.eclipse.contribution.junit/TestResult
```
public TestResult(IJavaProject project, String klass, String method,
    int status, long startTime) {
  this.project= project;
  this.klass= klass;
  this.method= method;
  this.status= status;
  this.startTime= startTime;
}
public void testFailed()  {
  status= FAILED;
}
public boolean isFailure()  {
  return status == FAILED;
}
```

```
public void testFinished()  {
  endTime= System.currentTimeMillis();
}
public long testDuration()  {
  return endTime-startTime;
}
```

23.2   The Test

Before we start with the UI-related work items, let's first write a test. As usual when developing test-first, once we have a fixture and the required helper methods in place, the rest of development is much simpler. First we create a test setup using our `TestProject` helper as we have done before. We create a test project with a single failing test:

org.eclipse.contribution.junit.test/TestReportTest
```
public class TestReportTest extends TestCase {
  private TestReportView view;
  private TestProject testProject;
  private IPackageFragment pack;
  private IType type;

  protected void setUp() throws Exception {
    testProject= new TestProject();
    testProject.addJar("org.junit", "junit.jar");
    pack= testProject.createPackage("pack1");
    type= testProject.createType(pack, "FailTest.java",
      "public class FailTest extends junit.framework.TestCase {"+
      " public void testFailure() {fail();}}");
  }
  protected void tearDown() throws Exception {
    testProject.dispose();
  }
}
```

In the actual test we first make sure that our view is visible. Then, we run the tests. After the tests run, the table should contain what we expect:

org.eclipse.contribution.junit.test/TestReportTest
```
public void testReportView() throws Exception {
  showView();
  JUnitPlugin.getPlugin().run(type);
  Table table= (Table)view.getViewer().getControl();
  assertEquals(1, table.getItemCount());
  TableItem item= table.getItem(0);
  assertEquals("testFailure - pack1.FailTest", item.getText(0));
}
```

The `showView()` method makes the `TestReportView` view visible in the current workbench page and keeps a reference to it in an instance variable of our test-case class:

org.eclipse.contribution.junit.test/TestReportTest
```
private void showView() throws PartInitException {
  view= (TestReportView) getPage().showView(
    "org.eclipse.contribution.junit.testReportView");
}
```

We introduce a helper method `getPage()` as we did in other tests to get the current workbench page. In the test we retrieve the underlying SWT `Table` widget from the view and ask it for its number of items, this corresponds to the number of rows in the table. Next we assert that the text of the first column in the first row corresponds to the presentation of the failed test. This presentation will be defined by the label provider as we will see in Section 23.4.

23.3   The View

To start, let's declare the test-report-view extension. We can either edit the *plugin.xml* directly or we can use PDE to guide us through the extension creation. An extension point should define its attributes and expected values in an *extension point schema*. PDE uses the schema information to both validate the manifest and guide you through extension point creation. Since we know which extension point we want to define and since we haven't used the PDE schema-based extension until now, let's use it to define the extension point for the test report view.

Open the *plugin.xml* in the manifest editor and switch to the **Extensions** tab, shown in Figure 23.3.

Figure 23.3

With the **Add...** button we can add the definition of a new extension. PDE offers wizards to define extensions that are either driven by the extension point's schema or custom extension templates, as shown in Figure 23.4. The templates are hand-crafted for a particular extension and can therefore generate a significant portion of the code. Browse the available extension templates and use them when they fit your needs.

Figure 23.4

We use the schema-based extension for creating our view extension. On the next page, select the `org.eclipse.ui.views` extension point and click **Finish** (the view extension point doesn't require a point identifier or name and you can leave the corresponding fields empty). This will create a new view extension definition that we can refine using the **New** action in the context menu and the **Properties** view. Double click an element to make its properties visible in the **Properties** view. To complete the views extension point, we add a new `view` element using the **New** action as shown in Figure 23.5.

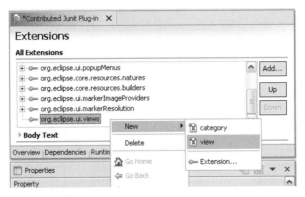

Figure 23.5

We also need to enter values for the `class`, `icon`, `id`, and `name` properties in the **Properties** view, shown in Figure 23.6. When entering the class name, you also have the option to generate the initial implementation of the class. The generated class conforms to the type specified in the schema information for the extension point. In our case, this is `ViewPart`. We won't use this feature now, so we can develop our view step-by-step.

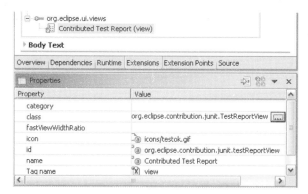

Figure 23.6

Having entered all this information, you should get the following extension point definition in the manifest editor's **Source** page:

org.eclipse.contribution.junit/plugin.xml
```
<extension point="org.eclipse.ui.views">
  <view
    name="Contributed Test Report"
    icon="icons/testok.gif"
    class="org.eclipse.contribution.junit.TestReportView"
    id="org.eclipse.contribution.junit.testReportView">
  </view>
</extension>
```

This is a lot of work to get a couple of lines of XML, so we typically edit the XML directly on the **Source** page when defining a new extension point. For beginners, though, the reduction in errors is likely worth the extra work.

We have assigned an icon to the view. The workbench uses this icon to present the view more attractively in view choosers. We chose an icon we added to the icons folder of our plug-in. We'll see later in this chapter how to define and use icons in our code.

Now that we're done with the declaration of TestReportView, we can work on its implementation. We derive from ViewPart and keep a reference to the JFace table viewer in an instance variable.

org.eclipse.contribution.junit/TestReportView
```
public class TestReportView extends ViewPart {
  private TableViewer viewer;
        // ...
  public TableViewer getViewer() {
    return viewer;
  }
}
```

The most important method of the view is `createPartControl()`, where we create and initialize the SWT `Table` and connect it with a JFace viewer. Let's start with the creation of the two-column SWT table:

org.eclipse.contribution.junit/TestReportView
```
public void createPartControl(Composite parent) {
  Table table= new Table(parent, SWT.SINGLE | SWT.H_SCROLL |
    SWT.V_SCROLL | SWT.FULL_SELECTION);

  table.setHeaderVisible(true);
  table.setLinesVisible(true);

  TableColumn column= new TableColumn(table, SWT.NONE, 0);
  column.setText("Test");
  column.setWidth(300);
  column.setAlignment(SWT.LEFT);

  column= new TableColumn(table, SWT.NONE, 1);
  column.setText("Time(ms)");
  column.setWidth(100);
  column.setAlignment(SWT.RIGHT);
  //...
}
```

We initialize the settings of the table in the constructor. SWT requires style bits when creating a table. These are settings that cannot be changed after the table has been created. For the report view we want a single selection, both horizontal and vertical scrolling, and we want the selection to cover all the columns. We don't set the border style bit (`SWT.BORDER`) since tables draw their own border.

Until now no JFace code is involved. These are all plain SWT calls. This illustrates the goal of JFace not to hide SWT from clients but to add value on top of it. Let's look at the JFace viewer configuration part of `createPart-Control()`:

org.eclipse.contribution.junit/TestReportView
```
public void createPartControl(Composite parent) {
  //...
  viewer= new TableViewer(table);
  viewer.setLabelProvider(new TestReportLabelProvider());
  viewer.setContentProvider(new TestReportContentProvider());
  viewer.setInput(new ArrayList());
}
```

The `TableViewer` isn't required to be subclassed for reuse. All that is needed is to configure it with a label and content provider.

First the viewer is connected with `table` by passing the `table` widget in the `TableViewer`'s constructor. Next we use a list of `TestResult` objects as the domain model for the viewer. Initially the list is empty, and we therefore pass an empty list as the input of the viewer.

View parts need to define their focus control. We do this by overriding `setFocus()`:

org.eclipse.contribution.junit/TestReportView
```
public void setFocus() {
  viewer.getControl().setFocus();
}
```

How does a viewer populate the `Table` widget with table items? Starting from the viewer's input, the content provider is asked for domain objects. How this is done depends on the viewer. For a tree viewer the domain is traversed by asking the content provider for the children of a domain object. For a table, the domain is asked for the elements corresponding to the domain object. JFace provides different content-provider interfaces for the different viewers. The domain objects returned from the content provider are then passed to the label provider. The label provider assigns a text and an icon to a domain object. All these interactions are done in terms of the type `Object`. The content and label providers know the domain and can therefore safely cast `Object` to the corresponding domain type.

23.4 TestReportLabelProvider

The basic `ILabelProvider` interface has just two methods:

org.eclipse.jface.viewers/ILabelProvider
```
public interface ILabelProvider extends IBaseLabelProvider {
  public Image getImage(Object element);
  public String getText(Object element);
}
```

As described above, the common currency for viewers is the type `Object`. The label provider returns an image and a text for such a domain object. In the case of `Table`, the label provider interface is extended to return images and text corresponding to table columns. The `TestReportLabelProvider` is therefore positioned in the label provider type hierarchy, as shown in Figure 23.7.

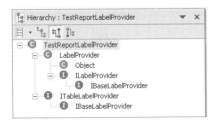

Figure 23.7

org.eclipse.contribution.junit/TestReportLabelProvider
```
public class TestReportLabelProvider extends LabelProvider
    implements ITableLabelProvider {
  //...
}
```

The `getColumnText()` method returns the text corresponding to a column in a table. For the `TestReportView` the first column shows the test name and the second column the test duration:

org.eclipse.contribution.junit/TestReportLabelProvider
```
public String getColumnText(Object element, int columnIndex) {
  TestResult result= (TestResult)element;
  switch (columnIndex) {
  case 0:
    return result.method+" - "+result.klass;
  case 1:
    return Long.toString(result.testDuration());
  }
  return null;
}
```

The element we receive as an argument corresponds to a `TestResult` that we cast accordingly.

Before we can implement the corresponding `getColumnImage()` method, we have to make a short digression into managing images. Images are an SWT resource that need to be loaded and disposed of when no longer needed. To simplify the management of images, JFace provides image descriptors. An `ImageDescriptor` knows how to create an image from different sources. We store our images in an icon folder of our plug-in, shown in Figure 23.8.

Figure 23.8

This allows us to use icons in both the *plugin.xml* (see the View extension definition above) and the Java code. We want to use a relative path to fetch icons. Here is the helper method to create an image using a relative path:

org.eclipse.contribution.junit/TestReportLabelProvider
```
private static Image createImage(String path) {
  URL url= JUnitPlugin.getPlugin().getDescriptor().getInstallURL();
  ImageDescriptor descriptor= null;
  try {
    descriptor= ImageDescriptor.createFromURL(new URL(url, path));
  } catch (MalformedURLException e) {
    descriptor= ImageDescriptor.getMissingImageDescriptor();
  }
  return descriptor.createImage();
}
```

We call `createImage()` with an image path relative to the plug-in, for example *icons/testok.gif*. The method first retrieves the install location of the `JUnitPlugin` and then creates an `ImageDescriptor` that refers to the requested path. This is all done with URLs. The `ImageDescriptor` can create an SWT image from this URL. If this fails, we just use the missing image descriptor that returns an ugly little red square icon. With the help of `createImage()` we create the images required for our label provider. We need an image for both a successful and a failed test. We keep them in an array that we initialize in the constructor. Using an array allows us to access the images easily by the test status stored in the `TestResult`.

org.eclipse.contribution.junit/TestReportLabelProvider
```
public TestReportLabelProvider() {
  images= new Image[2];
  images[TestResult.OK]= createImage("icons/testok.gif");
  images[TestResult.FAILED]= createImage("icons/testerr.gif");
}
```

Now we are ready to implement `getColumnImage()`:

org.eclipse.contribution.junit/TestReportLabelProvider
```
public Image getColumnImage(Object element, int columnIndex) {
  if (columnIndex == 0)
    return images[((TestResult)element).status];
  return null;
}
```

Only the first column has an image. After casting the passed-in element to `TestResult`, we return the image corresponding to the test result's status.

We override the `dispose()` method, which JFace calls to enable clients to free resources.

org.eclipse.contribution.junit/TestReportLabelProvider
```
public void dispose() {
  for (int i= 0; i < images.length; i++)
    images[i].dispose();
}
```

Finally, to emphasize failed tests in the table we want to render them in red. We can add `IColorProvider` to the label provider to define the color representation. Therefore, to render a failed test we add the `IColorProvider` interface and implement its methods:

org.eclipse.contribution.junit/TestReportLabelProvider
```
public class TestReportLabelProvider
    extends LabelProvider
    implements ITableLabelProvider, IColorProvider {
  public Color getForeground(Object element) {
    if (((TestResult)element).isFailure())
      return Display.getDefault().
        getSystemColor(SWT.COLOR_RED);
    return null;
  }
  public Color getBackground(Object element) {
    return null;
  }
}
```

Next we implement the content provider, which typically is the most involved piece of a viewer.

23.5   TestReportContentProvider

A content provider has two responsibilities. First, it knows how to access and navigate the domain. Second, it observes the domain for changes and updates the viewer accordingly.

Accessing the domain is simpler, so let's start with that. The `TestContentProvider` implements `IStructuredContentProvider`. It defines the interface for accessing a *structured domain*, that is, a domain that consists of a collection of elements. It has a single method, `getElements()`. This method is responsible for returning the domain objects corresponding to the passed-in object. The implementation of `getElements()` is:

org.eclipse.contribution.junit/TestReportContentProvider
```
class TestReportContentProvider
    implements IStructuredContentProvider
  public Object[] getElements(Object inputElement) {
    return ((List)inputElement).toArray();
  }
}
```

The method `getElements()` receives the input element as an argument and returns an array of domain objects that correspond to this element. In our case, the input is a `List` of `TestResult`s and all that needs to be done is to convert the `List` into an array. Returning an array is consistent with the Eclipse convention to use arrays in the API wherever possible.

Let's move on to the update part of the task. As test results are reported we want to update the table. For this reason the `TestReportContentProvider` is also an `ITestRunListener`, as shown in Figure 23.9.

Figure 23.9

The `TestReportContentProvider` registers as a dynamic listener in its constructor and deregisters in the `dispose()` method.

org.eclipse.contribution.junit/TestReportContentProvider
```
class TestReportContentProvider
    implements IStructuredContentProvider, ITestRunListener {

  public TestReportContentProvider() {
    JUnitPlugin.getPlugin().addTestListener(this);
  }

  public void dispose() {
    JUnitPlugin.getPlugin().removeTestListener(this);
  }
}
```

To update the viewer when the domain model changes, the content provider needs a reference to the viewer. Whenever the input of the viewer changes the content provider is informed with `inputChanged()`. In addition to the new and old inputs the viewer is passed in and we can grab a reference to the viewer from there:

org.eclipse.contribution.junit/TestReportContentProvider
```
private TableViewer viewer;
public void inputChanged(Viewer tableViewer, Object oldInput,
    Object newInput) {
  viewer= (TableViewer)tableViewer;
}
```

The content provider gets informed about test progress, so it can now update the view. The scheme we will use is that we store the `TestResult` object of the test run in progress. We update the current result as we receive test notifications. The first notification we will get is that the tests have started:

org.eclipse.contribution.junit/TestReportContentProvider
```
public void testsStarted(IJavaProject project, int testCount) {
  ((List)viewer.getInput()).clear();
  currentResult= null;
  viewer.refresh();
}
```

From the viewer's input, we get at our list and clear it. To update the viewer we call the `refresh()` method. This method does a full refresh of the viewer from the domain model. JFace viewers provide different methods to sync the widget with the domain. The `refresh()` method is the most expensive one. There are also methods to refresh single items. Finally, we reset the `currentResult` to `null`. Before we proceed, let's use the **Extract Method** refactoring to extract the cast into a separate method:

org.eclipse.contribution.junit/TestReportContentProvider
```
private List getTestResults() {
  return (List) viewer.getInput();
}
```

When a test starts, we add the `currentResult` to the list and create a new `TestResult`:

org.eclipse.contribution.junit/TestReportContentProvider
```
public void testStarted(IJavaProject project, String klass,
    String methodName) {
  addLastResult();
  currentResult= new TestResult(project, klass,
    methodName, 0, System.currentTimeMillis());
}
```

When a test fails, we update the current test result:

org.eclipse.contribution.junit/TestReportContentProvider
```
public void testFailed(IJavaProject project, String klass,
    String method, String trace) {
  currentResult.testFailed();
}
```

Finally, when the test run is finished, we add the last result:

org.eclipse.contribution.junit/TestReportContentProvider
```
public void testsFinished(IJavaProject project) {
  addLastResult();
}
```

The only method left to look at is addLastResult(). It updates our domain model and adds the result. Next it appends the result to the viewer by calling insert(). Insert() takes the domain object we want to add and the index where it should be added to the table. We pass -1 to indicate that it should be appended at the end. Notice that communication with the viewer is always in terms of the domain objects and not in terms of SWT items. Updating the corresponding SWT items is done in an optimized way inside the viewer and you don't have to worry about it.

org.eclipse.contribution.junit/TestReportContentProvider
```
private void addLastResult() {
  if (currentResult != null)  {
    currentResult.testFinished();
    getTestResults().add(currentResult);
    viewer.insert(currentResult, -1);
  }
}
```

Now is a good time to run our test. The test is green. We have the functionality we expected.

Let's also try the test report in auto-test mode. We start our workbench, add the TestReportView with **Window > Show View,** and make a change. A rebuild is triggered, but unfortunately, we get an exception:

```
org.eclipse.swt.SWTException: Invalid thread access
  at org.eclipse.swt.SWT.error(SWT.java:2350)
  at org.eclipse.swt.SWT.error(SWT.java:2280)
  at org.eclipse.swt.widgets.Widget.error(Widget.java:389)
  at org.eclipse.swt.widgets.Widget.checkWidget(Widget.java:319)
  at org.eclipse.swt.widgets.Table.getItemCount(Table.java:823)
  at org.eclipse.jface.viewers.TableViewer.insert(
    TableViewer.java:424)
  at org.eclipse.contribution.junit.
    TestReportContentProvider.addLastResult(
    TestReportContentProvider.java:74)
```

Why do we fail with this exception? The build operation takes a while. To keep the UI responsive during such a long-running operation, Eclipse runs it in a separate thread. SWT is not thread-safe. It only allows a widget to be accessed from the thread that created it. In our case, the widgets were created in the main thread. When we tell the viewer to update, JFace will attempt to interact with the SWT widgets and the exception is thrown. Fortunately, SWT is friendly enough to check whether its widgets are accessed from the correct thread. Setting a breakpoint in `testsStarted()` illustrates the problem. In the debug view shown in Figure 23.10, we can see that our listener method doesn't get called in the main thread. Instead, it is called from a `ModalContext` thread, which is part of the Eclipse support for long-running operations.

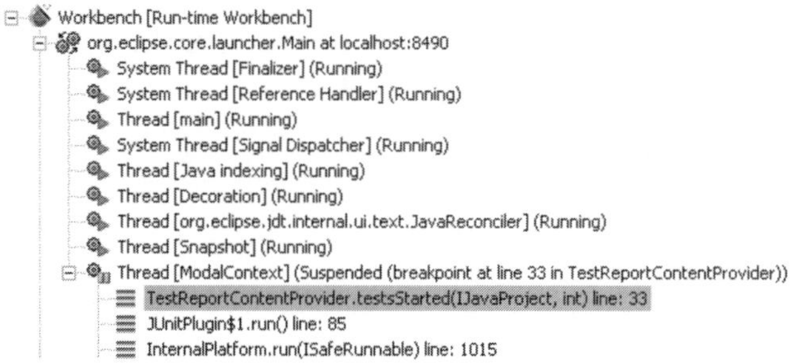

Figure 23.10

We therefore have to make sure that we call the viewer update methods in the main thread. SWT supports posting an event that then gets processed by the correct thread. Here is the `addLastResult()` method enriched with the posting logic:

org.eclipse.contribution.junit/TestReportContentProvider
```
private void addLastResult() {
  if (currentResult != null)  {
    currentResult.testFinished();
    getTestResults().add(currentResult);
    Control ctrl= viewer.getControl();
    if (ctrl == null || ctrl.isDisposed())
      return;
    ctrl.getDisplay().syncExec(new Runnable() {
      public void run() {
        if (!viewer.getControl().isDisposed())
          viewer.insert(currentResult, -1);
      }
    });
  }
}
```

This is a lot of checking code just to post an event. However, we have to keep in mind that we are in a different thread and the world can change under us while our code executes. In particular, the viewer might get disposed at any time. We check whether the viewer still exists before we send the event, represented

as a `Runnable`. The method to post an event is provided by the SWT `Display`
class. With `syncExec()` we can post a `Runnable` that is executed in the main
thread. Inside the `Runnable` we have to check again that the viewer wasn't disposed in the meantime. If the viewer still exists, we finally call the `insert()`
method to update the viewer. We have to do the same dance in the `tests-`
`Started()` method as well, since it calls the viewer's `refresh()` method.

As an alternative to `syncExec()`, we could have also used `asyncExec()`.
The method `syncExec()` blocks the calling thread until the runnable is executed. `AsyncExec()` doesn't block the calling thread and it will continue
immediately. Use `syncExec()` if possible because it provides more determin-
istic behavior. However, `syncExec()` always has deadlock potential and you
need to know whether it is safe to block or not.

The `TestReportView` is not the only view part we have implemented. We
started this circle with the simpler `ResultView`. It has the same illegal-thread-
access problem. We use the same approach as in `TestReportView` to fix the
problem and post the redraw request via `syncExec()` to the main thread. This
is done in a `changeColor()` helper method:

org.eclipse.contribution.junit/ResultView
```
private void changeColor(final boolean success) {
  Display display= getSite().getShell().getDisplay();
  display.syncExec(new Runnable() {
    public void run() {
      if (control.isDisposed())
        return;
      if (success) {
        Display display= control.getDisplay();
        Color green= display.getSystemColor(SWT.COLOR_GREEN);
        control.setBackground(green);
      } else  {
        Color red= display.getSystemColor(SWT.COLOR_RED);
        control.setBackground(red);
      }
    }
  });
}
```

Because we are in a view part, we can use the site to get access to a display for
posting our runnable. As in the last section, we check that the control didn't
get destroyed in the meantime.

With the `changeColor()` helper method we can now change the listener
method implementations:

org.eclipse.contribution.junit/ResultView$Listener
```
public void testsFinished(IJavaProject project) {
  changeColor(success);
}
public void testFailed(IJavaProject project, String klass,
```

```
    String method, String trace) {
  success= false;
  changeColor(success);
}
```

23.6   Handling Events

The last feature we want to add to our view is the ability to open the corresponding test case in an editor. To start on this feature we add another test to `TestReportTest`. The test verifies that the expected editor is open after the call to an event-handling method we have not yet implemented.

org.eclipse.contribution.junit.test.junit/TestReportTest
```
public void testOpenEditor() throws Exception {
  showView();
  JUnitPlugin.getPlugin().run(type);
  Table table= (Table)view.getViewer().getControl();
  table.select(0);
  view.handleDefaultSelected();
  IEditorReference editor= assertEditorOpen();
  assertEditorInput(editor);
}
```

We trigger a test run and then programmatically select the first row of the SWT table widget. Next we call the to-be-implemented method `handle-DefaultSelected()`, which will handle the double click and open the editor. Notice that the call to `table.select(0)` doesn't trigger a call to the listener. The SWT listeners are usually only called when the change is user-initiated. For this reason, we call the event-handling method `handleDefault-Selected()` manually.

The Java editor will immediately flag the missing method as an error. However, if we really want to start with a test failure, now we could run this test. This is possible because Eclipse allows us to run code even when it has errors. In other words, the Eclipse compiler can generate code for compilation units having errors. To illustrate this possibility, let's run the test now and we get the failure shown in Figure 23.11.

Figure 23.11

At this point we can use the Java editor's quick-fix function to create the method in `TestReportView`. After the call of the event handling method, we call a helper method, `assertEditorOpen()`, that tests whether any editor is open:

org.eclipse.contribution.junit.test.junit/TestReportTest
```
private IEditorReference assertEditorOpen() {
  IWorkbenchPage page= getPage();
  IEditorReference[] editors= page.getEditorReferences();
  assertEquals(1, editors.length);
  return editors[0];
}
```

Because our test starts in a fresh workbench with no editors open, towards the end of the test we can fetch all editors and assert that now a single editor is open. The editors we get back from `getEditorReferences()` are actually just references to the editors and not the real editor parts. The workbench uses the indirection through a proxy so that it can lazily create editors only when they become visible. This is important for the start-up performance. Imagine restarting a workbench with a dozen open editors. Using references enables Eclipse to create only the top-most visible editor during start-up instead of all editors. Because we need the open editor for our next step, we return it from `assertEditorOpen()`.

Next we verify that the editor corresponding to *FailTest.java* is opened. This is done in another helper method, `assertEditorInput()`:

org.eclipse.contribution.junit.test.junit/TestReportTest
```
private void assertEditorInput(IEditorReference editor)
    throws JavaModelException {
  IEditorInput expected= new FileEditorInput(
    (IFile)type.getUnderlyingResource());
  IEditorPart part= editor.getEditor(true);
  assertEquals(expected, part.getEditorInput());
}
```

The content of an editor is described by an `IEditorInput`, a lightweight description of an input source for an editor (not necessarily just a file). The different sources have to implement `IEditorInput`. In our case, the editor's input is the file *FailTest.java*. We therefore create a `FileEditorInput` for the file corresponding to the type `FailTest`. This gives us the expected value we compare with the input of the editor. To retrieve the input of the editor we have to fetch the real editor part from the reference.

Finally, we have to reset the state of the workbench after each test and we add a call to `closeAllEditors()` to `tearDown()`.

org.eclipse.contribution.junit.test.junit/TestReportTest
```
protected void tearDown() throws Exception {
  getPage().closeAllEditors(false);
  testProject.dispose();
}
```

Now, let's make this test pass. When a selection occurs, SWT fires a selection event. We register a selection listener with the `table` widget and add the following code to `createPartControl()`:

org.eclipse.contribution.junit/TestReportView.createPartControl()
```
table.addSelectionListener(new SelectionAdapter() {
  public void widgetDefaultSelected(SelectionEvent e) {
    handleDefaultSelected();
  }
});
```

We implement the `SelectionListener` with the help of `SelectionAdapter`. `SelectionAdapter` provides default implementations for the selection-handling methods defined in `SelectionListener`. We need only override the methods we are interested in. Here we are only interested in the double click event. SWT refers to this event in a more abstract way and calls it the default selection. We therefore override `widgetDefaultSelected()` and call our event-handling method `handleDefaultSelected()`.

org.eclipse.contribution.junit/TestReportView
```
public void handleDefaultSelected() {
  IStructuredSelection s=
    (IStructuredSelection)viewer.getSelection();
  Object firstElement= s.getFirstElement();
  if (firstElement != null)
    openTest((TestResult)firstElement);
}
```

We declare the method public so that our test can call it as well. A table viewer is a structure-oriented viewer like a tree or a list and it therefore maintains a structured selection. When we request the current selection from the viewer, we can therefore safely downcast it to an `IStructuredSelection`. From the selection, we are only interested in the first element and we know that our table shows `TestResults`. Therefore, we cast the first selected element to `TestResult` and call another helper method to open the result in the Java editor:

org.eclipse.contribution.junit/TestReportView
```
private void openTest(TestResult result) {
  try {
    IType type= result.project.findType(result.klass);
```

```
        IJavaElement testMethod= type.getMethod(result.method,
          new String[0]);
        IEditorPart part= JavaUI.openInEditor(type);
        JavaUI.revealInEditor(part, testMethod);
      } catch (CoreException e) {
        // TODO error handling
      }
    }
```

The class `JavaUI` is defined in `org.eclipse.jdt.ui`. We have to add this plug-in to the list of required plug-ins in the manifest. `JavaUI` is a Façade for Java user-interface related functionality. It provides the methods `openInEditor()` to open a Java element in an editor and `revealInEditor()` to select and reveal a Java element in an editor. We convert the test result into a type and method. We have already done this in the `MarkerCreator`. We use the same methods for the conversion. Once we have the Java elements we can use the `JavaUI` methods to open and reveal the selected test.

To finish this chapter, let's make the open-in-editor function also available from the view's toolbar, as shown in Figure 23.12.

Figure 23.12

Here is the test we wrote for this feature. It asserts that the view's toolbar has a single item:

org.eclipse.contribution.junit.test/TestReportTest
```
public void testActionInToolbar() throws Exception {
  showView();
  IActionBars actionBars= view.getViewSite().getActionBars();
  IToolBarManager manager=
    actionBars.getToolBarManager();
  assertEquals(1, manager.getItems().length);
}
```

To make this test pass, we implement a JFace action that we then contribute to the local toolbar. A JFace action allows us to define the response to a user event. When using a JFace action we don't have to handle the SWT event directly, JFace does this for us. This is useful because it allows us to implement actions independent of the widget that triggered the event. We implement a `GotoTestAction` as an inner class of `TestReportView`.

org.eclipse.contribution.junit/TestReportView$GotoTestAction
```
private class GotoTestAction extends Action {
  private GotoTestAction() {
```

```
      setText("Go to Test");
      setToolTipText("Go to the Selected Test");
      ImageDescriptor descriptor=
         PlatformUI.getWorkbench().getSharedImages().
           getImageDescriptor(ISharedImages.IMG_OPEN_MARKER);
      setImageDescriptor(descriptor);
    }
  public void run(){
    handleDefaultSelected();
  }
}
```

We configure the action with all the UI information—an image, tooltip, and label—so that the action can be associated with buttons, menu items, or toolbar items. All this information is defined in the action's constructor. The action's text and the tooltip should use book title capitalization. Incorrect capitalization is a common source of UI inconsistencies. For the action's image we can use a shared image that is provided by the workbench. The workbench and the Java development tools provide a set of shared images other plug-ins can reuse. Constants for the available images are defined in `org.eclipse.ui.ISharedImages` for the workbench and in `org.eclipse.jdt.ui.IShared-Images` for the Java development tools. Using a shared image ensures visual consistency, and even better, we don't have to manage these images ourselves.

The action's `run()` method implements the response to the user event. This is the same response as when the user double clicked a test result. We can therefore simply call `handleDefaultSelected()` as we did for the double click event.

The last thing to do is install the action in the view's toolbar. We extend the view's `createPartControl()` as follows:

org.eclipse.contribution.junit/TestReportView
```
public void createPartControl(Composite parent) {
  //...
  IActionBars actionBars= getViewSite().getActionBars();
  actionBars.getToolBarManager().add(new GotoTestAction());
}
```

A view gets access to its menu, toolbar, and status line through the `IAction-Bars` interface that we retrieve from the view's site.

We are done with a basic `TestReportView` and have also fixed the `ResultView`. We could do more, for example

❍ Showing the stack trace of a selected failure

❍ Adding an option to bring the view to front at the beginning of a test run

Reviewing this chapter, we have

❍ Used JFace to implement a tabular `TestReportView`

❍ Implemented a simple domain model and a corresponding label provider and content provider

❍ Shown how to use the `syncExec()` method to handle the case when you need to interact with SWT widgets but you are not in the main thread

❍ Used a selection listener to handle double clicks

❍ Contributed an action to the view's toolbar

In the next chapter we will implement a simple editor to exclude tests from auto-testing.

23.7   **Forward Pointers**

❍ *Sorters and filters*—You can configure JFace viewers with sorters and filters. For example, we could provide a filter that only shows test failures.

❍ *Shared images*—For images that are frequently used it is recommended to store them only once in an `ImageRegistry` as provided by JFace. The UI plug-ins can override a corresponding method for this purpose (see the method `AbstractUIPlugin.createImageRegistry()`). For more information on image management refer to: *www.eclipse.org/articles/ Article-Using Images In Eclipse/Using Images In Eclipse.html*

❍ *Structured views*—Structured views can optionally maintain the elements in a hash table. This speeds up the viewer update if a viewer has many items that frequently change. See the method `StructuredViewer.set-UseHashLookup()`.

❍ *Providing the current selection*—To enable the workbench to track your view part's selection, you register a selection provider with the part's site. JFace viewers provide a selection and implement the `ISelection-Provider` interface. Here is how you can register a viewer with the Workbench: `getSite().setSelectionProvider(viewer)`.

❍ *Tracking the current selection (selection linking) in a view*—To track the current selection as is done, for example, in the **Properties** view, you register the view as a selection changed listener with the current workbench page. You can retrieve the workbench page from the view's site: `getSite().getPage().addSelectionListener(this)`.

○ *Updating views*—Updating a view can be expensive and you might only
  want to update a view when it is visible. By registering as an
  `IPartListener2` with the `WorkbenchPage`, you can track the visibility
  state of a view and only update the view when it is visible or becomes
  visible again.

○ *JavaUI*—The Façade to the Java-related UI functionality also provides
  access to a set of dialogs for selecting Java elements like packages or
  types.

○ *Global actions*—Actions like cut, copy, paste, or select all are *global
  actions*. They are defined and presented by the workbench, but the handling of a global action is forwarded to the active part. To handle a global action, a part registers an action handler for a predefined action
  constant. The action handler is an ordinary JFace action. The action
  handler is registered with the `IActionBar` interface we have encountered
  previously. Here is a snippet for how to handle the global **Select All**
  action with an action defined by a part:

```
IAction selectAllAction;
IActionBars actionBars= getViewSite().getActionBars();
actionBars.setGlobalActionHandler(
    IWorkbenchActionConstants.SELECT_ALL,
    selectAllAction);
```

CHAPTER 24

A Simple Editor to Exclude Tests

Auto-test runs all tests it finds inside a project. This is simple, but sometimes a user may want some control over the tests to be executed. In this chapter we will add support for excluding test cases from an auto-test run. We will implement a simple editor to define test cases that should be excluded. Editors are similar to views, but different enough to deserve a chapter of their own. We will see how to

○ Contribute an editor

○ Contribute an action to an editor

To support the exclusion feature, we need to permanently store a list of test cases associated with a project. Let's consider the different options Eclipse offers us to store state:

○ *Preferences*—Each plug-in has a preferences store accessed with `Plugin.getPreferences()`. Preferences map property names to primitive values. You change preference settings with preference pages contributed to the preferences dialog. Since preferences are not associated with a particular resource, they are global to the entire workspace. Preferences are therefore not an appropriate place to store a project's excluded tests.

○ *Properties*—Resources have properties keyed by a qualified name. There are two kinds of properties: session properties retrieved by `IResource.getSessionProperty()` and persistent properties retrieved by `getPersistentProperty()`. Persistent properties are intended to store resource-specific information that needs to persist across sessions.

217

They could be used for exclusion lists. However, they have the limitation that they cannot be released to a repository. Their values cannot be shared with other members in the team. When we exclude a test case from an auto-test, the exclusion should be shared with other team members.

○ *Plug-in metadata*—The platform maintains a metadata area where a plug-in can store additional data. You retrieve the location of this area with `Plugin.getStateLocation()`. In the returned location you are free to create files and directories, but you are responsible for managing them. For example the Java core plug-in stores its source indices in this location. We could store information about excluded tests in this location. However, the metadata area isn't shareable across a team.

○ *Files*—Files are the simplest and most flexible way to store data. Files can easily be shared with other team members. We therefore use a simple file to store the exclusion list.

Excluded test cases will be defined in a file *test.exclusion* stored at the top-level of a project. The file lists the fully qualified names of the excluded tests, one per line. We'll create a test-filter editor to simplify the entry of the test names. It provides a command to show a dialog with all available tests inside the project. From this list the user selects a test case to be inserted into the exclusion list. Figure 24.1 shows the test-filter editor in action.

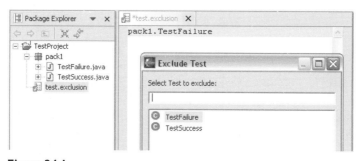

Figure 24.1

Let's start with a test case that specifies our desired behavior. When a failing test is excluded from auto-test, there should be no test failures. We add the test that captures this behavior to our builder tests:

org.eclipse.contribution.junit.test/BuilderTest

```
public void testAutoTestingFilter() throws Exception {
  IWorkspaceRunnable runnable= new IWorkspaceRunnable() {
    public void run(IProgressMonitor pm) throws CoreException {
      JUnitPlugin.getPlugin().addAutoBuildNature(
        testProject.getProject());
```

```
      IFile file= testProject.getProject().getFile(
        new Path("test.exclusions"));
      file.create(new ByteArrayInputStream(
        "pack1.FailTest".getBytes()), true, null);
      IPackageFragment pack= testProject.createPackage("pack1");
      testProject.createType(pack, "FailTest.java",
        "public class FailTest " +
        "extends junit.framework.TestCase {" +
        "    public void testFailure() {fail();}}");
    }
  };
  ResourcesPlugin.getWorkspace().run(runnable, null);
  IMarker[] markers= getFailureMarkers();
  assertEquals(0, markers.length);
}
```

We use the resources API to create the filter file and set its contents to the name of the failing test case. To make this test green, we augment the `AutoTest-Builder` with a call to a filter method that removes the types specified in the *test.exclusion* file:

org.eclipse.contribution.junit/AutoTestBuilder
```
protected IProject[] build(int kind, Map args,
    IProgressMonitor monitor) throws CoreException {
  if (hasBuildErrors() || !enabled)
    return null;
  IJavaProject javaProject= JavaCore.create(getProject());
  IType[] types= new TestSearcher().findAll(javaProject, monitor);
  types= exclude(types);
  if (trace)
    printTestTypes(types);
  JUnitPlugin.getPlugin().run(types, javaProject);
  return null;
}
```

The implementation of the filter doesn't provide us with any additional interesting Eclipse insights. It is therefore included in Appendix C.

Where does the exclusion file *test.exclusion* come from? We could contribute a choice to the **New Dialog** using the `org.eclipse.ui.newWizard` extension point. However, to keep things simple the user would have to create the file using the standard new file wizard.

24.1 Contributing an Editor

Now let's make working with the exclusion file a bit friendlier by contributing a custom editor.

We want to use the Java editor contribution as an example. A quick search for "JavaEditor" with the **Open Type** dialog shows us that the Java editor is included in the `org.eclipse.jdt.ui` plug-in. We find the following definition in the *plugin.xml*:

org.eclipse.jdt.ui/plugin.xml
```
<extension point= "org.eclipse.ui.editors"
  id= "org.eclipse.jdt.ui.javaeditor">
  <editor
    id="org.eclipse.jdt.ui.CompilationUnitEditor"
    icon="icons/full/obj16/jcu_obj.gif"
    name="%JavaEditor.label"
    extensions="java"
    class="org.eclipse.jdt.internal.ui.javaeditor.
      CompilationUnitEditor"
    contributorClass="org.eclipse.jdt.internal.ui.javaeditor.
      CompilationUnitEditorActionContributor"
    default="true">
  </editor>
</extension>
```

The Java editor is contributed to files with the extension "java".

An editor contribution requires two implementation classes. The `class` attribute defines the implementation of the editor part and the `contributor-Class` specifies a separate class defining menu and toolbar contributions. This is a major difference between editors and views. A view has a single implementation class and this class handles toolbar contributions internally. Why are editor contributions factored out into a separate class? More than one editor of a particular kind can be open inside a workbench page. All open editors share the global menu and toolbar. Having a separate class for the object contributions allows the Eclipse workbench to share the editor contributions among editors of the same kind. Figure 24.2 illustrates this. It shows two open Java compilation unit editors and a text editor. The `CompilationUnitEditor-ActionContributor` is shared between the compilation unit editors.

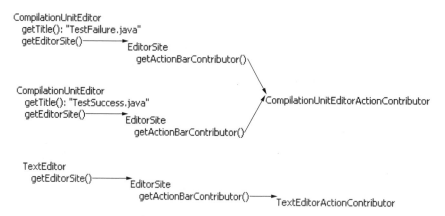

Figure 24.2   Shared ActionContributor

Views vs. Editors

Views and editors are both visual components shown inside a workbench page. There are several distinctions between views and editors:

○ *Saving*—Changes in views are immediately reflected in the workspace. Editors have an open-modify-save life cycle. In editors changes are permanently stored once the user has explicitly saved them.

○ *Input*—Editors are opened by the user on a particular element. This element becomes the input for the editor. Views have no predefined input. Each view decides where to fetch its input.

○ *User interface*—A view has its own local toolbar. Editors contribute to the global toolbar. Editors are constrained to appear within the main editor area. Views can be freely rearranged and stacked inside the workbench, except on top of or behind editors.

○ *Instance count*—A view of a particular kind occurs at most once inside a workbench page. Multiple editors of the same kind can be opened on different inputs inside the same workbench page.

Editors are typically used to edit resources whereas views are used for various purposes. The views that come with Eclipse illustrate the different ways to use views. We can categorize views as follows:

○ *Navigator views*—Present the hierarchical structure of a particular domain and support to open editors. Examples: **Navigator** (resource hierarchy), **Package Explorer** (Java element hierarchy), **Type Hierarchy** (the type hierarchy).

○ *Outline view*—Presents the structure of the contents of the active editor. There is a single generic **Outline** view provided by the workbench that can be reused for any kind of editor.

○ *Result/Output views*—Show the result or output of an operation. Examples: **Search** (results of a search), **Synchronize** (result of a synchronize operation), **Console** (output of a process), **JUnit** (results of a test run).

○ *Information/Detail views*—Provide additional information about the currently selected object. These views typically track the current selection. Examples: **Properties** shows generic properties of a selected object, **Variables** shows details about the selected stack frame in the debugger.

○ *Collector views*—Collect particular artifacts. Examples: **Tasks** (the pending tasks and problems), **Bookmarks** (assigned bookmarks), **Breakpoints** (defined breakpoints).

There are also a lot of commonalities between views and editors. They are captured in the `IWorkbenchPart` interface, the common interface between `IEditorPart` and `IViewPart`. Finally, when implementing either a view or an editor, you can leverage JFace. JFace viewers can be used to implement both views and editors.

The declaration of the Java editor contribution sets an attribute `default` to `true`. This is a hint that the contributed editor should be the default editor for **.java* files. Consistent with the Diversity Rule, more than one editor can be contributed for a particular element. However, when opening a file, only a single editor should be opened. Eclipse handles the ambiguity by giving the user the option to open any of the registered editors in the **Open With** menu, but it makes it convenient to open the default editor directly, as shown in Figure 24.3.

Figure 24.3

This illustrates another rule:

> **USER ARBITRATION RULE** When there are multiple applicable contributions, let the user decide which one to use.

So let's make our editor contribution for the *test.excludes* file. Since the file has a fixed name, we don't contribute the editor to the suffix only but to the entire file name. This is consistent with the Relevance Rule. We want to make our contribution as specific as possible. Instead of implementing a text editor from scratch we reuse the default text editor, but we contribute a custom `contributorClass`:

org.eclipse.contribution.junit/plugin.xml
```
<extension point="org.eclipse.ui.editors">
  <editor
    id="org.eclipse.contribution.junit.TestExclusionEditor"
    icon="icons/testok.gif"
    name="Test Exclusions Editor"
    filenames="test.exclusion"
    class="org.eclipse.ui.editors.text.TextEditor"
    default="true"
    contributorClass="org.eclipse.contribution.junit.
      TestExclusionEditorActionContributor">
  </editor>
</extension>
```

Eclipse allows the user to modify the file-editor associations in the preferences. If we start up the run-time workbench after the above change, our editor shows up in the **File Associations** preference page, as shown in Figure 24.4.

Figure 24.4

Even though we don't have to implement the editor ourselves, let's look at how its implementation differs from a view. An editor is opened on a particular element that becomes its input. An editor input is a lightweight description of the element. When a text editor is opened on a file, its input is an `IFileEditorInput`, as illustrated in Figure 24.5.

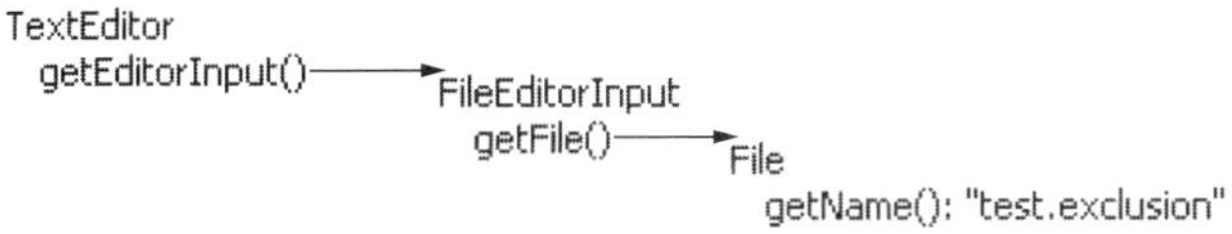

```
TextEditor
   getEditorInput()──────▶
                           FileEditorInput
                              getFile()──────▶
                                               File
                                   getName(): "test.exclusion"
```

Figure 24.5   FileEditorInput Represents an IFile

The input is passed to an editor part together with its site in the `init()` method.

In contrast to views, editors follow an open-modify-save cycle. The methods supporting saving are captured in the `ISaveablePart` interface. It defines methods like `isDirty()`, `doSave()` and `doSaveAs()`. When the dirty state of an editor changes we have to notify interested parties with `fireProperty-Change(PROP_DIRTY)`.

Next we'll implement the contributor class to add the actions for our editor.

24.2   Contributing a Contributor

Our contributor class extends the `BasicTextEditorActionContributor` and contributes an action, `ExcludeTestAction`, to append a test to be excluded.

Here is the test to verify that the action is contributed when our editor is opened. As for most of our other tests, the test is creating a `TestProject` in `setUp()` that is then disposed in `tearDown()`.

org.eclipse.contribution.junit.test/ExclusionEditorTest
```
public class ExclusionEditorTest extends TestCase {
  private TestProject testProject;

  protected void setUp() throws Exception {
    testProject= new TestProject();
  }

  protected void tearDown() throws Exception {
    getPage().closeAllEditors(false);
    testProject.dispose();
  }
}
```

The actual test creates a *test.exclusion* file and opens it in the editor.

org.eclipse.contribution.junit.test/ExclusionEditorTest
```
public void testEditorContribution() throws CoreException {
  IFile file= testProject.getProject().getFile(
    new Path("test.exclusion"));
  file.create(new ByteArrayInputStream("".getBytes()), true, null);
  IEditorPart part= getPage().openEditor(file);
  assertTrue(findContributedAction(part));
}
```

To verify that the `ExcludeTestAction` is contributed to the toolbar, we have to reach into the toolbar manager and look for our contributed action:

org.eclipse.contribution.junit.test/ExclusionEditorTest
```
private boolean findContributedAction(IEditorPart part) {
  IActionBars actionBars= part.getEditorSite().getActionBars();
  IToolBarManager manager= actionBars.getToolBarManager();
  IContributionItem[] items= manager.getItems();
  for (int i= 0; i < items.length; i++) {
    IContributionItem item= items[i];
    if (item instanceof ActionContributionItem) {
      IAction a=((ActionContributionItem)item).getAction();
      if (a.getClass().equals(ExcludeTestAction.class))
        return true;
    }
  }
  return false;
}
```

Now let's implement the contributor class. It manages the action we want to contribute:

org.eclipse.contribution.junit/TestExclusionEditorActionContributor

```
public class TestExclusionEditorActionContributor
    extends BasicTextEditorActionContributor {
  private ExcludeTestAction excludeAction;

  public TestExclusionEditorActionContributor() {
    excludeAction= new ExcludeTestAction();
  }
...
```

We contribute the `excludeAction` to the **Edit** menu and append it to the local toolbar by extending the corresponding contribution methods:

org.eclipse.contribution.junit/TestExclusionEditorActionContributor

```
public void contributeToToolBar(IToolBarManager manager) {
  super.contributeToToolBar(manager);
  manager.add(new Separator());
  manager.add(excludeAction);
}

public void contributeToMenu(IMenuManager menu) {
  super.contributeToMenu(menu);
  IMenuManager editMenu= menu.findMenuUsingPath(
    IWorkbenchActionConstants.M_EDIT);
  if (editMenu != null) {
    editMenu.add(new Separator());
    editMenu.add(excludeAction);
  }
}
```

Notice that we contribute the same action object to both the menu and the toolbar. When changing an attribute of an action (for example, its enabled state), both the menu and toolbar are automatically updated.

Since the contributor is shared among editors of the same kind we have to implement `setActiveEditor()`. This method is called whenever the contributor's editor has changed. We check that the new editor is a `TextEditor` and inform our action that it should now target a different editor:

org.eclipse.contribution.junit/TestExclusionEditorActionContributor

```
public void setActiveEditor(IEditorPart target) {
  super.setActiveEditor(target);
  ITextEditor editor= null;
  if (target instanceof ITextEditor)
    editor= (ITextEditor)target;
  excludeAction.setActiveEditor(editor);
}
```

Finally, to enable early garbage collection of editors when the contributor is disposed, we make sure that the action clears the reference to the active editor:

org.eclipse.contribution.junit/TestExclusionEditorActionContributor
```
public void dispose() {
  super.dispose();
  excludeAction.setActiveEditor(null);
}
```

Next, let's implement the `ExcludeTestAction`. It is an ordinary JFace action and it keeps a reference to its target editor:

org.eclipse.contribution.junit/ExcludeTestAction
```
public class ExcludeTestAction extends Action {
  private ITextEditor editor;
  public ExcludeTestAction() {
    setText("Exclude Test");
    setToolTipText("Exclude a Test Case");
    setImageDescriptor(createImage("icons/test.gif"));
  }

  public void setActiveEditor(ITextEditor target) {
    editor= target;
  }
  //...
}
```

We create the images in the helper method `createImage()` which retrieves the images relative to the installed plug-in location:

org.eclipse.contribution.junit/ExcludeTestAction
```
private ImageDescriptor createImage(String path) {
  URL url= JUnitPlugin.getPlugin().getDescriptor().getInstallURL();
  ImageDescriptor descriptor= null;
  try {
    descriptor= ImageDescriptor.createFromURL(new URL(url, path));
  } catch (MalformedURLException e) {
    descriptor= ImageDescriptor.getMissingImageDescriptor();
  }
  return descriptor;
}
```

When the action is run, it allows the user to select a test. Once the user makes a choice, it appends the selected test name to the active editor:

org.eclipse.contribution.junit/ExcludeTestAction
```
public void run() {
  IType type= selectTest();
  if (type != null)
    appendTest(type.getFullyQualifiedName());
}
```

The method `selectTest()` uses the `TestSearcher` to find all the tests inside the project and presents the list in a dialog. As we have seen above, the input to a text editor is a `IFileEditorInput` from which we can navigate to the containing Java project:

org.eclipse.contribution.junit/ExcludeTestAction
```
private IType selectTest() {
  IEditorInput input= editor.getEditorInput();
  if (input instanceof IFileEditorInput) {
    IFile file= ((IFileEditorInput)input).getFile();
    IJavaProject jproject= JavaCore.create(file.getProject());
    try {
      IType[] types= new TestSearcher().findAll(jproject,
        new NullProgressMonitor());
      return showDialog(types);
    } catch (JavaModelException e) {
    }
  }
  return null;
}
```

To show the list of tests, we use an `ElementListSelectionDialog` with a JFace label provider to define the appearance of the elements in the dialog. The Java development tools provide a standard `JavaElementLabelProvider` that we use to render the types.

org.eclipse.contribution.junit/ExcludeTestAction
```
private IType showDialog(IType[] types) {
  ElementListSelectionDialog dialog=
    new ElementListSelectionDialog(
      editor.getSite().getShell(),
      new JavaElementLabelProvider());
  dialog.setTitle("Exclude Test");
  dialog.setMessage("Select Test to exclude:");
  dialog.setElements(types);
  if (dialog.open() == Window.OK)
    return (IType)dialog.getFirstResult();
  return null;
}
```

Finally, we are ready to insert the fully qualified type name into the editor. Eclipse editors use `IDocument`s to store their contents. A text editor has a document provider. It knows which document is associated with a particular editor input. Once we have the document we can insert the text:

org.eclipse.contribution.junit/ExcludeTestAction
```
private void appendTest(String testName) {
  IDocumentProvider provider= editor.getDocumentProvider();
  IEditorInput input= editor.getEditorInput();
```

```
IDocument document= provider.getDocument(input);
if (document == null)
  return;
try {
  document.replace(document.getLength(), 0, testName+"\n");
} catch (BadLocationException e) {
}
}
```

This concludes the implementation of our simple editor. Let's review this chapter:

❍ We have contributed a text editor for the exclusion file.

❍ We have shown how contributions in editors are done and how they differ from contribution to views.

In the next chapter we will revisit the `ResultView`.

24.3   Forward Pointers

❍ *Assigning shortcuts*—To assign a user-configurable keyboard shortcut to an editor action, you use the `org.eclipse.ui.commands` extension point.

❍ *Action set part associations*—Some actions should be applicable in both views and editors. For example, most Java actions manipulating the source code are available from both the Java views and the Java editors. You can contribute such actions in an action set and then define in which workbench parts the action set should be visible. See the `org.eclipse.ui.actionSetPartAssociations` extension point.

❍ *Content outline*—For editors with more complex contents you want to populate the content outline. To do so, you have to implement `getAdapter()` and return a outline page when the `getAdapter()` is called with `IContentOutlinePage.class`.

❍ *Navigation history*—Workbench editors keep a navigation history so that you can navigate back and forth between your open editors. If you implement a custom editor you also want to support the navigation history by implementing `INavigationLocationProvider`.

❍ *Multi-page editors*—`MultiPageEditorPart` provides support for creating an editor with multiple pages, where each page contains an editor.

❍ *New wizards*—Use the extension point `org.eclipse.ui.newWizards` to register wizards for creating new things like files, folders or projects with the **New Dialog**.

○ *JFace text*— Provides a framework, `org.eclipse.jface.text.*`, for manipulating text syntactically. It offers support for syntax coloring, content assistance, formatting, etc. For example, we could leverage JFace text to replace our dialog to select a test to exclude with a much more convenient code-assist style user interface as used in the Java editor to complete code (Figure 24.6).

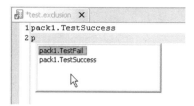

Figure 24.6

To do so you implement a `TextEditor` subclass that is configured with a `SourceViewerConfiguration` that defines a custom content assistant. The content assistant uses an `IContentAssistProcessor` that knows how to complete test class names.

○ `Org.eclipse.ui.texteditor.*`—Provides a framework for text editors.

○ *Contributing to an editor's menu and toolbar actions*—The extension point `org.eclipse.ui.editorActions` allows you to contribute to the menu and toolbar of an existing editor. For example, to contribute an action to our exclusion editor's toolbar you add the following declaration to the manifest:

```
<extension point="org.eclipse.ui.editorActions">
  <editorContribution
    targetID="org.eclipse.contribution.junit.
      TestExclusionEditor"
    id="contributedId">
    <action
      label= "..."
      class= "..."
      toolbarPath= "..." >
    </action>
  </editorContribution>
</extension>
```

CHAPTER 25

ResultView Revisited— Observing Changes

Our old `ResultView` will keep displaying red or green even if the underlying Java code changes. We would like the color to be accurate—red if a test fails, green if all tests succeed, and neutral if we don't know. In this chapter we revisit the `ResultView` to clear the red/green result indication as soon as a Java resource has changed and we no longer know whether the tests will succeed or not. This will allow us to illustrate how to listen to changes to Java elements.

In this chapter, we'll see how to

○ Listen to changes to Java elements

○ Process Java element deltas

25.1 Testing Color

Let's start with the corresponding test case. We add the following test to `ViewColorTest`:

org.eclipse.contribution.junit.test/ViewColorTest
```
public void testResultViewColorReset() throws Exception {
  view.getListener().testsStarted(null, 0);
  view.getListener().testFailed(null, "class", "method", "trace");
  view.getListener().testsFinished(null);
  Display display= view.getControl().getDisplay();
  Color red= display.getSystemColor(SWT.COLOR_RED);
  assertEquals(red, view.getControl().getBackground());
  Color background= display.getSystemColor(
    SWT.COLOR_WIDGET_BACKGROUND);
```

```
  changeWorkspace();
  assertEquals(background, view.getControl().getBackground());
}
```

We simulate the messages broadcast when a test fails. The view should be red. Then we change the workspace and assert that the view color is reset. We implement `changeWorkspace()` by adding and removing a project using the `TestProject` fixture.

org.eclipse.contribution.junit.test/ViewColorTest
```
public void changeWorkspace() throws Exception {
  TestProject project= new TestProject();
  project.createPackage("pack1");
  project.dispose();
}
```

25.2 Observing Changes

How do we observe changes in Eclipse? The **Navigator** and **Package Explorer** are good examples for how views handle change. They both present the workspace and update themselves as the workspace changes. As we have seen in Chapter 23, one responsibility of a JFace content provider is to observe the changes in their domain model. Figure 25.1 shows the content providers underlying these Eclipse views.

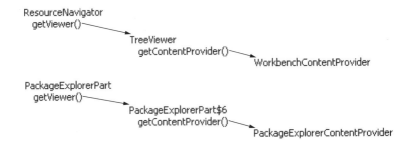

Figure 25.1   ContentProvider Observes Changes

When analyzing the code we find that the `WorkbenchContentProvider` listens to resource changes:

org.eclipse.ui.model/WorkbenchContentProvider
```
public class WorkbenchContentProvider
  implements IResourceChangeListener {
  ...
```

```
newWorkspace.addResourceChangeListener(this,
   ResourceChangeEvent.POST_CHANGE);
```

The `PackageExploreContentProvider` listens to Java element changes:

org.eclipse.jdt.ui/PackageExplorerContentProvider
```
class PackageExplorerContentProvider
   implements IElementChangedListener {
...
   JavaCore.addElementChangedListener(this);
```

Both mechanisms are very similar and are listener-based. A listener is informed of changes by a change event. The change event carries a hierarchical delta describing the changes. A resource-change listener receives the change notification in terms of resources and a Java-element-change listener in terms of Java elements. The event object a listener receives is only valid for the duration of the event method. See Table 25.1 for a comparison of resource and Java element-based notifications.

Table 25.1   Observing Changes to Resources vs. Java Elements

Observing changes in	Resources	JavaElements
Listener interface	IResourceChangeListener	IElementChangedListener
Change event	IResourceChangeEvent	ElementChangedEvent
Delta	IResourceDelta	IJavaElementDelta
Register listener with	IWorkspace	JavaCore

Java elements provide a Java-specific view of the underlying resources as defined by a project's build class path. This means folders on the build class path become packages, and so on. We have to choose between general resource changes and Java-specific changes. Since we are only interested in Java changes, we implement a listener for Java element deltas. Let's first understand Java element deltas better.

We set a break point in the `PackageExplorerContentProvider` and examine the `ElementChangedEvent` in the **Variables** view. Fortunately, Java core politely implements `toString()`, showing the contents of a delta. In Figure 25.2 we see the delta that results from changing the contents of the compilation unit `FailTest.java` in the package `pack1` in the project `TestProject1`.

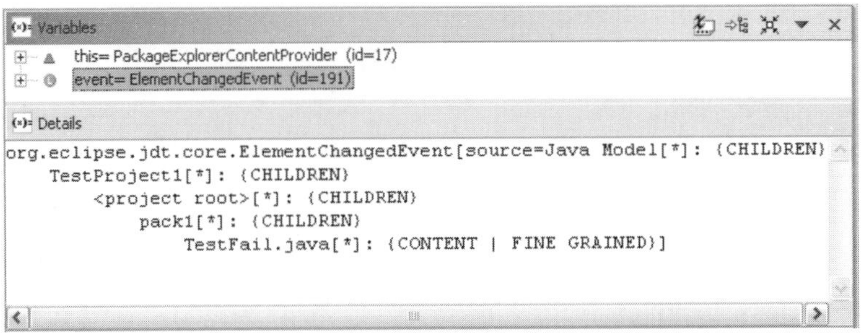

Figure 25.2

In the `toString()` representation we see that the delta starts at the `Java-Model` and then includes a path to the changed node `FailTest.java`. This delta describes a single change only, but deltas can include more than one change. The kind of change is encoded as changed = *, added = +, removed = -.

First we define a `DirtyListener` inner class in the `ResultView`. It implements `IElementChangedListener` and its event handling method `elementChanged()`. We register a `DirtyListener` with the `JavaModel` in `createPartControl()` and deregister it in `dispose()`. Since `dispose()` can be called without a matching call to `createPartControl()`, we have to check that the listener got registered.

org.eclipse.contribution.junit/ResultView$DirtyListener
```
private DirtyListener dirtyListener;
private class DirtyListener implements IElementChangedListener {
  public void elementChanged(ElementChangedEvent event) {
    processDelta(event.getDelta());
  }
}
```

org.eclipse.contribution.junit.ResultView
```
public void createPartControl(Composite parent) {
  listener= new Listener();
  JUnitPlugin.getPlugin().addTestListener(listener);
  dirtyListener= new DirtyListener();
  JavaCore.addElementChangedListener(
    dirtyListener,
    ElementChangedEvent.PRE_AUTO_BUILD);
  control= new Label(parent, SWT.NONE);
}

public void dispose() {
  if (listener != null)
    JUnitPlugin.getPlugin().removeTestListener(listener);
  if (dirtyListener != null)
    JavaCore.removeElementChangedListener(dirtyListener);
  listener= null;
  dirtyListener= null;
}
```

The method `addElementChangedListener()` supports an event mask as its second argument. The event mask allows us to specify the events we are interested in. We use `ElementChangeEvent.PRE_AUTO_BUILD` as the event mask to indicate that we want to receive change notifications before the auto-build starts. With auto-testing enabled, tests are run as part of an auto-build and we want to reset the notification before the tests start. Otherwise our listener would not correctly reset the color indication for auto-test builds.

25.3 Reacting to Changes

We want to reset the color in the view when one of the following changes occurs:

○ Adding/removing a Java element inside the workspace, a project, a source folder, or package

○ Changing the contents of a compilation unit

We process a delta in the method `processDelta()`. It recursively traverses the delta and returns true when the traversal should continue:

org.eclipse.contribution.junit/ResultView$DirtyListener
```
private boolean processDelta(IJavaElementDelta delta) {

  // analyze delta see below

  IJavaElementDelta[] affectedChildren=
    delta.getAffectedChildren();
  for (int i= 0; i < affectedChildren.length; i++)
    if (!processDelta(affectedChildren[i]))
      return false;
    return true;
}
```

Each delta node provides access to its affected children. These are the deltas for added, removed, or changed children. Next let's look into the delta analysis. Each delta node has a change kind—added, removed, changed—and a corresponding Java element. If the user adds or removes Java elements above compilation units, we reset the view. Similarly, any change to a compilation unit invalidates the view color. This is the corresponding delta analysis code:

org.eclipse.contribution.junit/ResultView$DirtyListener.processDelta()
```
int kind= delta.getKind();
int type= delta.getElement().getElementType();
switch (type) {
  case IJavaElement.JAVA_MODEL:
```

```
case IJavaElement.JAVA_PROJECT:
case IJavaElement.PACKAGE_FRAGMENT_ROOT:
case IJavaElement.PACKAGE_FRAGMENT:
  if (kind == IJavaElementDelta.ADDED ||
      kind == IJavaElementDelta.REMOVED)
    return testResultDirty();
  break;
case IJavaElement.COMPILATION_UNIT:
  return testResultDirty();
}
```

Finally, here is the implementation of `ResultView.testResultDirty()`. We have to post the color change to the main thread since the delta can be sent out from another thread.

org.eclipse.contribution.junit/ResultView
```
private boolean testResultDirty() {
  final Display display= getSite().getShell().getDisplay();
  display.syncExec(new Runnable() {
    public void run() {
      if (!control.isDisposed()) {
        Color background= display.
          getSystemColor(SWT.COLOR_WIDGET_BACKGROUND);
        control.setBackground(background);
      }
    }
  });
  return false;
}
```

Working Copies

A working copy is a concept introduced by the Eclipse JDT. You can't update the whole Java model on every keystroke, so JDT only updates the model when a compilation unit is saved. A working copy is an in-memory copy of the original compilation unit. When you change a working copy the changes are not immediately reflected in the file system or the Java model. The Java editor creates a working copy for a compilation unit when you open it. When the compilation unit is saved, it is committed to the file system and the changes to the compilation unit are reported as Java-element deltas. Changes made while typing are reported as Java element deltas rooted at the working copy element.

Working copies are an important concept when you want to programmatically manipulate a compilation unit. You do not manipulate a compilation unit directly. Instead, you create a working copy and change its buffer. You can retrieve the working copy created by the Java editor from the working copy manager: `JavaUI.getWorkingCopyManager()`.

With these additions the test passes. Unfortunately the color resets when we open or close a compilation unit in an editor. To understand what is going on, let's enable the tracing option for Java element deltas. To do so, we switch to the **trace option** tab of the launch configuration for our workbench and enable the **javadelta** tracing option, as shown in Figure 25.3.

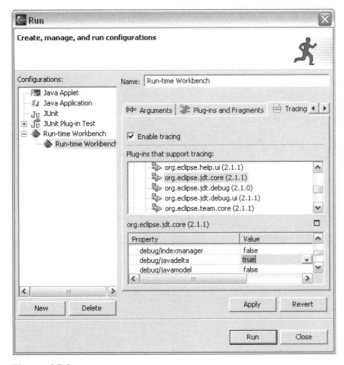

Figure 25.3

When this tracing option is set, all delta notifications are logged to the console. In addition, you can see how much time each listener takes. When opening the compilation unit FailTest.java, we get the following trace:

```
FIRING POST_CHANGE Delta [Thread[main,5,main]]:
Java Model[*]: {CHILDREN}
  TestProject1[*]: {CHILDREN}
    src[*]: {CHILDREN}
      pack1[*]: {CHILDREN}
        [Working copy] FailTest.java[+]: {}
Listener#1=...PackageExplorerContentProvider@139491b->0ms
Listener#2=...ResultView$DirtyListener@16db492 -> 0ms
```

The trace indicates that a working copy was added in `pack1`. We don't want to reset the result color when merely opening a compilation unit, so we filter out working copy changes in the `processDelta()` method:

org.eclipse.contribution.junit/ResultView#DirtyListener.processDelta()
```
//...
case IJavaElement.COMPILATION_UNIT:
  ICompilationUnit unit= (ICompilationUnit)delta.getElement();
  if (unit.isWorkingCopy())
    return true;
  return testResultDirty();
```

The `ResultView` now more accurately reflects the current state of the tests. Reviewing this chapter

- We have used `JavaElementChangedListener`s to observe changes to Java elements.
- We have shown how to analyze a `JavaElementDelta`.
- We have seen how to trace the broadcast of Java element deltas.

25.4   Forward Pointers

- When registering the listener you can specify an event mask in both the resource and Java element worlds. In the event mask you can specify which events you are interested in, for example, `POST_CHANGE`, `PRE_CLOSE`, `PRE_AUTOBUILD`, etc.
- Resource deltas not only carry information about the changed resources, but also about the changed markers.
- For more information about resource deltas, refer to: *www.eclipse.org/articles/Article-Resource-deltas/resource-deltas.html*.

CHAPTER 26

Perspectives

Contributions are a double-edged sword. If you are not careful with how you make contributions, you end up with a contribution mess—long context menus, crowded toolbars, lots of views. Up to now we have contributed views without paying a lot of attention to how they appear in the workbench. In this chapter we will smoothly integrate our views into Eclipse. We will see how to

○ Extend an existing perspective

○ Make our views easily accessible for the user

26.1 Views in Perspective

A perspective defines how a set of views and editors are arranged. The current layout of a workbench page is defined by its active perspective, as shown in Figure 26.1.

Figure 26.1

We have defined two testing-related views so far. Why not define a test perspective? The perspective could contain our views as a way of introducing JUnit into Eclipse. A perspective is intended to be a context for solving a whole problem. Thus, there is the Java perspective, which helps in manipulating Java programs and a debug perspective for diagnosing problems. If we were to provide an environment for project management, we would likely create a project management perspective. The resources used in project management are strongly connected to each other, but only weakly connected to programming resources.

Since JUnit testing is expected to be part of programming, we want to integrate into existing perspectives rather than define a new perspective. Following the Integration Rule we integrate our contributions into the existing Java perspective.

A perspective determines what views are visible. If the user opens a view that isn't visible yet, then Eclipse opens it in a default location. We want the views to appear at a reasonable location without further intervention. The user should not have to arrange the views manually when they become visible. Figure 26.2 shows the arrangement we would like.

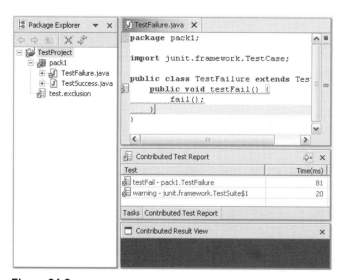

Figure 26.2

The workbench defines an `org.eclipse.ui.perspectiveExtensions` extension point.

With a plug-in search for `perspectiveExtensions` we find plenty of references we can mimic. We pick `org.eclipse.jdt.debug.ui`, as shown in Figure 26.3.

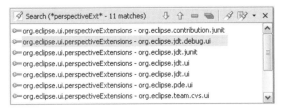

Figure 26.3

In its manifest we find a good example of a perspective extension:

org.eclipse.jdt.debug.ui/plugin.xml
```
<perspectiveExtension
  targetID="org.eclipse.debug.ui.DebugPerspective">
    ...
  <view
     id="org.eclipse.jdt.ui.PackageExplorer">
     relative="org.eclipse.debug.ui.DebugView"
     visible="false"
     relationship="stack">
  </view>
</perspectiveExtension>
```

This definition specifies that in the **Debug** perspective, the **Package Explorer** should be stacked on top of the **Debug** view and that the **Package Explorer** is initially not visible. To get to our target layout, we want to stack the test report view on top of the task list in the Java perspective. First we have to find out the ids of the Java perspective and the task list. We can look them up in the *plugin.xml* of their contributing plug-ins. If we don't know which plug-in defines them, we can do a plug-in search for references to the perspectives and views extension points. With the ids we can add the following definition to our manifest:

org.eclipse.contribution.junit/plugin.xml
```
<extension point="org.eclipse.ui.perspectiveExtensions">
  <perspectiveExtension
    targetID="org.eclipse.jdt.ui.JavaPerspective">
    <view
      id="org.eclipse.contribution.junit.testReportView">
      relative="org.eclipse.ui.views.TaskList"
      visible="false"
      relationship="stack">
    </view>
  </perspectiveExtension>
</extension>
```

We add another perspective extension for the result view. Say we want the result view to be smaller than the task list because it contains less information. We can set the ratio to 60 (60 percent task list, 40 percent result view):

org.eclipse.contribution.junit/plugin.xml
```
<perspectiveExtension
  targetID="org.eclipse.jdt.ui.JavaPerspective">
  <view
    relative="org.eclipse.ui.views.TaskList"
    visible="false"
    relationship="bottom"
    ratio="0.6"
    id="org.eclipse.contribution.junit.resultView">
  </view>
</perspectiveExtension>
```

26.2   Show View Menu

We now have a reasonable layout, but it is still cumbersome for the user to open the test views. Users have to go through the **Other...** dialog when choosing **Window > Show View,** as shown in Figure 26.4. We would like to give the test views the same first-class status as other important views. The use of the **Other...** menu item is an example of the Other Rule:

> **OTHER RULE**   Make all contributions available, but the ones that don't typically apply to the current perspective appear in an **Other...** dialog.

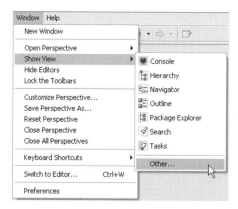

Figure 26.4

To add a view to the perspective's **Show View** submenu of the **Window** menu, we use the `viewShortcut` perspective extension:

org.eclipse.contribution.junit/plugin.xml
```
<perspectiveExtension
  targetID="org.eclipse.jdt.ui.JavaPerspective">
  <viewShortcut id="org.eclipse.contribution.junit.
    testReportView"/>
```

```
<viewShortcut id="org.eclipse.contribution.junit.resultView"/>
</perspectiveExtension>
```

Once we have added the view shortcut, our views appear as first-class views in the **View** menu, as shown in Figure 26.5.

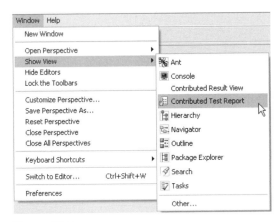

Figure 26.5

When experimenting with perspective extensions, keep in mind that the extensions are only processed when a perspective is created. Therefore, to see the effect of a perspective extension for an existing perspective, you have to first reset it (**Window > Reset Perspective**).

We are still not fully compliant with the Integration Rule for our views. The views don't integrate nicely into the **Show View** dialog. They show up in the "Other" category, as shown in Figure 26.6.

Figure 26.6

Our views are relevant for Java development, and we therefore want to contribute them to the Java category (Relevance Rule). In the *plugin.xml* of `org.eclipse.jdt.ui` we find the corresponding `category` definition:

org.eclipse.jdt.ui/plugin.xml
```
<extension point="org.eclipse.ui.views">
 <category
   id="org.eclipse.jdt.ui.java"
   name="%viewCategoryName">
 </category>
 ...
```

We contribute our views to the `org.eclipse.jdt.ui.java` category by adding a corresponding `category` attribute in their definition:

org.eclipse.contribution.junit/plugin.xml
```
<view
  id="org.eclipse.contribution.junit.resultView"
  name="Contributed Result View"
  class="org.eclipse.contribution.junit.ResultView"
  category="org.eclipse.jdt.ui.java">
</view>
```

Next we'll add on-line help for our contributed test runner. In this chapter we have

○ Defined perspective extensions for the test views and view shortcuts in the Java perspective

○ Contributed our views to an existing category

26.3   Forward Pointers

○ To define your own perspective, you use the `org.eclipse.ui.perspectives` extension point and implement an `IPerspectiveFactory`. The factory defines the initial layout and shortcuts for a perspective.

○ When a view appears in a perspective, it can ask the perspective for an "input" to help determine its initial contents.

○ In addition to view shortcuts you can define shortcuts for the following perspective contributions:

   – `actionSet`—The action sets initially visible in a perspective

   – `perspectiveShortcut`—The perspectives shown in the **Window > Open Perspective** submenu

- – `newWizardShortcut`—The new wizards shown in the **New** drop down

- – `showInPart`—Views to be added to the perspective's **Navigate > Show in** submenu

○ For more information on the use of perspectives, see: Using Perspectives in the Eclipse UI, *www.eclipse.org/articles/using-perspectives/ PerspectiveArticle.html.*

CHAPTER 27

Help

Another way of reducing the cost of service for your plug-ins is to provide on-line help. In Eclipse, help contents are structured as extensions to the `help` extension point. In this chapter we'll see how to

- ○ Add our own help contents
- ○ Link to our help contents from the user interface (context sensitive help)

There are several places we might want to integrate our help:

- ○ Stand-alone help
- ○ An "infopop" on the `ResultView` and the `TestReportView`
- ○ The auto-test property page
- ○ The run test action

27.1 Top-Level Help

All of the help contents in Eclipse follow the Contribution Rule. Every plug-in has the opportunity to contribute help. The help window is the only place you can see all the help together.

The basic unit of help is the table of contents, or toc. A toc is a tree containing other tocs or topics. Each toc or topic can have an html file associated with it. Figure 27.1 shows part of the help for the Plug-In Development Environment.

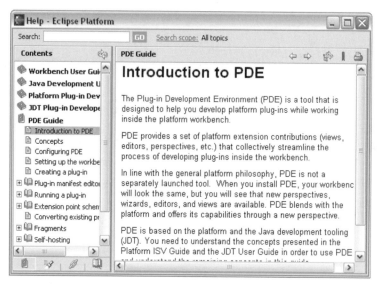

Figure 27.1

A contribution to the table of contents is represented in Eclipse as an extension to the extension point `org.eclipse.help.toc`. The user documentation for PDE is contributed in the separate plug-in `org.eclipse.pde.doc.user`. This plug-in only contains documentation and no code:

org.eclipse.pde.doc.user/plugin.xml
```
<extension point="org.eclipse.help.toc">
  <toc file="toc.xml" primary="true">
  </toc>
</extension>
```

This extension states that the table of contents will be found in a file called *toc.xml* (by convention, the root of the table of contents is always in *toc.xml*). Looking in *toc.xml*, we see the declaration of the structure above:

org.eclipse.pde.doc.user/toc.xml
```
<toc label="PDE Guide">
  <topic label="Introduction to PDE" href="guide/pde.htm"/>
  <topic label="Concepts" href="guide/pde_concepts.htm"/>
  <topic label="Configuring PDE" href="guide/pde_configuring.htm"/>
  <topic label="Setting up the workbench"
    href="guide/pde_setup.htm"/>
  <topic label="Creating a plug-in" href="guide/pde_creating.htm"/>
  <topic label="Plug-in manifest editor"
    href="guide/pde_manifest.htm">
  <topic label="Welcome page"
    href="guide/pde_manifest_welcome.htm" />
  <topic label="Overview page"
```

```
        href="guide/pde_manifest_overview.htm" />
      ...
    </topic>
  ...
</toc>
```

The topic elements nest inside the toc element, and each topic has an associated file as well as a label. When a topic is selected in the left-hand pane of the help window, the associated file is shown in the right-hand pane.

We'll put our help in the same plug-in as our code. Often, help comes in its own plug-in as we have seen above in org.eclipse.pde.doc.user, making it easy for a documentation team to work independently of the development team. First we need to make our plug-in dependent on the help plug-in, so we can see the toc extension point, then we'll make our extension:

org.eclipse.contribution.junit/plugin.xml
```
<requires>
  ...
  <import plugin="org.eclipse.help"/>
</requires>
<extension point="org.eclipse.help.toc">
  <toc file="toc.xml" primary="true" />
</extension>
```

Our help topic isn't referenced from anywhere. We therefore set the primary attribute to true so that it shows up in the top-level list of topics. For the moment, our table of contents will only have one topic, linked to a file called *help.html*:

org.eclipse.contribution.junit/toc.xml
```
<?xml version="1.0" encoding="UTF-8"?>
<?NLS TYPE="org.eclipse.help.toc"?>
<toc label="Auto-testing">
  <topic label="Auto-testing" href="help.html"/>
</toc>
```

We add a file *help.html* to our plug-in, containing the (currently sketchy) help contents:

org.eclipse.contribution.junit/help.html
```
<!DOCTYPE HTML PUBLIC "-//W3C//DTD HTML 4.0//EN">
<html>
<head>
<title>Auto-testing</title>
<meta http-equiv=Content-Type content="text/html;
charset=ISO-8859-1">
</head>
<body lang="EN-US">
```

```
<h2>Introduction to Auto-Testing</h2>
<p>Auto-testing is the ability to automatically run
all the tests for a project every time the project is built.
Failing tests appear as text markers, similar to compile errors.</p>
<h2>Turning on Auto-Testing</h2>
<p>Open the properties for a Java project. You will see a page
labelled "Auto-testing". Click on it, and click on the "Auto-test"
check box.</p>
</body>
</html>
```

When we start up the run-time workbench and open help, we see our help contents, as shown in Figure 27.2.

Figure 27.2

27.2 Integrated Help

We don't actually want our discussion of auto-testing to occur at the same level as those other topics. Auto-testing is a refinement of the Java development features of Eclipse. Following the Integration Rule, we'd like our help to fit in nicely with the rest of the JDT help. Fortunately, help has its own version of the Invitation Rule called **anchors**. An anchor is a point in the help tree where new help can be introduced. We can look at the JDT help to see how anchors appear. In the file *topics_Concepts.xml*, we find a likely table of contents into which we can integrate our auto-test help:

org.eclipse.jdt.docs.user/topics_Concepts.xml
```
<toc label="Concepts" href="concepts/concepts-1.htm" >
  ...
  <topic label="Java builder" href="concepts/concepts-4.htm"/>
```

```
    <anchor id="c_javabuilder" />
    ...
</toc>
```

To splice our help into the help on Java programming concepts, we give our `toc` element the attribute `link_to`, and name the file and the anchor where we'd like to see our help appear:

org.eclipse.contribution.junit/toc.xml
```
<toc label="Auto-testing" link_to="../org.eclipse.jdt.doc.user/
    topics_Concepts.xml#c_javabuilder">
  <topic label="Auto-testing" href="help.html"/>
</toc>
```

Now when we look at the help in the run-time workbench, we see our help integrated with the rest of the help on Java, as shown in Figure 27.3.

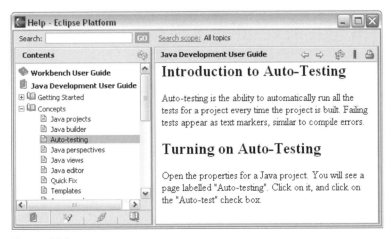

Figure 27.3

We'd also like to add a page to the section of Java help on Java project property pages, but unfortunately that `toc` tree doesn't declare any anchors. We can't add a page where we'd like it.

27.3 Context-Sensitive Help

Another kind of help is the context-sensitive help that appears when you click **F1** in a view. When we click **F1** in our test report view, we get the generic help, as shown in Figure 27.4.

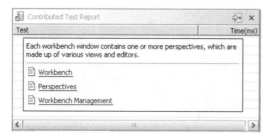

Figure 27.4

We'd like to see help on tests and auto-testing. Context-sensitive help is contributed by creating a help context extension and associating that context with a view.

We'll copy from the implementation of infopops in the search view, shown in Figure 27.5.

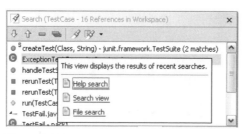

Figure 27.5

The class `WorkbenchHelp` provides an entry point for registering the availability of context-sensitive help. Help is associated with an SWT control. Looking at the class `SearchResultView`, we see that the help is registered when the view is created:

org.eclipse.search.internal.ui/SearchResultView
```
public void createPartControl(Composite parent) {
  ...
  WorkbenchHelp.setHelp(fViewer.getControl(),
    ISearchHelpContextIds.SEARCH_VIEW);
}
```

We add a similar line to `TestReportView.createPartControl()`:

org.eclipse.contribution.junit/TestReportView
```
public void createPartControl(Composite parent) {
  ...
  WorkbenchHelp.setHelp(viewer.getControl(),
    "org.eclipse.contribution.junit.autoTestContext");
}
```

For now we just add the context id in the code directly. Common practice in Eclipse is to centralize the help context ids in an interface I...HelpContext-Ids. There the context ids are categorized by the user-interface component (views, actions, wizards).

Nothing happens when we click **F1** because we haven't declared the help context extension. By searching for all references to the org.eclipse.help. contexts extension point we find the help context that applies to the search view:

org.eclipse.platform.doc.user/plugin.xml
```
<extension point="org.eclipse.help.contexts">
  <contexts file="contexts_Search.xml"
    plugin="org.eclipse.search"/>
</extension>
```

Because the documentation in Eclipse is organized into separate plug-ins, this declaration appears in org.eclipse.platform.doc.user instead of in org. eclipse.search where we expected it to be. Since we haven't separated help from the rest of our plug-in, we'll just declare the context in our plug-ins manifest:

org.eclipse.contribution.junit/plugin.xml
```
<extension point="org.eclipse.help.contexts">
  <contexts file="contexts.xml"
    plugin="org.eclipse.contribution.junit"/>
</extension>
```

Looking at the context file for search help, we see:

org.eclipse.platform.doc.user/contexts_Search.xml
```
<contexts>
  ...
  <context  id="search_view_context" >
    <description>This view displays the results
    of recent searches.</description>
    <topic label="Search view" href="reference/ref-26.htm"/>
    <topic label="File search" href="reference/ref-45.htm"/>
  </context>
  ...
</contexts>
```

We copy this to provide the infopop for the test results:

org.elipse.contribution.junit/contexts.xml
```
<contexts>
  <context id="autoTestContext">
    <description>These tests were run during
      auto-testing.</description>
    <topic label="Auto-testing" href="help.html" />
  </context>
</contexts>
```

We have defined the `plugin` name when we contributed to the `org.eclipse.help.contexts` extension point. The ID `autoTestContext` is now prefixed by this plug-in name. When we click **F1** in the **TestReportView,** we see our help, as shown in Figure 27.6.

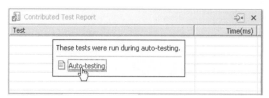

Figure 27.6

When adding help context IDs you want to cover the following UI elements:

- ○ Views
- ○ Editors
- ○ Actions
- ○ Dialogs
- ○ Wizards
- ○ Preference pages
- ○ Property pages

From this to-do list we can see that we should also assign a help context to the auto-test property page and to the `RunTestAction`. For the property page, we assign a help context in the same way as we did for the `TestReportView`. The `RunTestAction` is contributed in the plug-in manifest so we cannot define the help context in the code. Instead, we define the help context as an attribute in the *plugin.xml* definition. Here is how search defines a help context for one of its actions:

org.eclipse.search/plugin.xml
```
<action id="org.eclipse.search.OpenFileSearchPage"
  menubarPath="org.eclipse.search.menu/internalDialogGroup"
  label="%openFileSearchPageAction.label"
  icon="icons/full/obj16/tsearch_obj.gif"
  helpContextId="file_search_action_context"
  class="org.eclipse.search.internal.ui.OpenFileSearchPageAction"/>
```

We do the same for our `RunTestAction`:

org.eclipse.contribution.junit/plugin.xml
```
<action
  label="Run Test"
  class="org.eclipse.contribution.junit.RunTestAction"
```

```
    enablesFor="1"
    helpContextId="runTestActionContext"
    id="org.eclipse.contribution.junit.runtest.action">
</action>
```

Next we add a corresponding context:

org.eclipse.contribution.junit/contexts.xml
```
<contexts>
  <context id="runTestActionContext">
    <description>Runs all tests defined in the selected
      class.</description>
  </context>
</contexts>
```

When we click **F1** while the **Run Test** menu item is highlighted, we will see the context-sensitive help. **F1** help consists of only a description without a topic link, as shown in Figure 27.7.

Figure 27.7

We're nearing the end of the circle. In the next chapter, we'll internationalize our user interface. Reviewing this chapter, we

❍ Added a help topic by declaring an extension to `org.eclipse.help.toc` and creating a table-of-contents tree

❍ Spliced our help into the existing help by linking to an anchor

❍ Created an infopop help context by extending `org.eclipse.help.contexts` and creating the help contents and we connected to the context from our `TestReportView`

❍ Added a help context to the contributed `RunTestAction`

27.4 **Forward Pointers**

❍ *Putting help in a zip file*—To avoid the hassles of dealing with a large number of files in a plug-in, you can put all the help contents in a *doc.zip* file. Help first looks into the *doc.zip* file before looking into the plug-in directory.

❍ *Eclipse supports active help*—You can define links in your documentation that invoke code from a plug-in.

CHAPTER 28

Internationalization and Accessibility

Like any commercial-quality product, Eclipse is fully internationalizable and pays attention to accessibility requirements. When contributing to Eclipse we want to preserve this characteristic and make sure that our plug-in is usable by anybody. In this section we look into tasks related to internationalization and accessibility:

❍ Externalizing the strings from the *plugin.xml*

❍ Externalizing strings from Java code

❍ Paying attention to accessibility

All these tasks are highly mechanical, but need to be done. Let's start with externalizing the strings from the *plugin.xml*.

28.1 Externalizing Strings from the Manifest Files

Some strings in the *plugin.xml* are shown to the end user, the label of an action, for example. Others are shown to the plug-in developer through PDE, like the name of an extension point. All these strings need to be translatable and need to be externalized. PDE supports this with the look-aside file *plugin. properties*, shown in Figure 28.1.

Figure 28.1

A string prefixed with "%" in the *plugin.xml* is looked up in the *plugin. properties* file. We have to externalize all of the extension point names and all of the user-visible strings in our contributions. Here is an excerpt from the externalized *plugin.xml* file:

org.eclipse.contribution.junit/plugin.xml
```
<plugin
  ...
  name="%pluginName"
  ...">
  <extension-point id="listeners" name="%testListeners"/>
  <extension point="org.eclipse.ui.propertyPages">
    <page...
      name="%propertyPageName"
    </page>
  </extension>
  ...
</plugin>
```

The manifest file *feature.xml* describing a feature includes externalizable strings similar to the *plugin.xml*. The conventions to externalize these strings are the same as for the *plugin.xml*. The look-aside file for the *feature.xml* is named *feature.properties*.

28.2   Externalizing Strings from Code

Eclipse uses the standard Java resource bundle mechanism to externalize strings. The subpackages of `org.eclipse.ui.views` serve as good examples to illustrate the conventions:

❍ Introduce a resource bundle for each major component in a plug-in. In the case of `org.eclipse.views`, the components are the different views provided by the plug-in. Having a separate bundle for each component simplifies the bundle management and avoids having to merge conflicting changes when working in a team.

❍ For each resource bundle, add a properties file, for example, *messages. properties*, with the externalized strings. Use a helper class like `BookMark-ExplorerMessages` in `org.eclipse.ui.views.bookmarkexplorer` to access the bundle.

❍ Use qualified keys to ensure uniqueness, for example, `OpenBookmark. text`, `OpenBookmark.toolTip`, `OpenBookmark.errorTitle`.

Our contributed JUnit plug-in is simple enough that a single resource bundle is sufficient. To extract the strings, we use the string externalization support provided by the Eclipse Java tooling. **Source > Find Strings to Externalize** finds all the strings that are not yet marked as externalized. Eclipse uses the comment markers to tag externalized strings (//$NON-NLS-1$). The **Source > Externalize Strings** wizard extracts the strings and can create the bundle accessor class for us, as shown in Figure 28.2.

Figure 28.2

This is the generated helper class for accessing externalized strings:

org.eclipse.contribution.junit/JUnitMessages
```java
public class JUnitMessages {

  private static final String BUNDLE_NAME=
    "org.eclipse.contribution.junit.JUnitMessages"; //$NON-NLS-1$
  private static final ResourceBundle RESOURCE_BUNDLE=
    ResourceBundle.getBundle(BUNDLE_NAME);

  private JUnitMessages() {
  }
  public static String getString(String key) {
    try {
      return RESOURCE_BUNDLE.getString(key);
    } catch (MissingResourceException e) {
      return '!' + key + '!';
    }
  }
}
```

Here is an excerpt of code with externalized strings:

org.eclipse.contribution.junit/AutoTestPropertyPage
```java
...
Label label= new Label(composite, SWT.NONE);
```

```
label.setText(JUnitMessages.getString(
  "PropertyPage.description"));//$NON-NLS-1$
```

To verify that you have externalized all strings, you might want to turn on the **Usage of non-externalized strings** Java compiler option (**Window > Preferences > Java > Compiler**).

One problem with internationalization is you don't want to wait to ship your plug-ins until all the translations are ready. To ship translations separately, Eclipse provides *fragments*. A fragment allows you to add code or resources to an existing plug-in. Once the translations are ready, you can package them up into a fragment that extends your base plug-in.

Fragments

A plug-in fragment provides additional contents to an existing plug-in. The plug-in is already installed and should not be modified. A fragment is usually stored in the *plugins* directory together with the other plug-ins. When Eclipse detects a fragment its contents are merged with the existing plug-in.

In Eclipse fragments are used for two different purposes. One is to make additional translations available ("language packs"). The other use is to define platform-specific contents for an existing plug-in. For example, the fragment *org.eclipse.swt.win32* contains the win32-specific code of SWT.

Fragments come with a *fragment.xml* manifest. This is an example of a fragment for a language pack for the JDT UI plug-in (`org.eclipse.jdt.ui`) contributing translations in a `nl1.jar`:

```
<fragment
  name="Java Development Tools UI NL Support"
  id="org.eclipse.jdt.ui.nl1"
  version="2.0.0"
  plugin-id="org.eclipse.jdt.ui"
  plugin-version="2.0.0">
  <runtime>
    <library name="nl1.jar" />
  </runtime>
</fragment>
```

For fragments that do not contribute any code in the JAR files but resources only, there is another optimization you can make. If you change the library element to `<library name="nl1.jar" library=resource/>`, then the class loader only looks for resources in this library and not for classes.

28.3 Accessibility

While you externalize strings, it's a good time to give attention to accessibility issues. The primary accessibility issues you need to address in your plug-in are:

○ *Keyboard access*—Every action in the plug-in's UI needs to be accessible via the keyboard.

○ *Object information*—Enable screen readers. Associate labels with controls. Information contained in images should also be available as text.

○ *Display/sound*—Use color as an enhancement only. Support high contrast settings. Provide accessible alternatives for significant audio and video content.

In this chapter we will only touch on keyboard access and screen readers. The forward pointers contain guidelines for using color and sound.

An important requirement for an accessible application is that everything in an application can be reached with the keyboard. To make menu items and widgets in dialogs more easily accessible, we assign them mnemonics. This is done in both the *plugin.xml* and the code by prefixing the mnemonic letter with a "&". A mnemonic is shown with a letter underlined in menus and dialogs. When pressing the mnemonic letter, the selection or focus will jump to this item.

Currently, none of our menu items and dialog items has a mnemonic. We should try hard to come up with unique mnemonic letter choices. Since Eclipse menus are extensible, collisions can happen. The only consequence of a collision is that the user will have to press the mnemonic letter more than once. The object contribution to run a test and the auto test label in the property page both need a mnemonic, as shown in Figure 28.3.

Figure 28.3

org.eclipse.contribution.junit/plugin.properties
```
pluginName=Contributed Junit Plug-in
testListeners=Test Listeners
propertyPageName=Auto-test
runTestLabel=Run &Test
resultViewName=Contributed Result View
...
```

If you want to test whether your plug-in is accessible from the keyboard, use it while your mouse is unplugged.

Accessibility goes further than just defining mnemonics. For example, another requirement is that you have to accommodate screen readers. A screen reader can read the contents of widgets aloud. For example, our existing `ResultView` doesn't address this requirement. It only shows a red/green/grey color indication of a test's status. To make the view accessible, the color indication has to include some textual label like **OK, Failed, Unknown.**

In this chapter we have made our plug-in internationalized and accessible.

○ Externalized strings

○ Added mnemonics

The final bit of work on our plug-in in the next chapter is to explicitly publish its API.

28.4 **Forward Pointers**

○ *Testing your internationalized plug-ins*—Once you have externalized the strings, you also need to test how your dialogs look with longer strings on all the different platforms. For an in-depth article on testing an internationalized plug-in, refer to *www.eclipse.org/articles/Article-TVT/how2TestI18n. html.*

○ See *www.section508.gov/* for more information on accessibility requirements. IBM provides a detailed checklist for developers that is available at *www-3.ibm.com/able/guidelines/index.html.*

○ For information on how to fulfill accessibility requirements in Eclipse, refer to *www.eclipse.org/articles/Article-Accessibility/accessibility.html.*

○ SWT provides additional APIs for accessibility in the package `org. eclipse.swt.accessibility.`

○ For PDE support for creating projects representing a fragment, see **New > Plug-in Development > Fragment Projects.**

CHAPTER 29

Publishing a Plug-In for Other Programmers

We've talked a lot about how to communicate your intent to your computer through the wonders of Eclipse. Now it's time to talk about how you communicate with your fellow programmers. At this point we haven't made it explicit which classes of our plug-in we consider published and which ones we consider internal. Similarly, we haven't published our extension point. In this chapter we will look into publishing our plug-in and we'll see how to

○ Publish the plug-in API

○ Publish an extension point

29.1 Defining the API

Before diving into the details, let's first decide about what the API to our contributed JUnit plug-in should include:

○ Clients contributing a test run listener extension need to have access to the `ITestRunListener` interface (this is implied by the Conformance Rule).

○ Clients need a way to dynamically register a listener. This is required when a test run listener only needs to be temporarily registered. We have used this when we implemented views that track a test run. A view needs to be registered only when it is visible.

○ Clients need a way to start a test run.

The `ITestRunListener` is ready to be published. The support for dynamically registering a listener and running tests is provided by the `JUnitPlugin` class. However, the `JUnitPlugin` class includes several public methods that seem like implementation details (for example, methods like `addAutoBuild-Nature()` and `removeAutoBuildNature()`). We'd rather not publish these methods since they should only be used internally. We solve this problem by introducing an API Façade. `JUnitCore` is the entry point to the plug-in's core functionality. It provides static members only:

org.eclipse.contribution.junit/JUnitCore
```
public class JUnitCore {
  public static void addTestListener(ITestRunListener listener) {
    JUnitPlugin.getPlugin().getListeners().add(listener);
  }
  public static void removeTestListener(ITestRunListener listener){
    JUnitPlugin.getPlugin().getListeners().remove(listener);
  }
  public static void run(IType type) throws CoreException  {
    JUnitPlugin.getPlugin().run(type);
  }
  public static void run(IType[] types, IJavaProject project)
      throws CoreException {
    JUnitPlugin.getPlugin().run(types, project);
  }
}
```

Now that we have decided about the plug-in API, let's publish it.

29.2 Exporting Classes

The Eclipse runtime supports selectively exporting classes from a plug-in. By exporting only API classes you can limit what your clients see. In our case, this would correspond to the two classes `ITestRunListener` and `JUnitCore`. Any attempt to use a non-exported class would result in the class not being found at runtime.

In practice, the selective export of classes is not used in Eclipse. PDE does not yet support compile-time checking of class visibility. Not exporting a class is a harsh statement. It blocks a client from using a class at all. Not exporting any classes at all can be useful when your plug-in isn't intended to be extended. The style in Eclipse, though, is to open your contributions to further contribution, so all classes are usually exported.

Eclipse uses the defensive default that none of your classes are exported. To publish our classes, we have to adjust the `library` element of the manifest.

Since the plug-in is intended to be extended, we specify that we intend to export all the classes in `contribjunit.jar`. You adjust the library definition either with the PDE manifest editor in the **Runtime** tab (**Export the entire library**) or by editing the *plugin.xml* file directly:

org.eclipse.contribution.junit/plugin.xml
```
<runtime>
  <library name="contribjunit.jar">
    <export name = "*"/>
  </library>
</runtime>
```

By setting the export name pattern to "*" we are exporting all our classes.

Improving Class Loader Performance

For a production-quality plug-in you want to add the `package prefixes` element to the run-time section. This element was introduced in version 2.1 to improve the class loader performance. A plug-in's class loader is often asked to look up a class it doesn't contain. Performance can be improved by telling a class loader in advance which classes it will find. This is done by specifying the prefixes of the packages contained in the plug-in. In our case, the common prefix for both the internal and API packages is `org.eclipse.contribution.junit`. We therefore define the `prefixes` attribute as follows:

org.eclipse.contribution.junit/plugin.xml
```
<runtime>
  <library name="contribjunit.jar">
    <export name="*"/>
    <packages prefixes="org.eclipse.contribution.junit"/>
  </library>
</runtime>
```

With this additional information the plug-in class loader only starts the class look-up for its own classes when the class matches the prefix string. However, keep in mind that a typo in the prefix or forgetting to update the prefixes when adding a package with a new prefix will result in a `ClassNotFoundException`. Such exceptions can be tricky to debug. Therefore, when getting a `ClassNotFoundException`, you will want to check the `package prefixes` definition.

29.3   Separating Published from Internal Packages

We need to arrange our plug-in so readers will know what is important and what is not, what is stable and what is likely to change.

The Invitation Rule tells us to invite contributions. One way to invite contributions is to publish extension points, à la the Explicit Extension Rule. Another form of contribution is to expose some of your programmatic interface for others to use. Published APIs should also be explicit:

EXPLICIT API RULE   Separate the API from internals.

Designers need freedom. If you publish all functionality as potentially useful APIs, when you want to change the internal structure you break all clients. If you don't carefully define the API, you—as a designer—gradually lose your freedom to innovate.

STABILITY RULE   Once you invite others to contribute, don't change the rules.

Once you have published an API, it is rude to change it without a compelling reason. If I have written a plug-in based on your version 1.0, I'd like it to work without modification on your version 1.1. Keeping the API stable is to both of our benefits, except if it's wrong. The need to balance stability and growth leads us to the third API-related rule:

DEFENSIVE API RULE   Reveal only the API in which you have confidence, but be prepared to reveal more API as clients ask for it.

The convention for combining these rules in Eclipse is for every plug-in intended for external use to have two name spaces. If a package name contains `internal`, the classes it contains are not intended to be used outside the plug-in. Other packages can be considered published, available for subsequent extenders to use. The nice, short package name is for the API, the long name is for internals. Using package-private classes and interfaces is another way of satisfying the Explicit API Rule.

We have already chosen the API we want to publish. To follow the Eclipse convention we keep our API classes—`ITestRunListener` and `JUnitCore`—in `org.eclipse.contribution.junit`. We move all the other packages to the internal namespace: `org.eclipse.contribution.junit.internal.*`.

Refactoring and Updating the *plugin.xml*

When you define the API, you often have to move classes and rename packages. JDT provides refactoring support to do so. However, by default, Java source code is refactored. When doing plug-in development you have to remember that fully qualified class names also occur in the *plugin.xml* file. Therefore, when renaming or moving a Java element, these class references need to be updated as well. Fortunately, the **Rename** and **Move** refactorings provide an option to update fully qualified names in non-Java files. When doing plug-in development, add *plugin.xml* to the list of file name patterns to be considered during a refactoring. See the following dialog for an example.

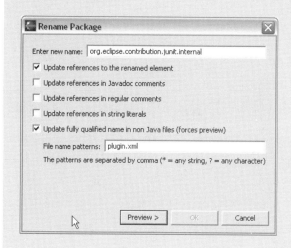

In the package restructuring we just did in `org.eclipse.contribution.junit` updating the *plugin.xml* wasn't sufficient. We are also referring to class names in strings. To update the references in strings you can check the **Update references in string literals**. There are two class references in strings:

○ The path to the resource bundle in `JUnitMessages.BUNDLE_NAME`.

○ The name of the main class to launch in the `TestRunner`.

29.4   Separating Core from UI

Large contributions have separate plug-ins for their core functionality and their user interface. This allows running the "headless" core functionality without having to load the UI plug-ins. Our plug-in isn't ready for this treatment. We can't imagine any of its functionality being useful when running headless. However, considering this split is always useful. Forcing yourself to separate the core from the user interface often illuminates design problems as you try to minimize the dependencies between plug-ins. No class in a core package should refer to a class in a UI package.

For now, we don't separate core and UI functionality into separate plug-ins, but we separate them into different packages. We come up with the package structure shown in Figure 29.1.

Figure 29.1

A reader can infer from this package structure that the only published API is `ITestRunListener` and `JUnitCore`. The non-UI-specific implementation of the functionality is in `internal.core`, and the user interface is in `internal.ui`.

29.5   Publishing an Extension Point—Extension Point Schemas

We have now published the API for the Java-based interface. What about specifying our extension point? PDE provides extension point schemas to specify the attributes and their expected values of an extension point. The overall goal of extension point schemas is to prevent users from making errors when defining extensions, as shown in Figure 29.2. PDE uses them to validate the *plugin.xml* in the manifest editor. Extension point validation is done by the plug-in manifest builder, which PDE adds to plug-in projects.

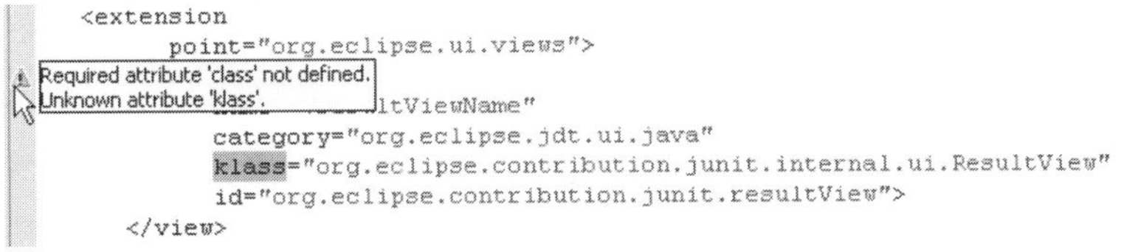

```
<extension
        point="org.eclipse.ui.views">
    Required attribute 'class' not defined.
    Unknown attribute 'klass'.           ltViewName"
            category="org.eclipse.jdt.ui.java"
            klass="org.eclipse.contribution.junit.internal.ui.ResultView"
            id="org.eclipse.contribution.junit.resultView">
    </view>
```

Figure 29.2

Schemas are also used in the PDE wizards to implement an extension point (see Chapter 23). Finally, a schema can contain embedded documentation similar to JavaDoc that is used for generating the extension point reference documentation.

We want to provide the same level of service for the `listeners` extension point we have defined for our plug-in. An extension point schema is a subset of an XML schema. Subset sounds simple, but it is still complex enough that you don't want to build it by hand. The PDE-provided schema editor is a big help.

A plug-in search for the declaration of the `views` extension point illustrates how schemas are associated with the extension point:

org.eclipse.ui/plugin.xml
```
<extension-point id="views" name="%ExtPoint.views"
    schema="schema/views.exsd"/>
```

By convention schemas are stored in a schema folder inside the plug-in project. There is a schema file for each extension point. A file has the same name as the extension point with the suffix *exsd*.[1]

We mimic this for our plug-in. First we associate a schema with the `listener` extension point definition:

org.eclipse.contribution.junit/plugin.xml
```
<extension-point id="listeners" name="%testListeners"
  schema="schema/listeners.exsd"/>
```

---

1. When renaming a package or class, you also want to include `*.exsd` to the list of filter patterns for non-Java resources that should be considered during the refactoring. This ensures that class names in schema files are updated as well.

We don't want to create a schema from scratch. We copy the *schema/views.exsd* into `org.eclipse.contribution.junit` and rename it *listeners.exsd*. A binary plug-in project doesn't include the schema files. We therefore have to reach into the source plug-in to find them. To enable shipping Eclipse without source, all the plug-in source is packaged into separate source plug-ins. To get at the source for the Eclipse platform feature, which includes the schema, we can use `eclipse/plugins/org.eclipse.platform.source_2.1.1/src/org.eclipse.ui_2.1.1/schema`.

Schema files have the PDE schema editor associated with them. After opening the schema, we see the screen shown in Figure 29.3.

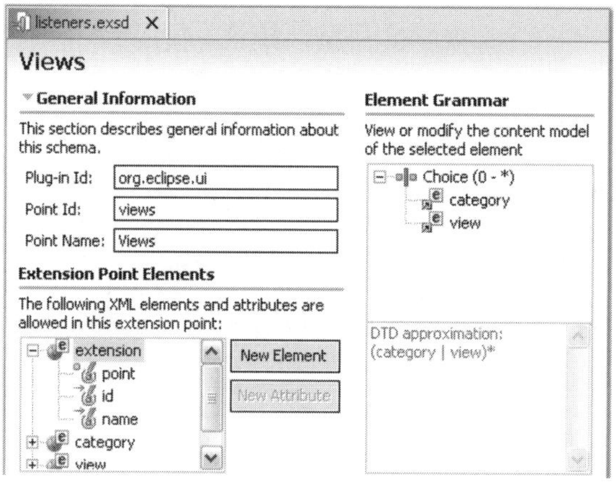

Figure 29.3

The **Extension Point Elements** tree on the left defines the elements and attributes of the schema and the **Element Grammar** tree on the right defines the structure of the selected element. The `view` extension point has two elements, `category` and `view`, in addition to the extension point element itself. The grammar for the extension point element is defined by a choice of either a `category` or a `view` element.

The schema for our listener extension point is simpler. It has a single element, `listener`, and the grammar of the extension point is a simple sequence with a reference to a `listener` element. We therefore tweak the schema to get the screen shown in Figure 29.4.

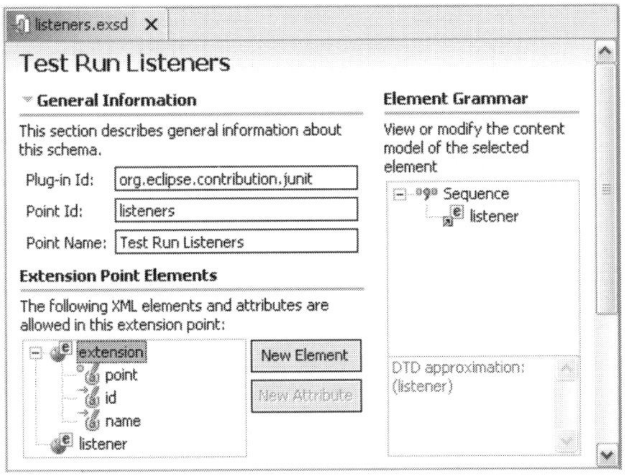

Figure 29.4

You define the properties of elements and attributes in the **Properties** view. The view is brought to the front when you double click an element in the schema editor. Entering the grammar deserves some explanation. First you have to create the element before you can use it in a grammar specification. We add a `listener` element. Once the `listener` element is defined, we create a sequence element in the grammar pane. Next we add a reference to the just-defined `listener` element, as shown in Figure 29.5.

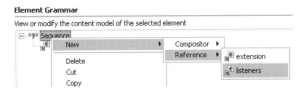

Figure 29.5

We have defined the element structure of the extension point. Now we can move on to define the expected attributes of the `listener` element. We add a single `class` attribute and edit its properties in the **Properties** view, as shown in Figure 29.6.

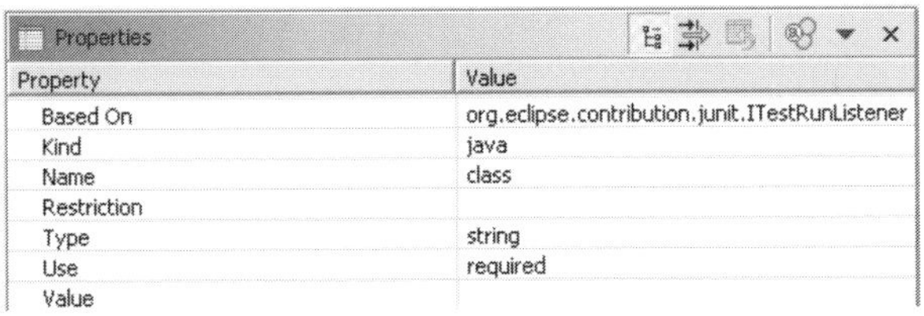

Property	Value
Based On	org.eclipse.contribution.junit.ITestRunListener
Kind	java
Name	class
Restriction	
Type	string
Use	required
Value	

Figure 29.6

We set the `Kind` property to `java`, to indicate that this attribute is Java-related. PDE can then leverage this knowledge and create a Java class for the user when defining an extension point. The kind of class is specified in the `Based On` property. In our case, the attribute must conform to `ITestRun-Listener`. Finally, we set the attribute `Use` to `required` since our extension point only makes sense with a `class` attribute.

The last step in completing the extension point schema is the addition of reference documentation. To do so, we switch to the documentation tab and use the `views` extension point documentation as a guide, as shown in Figure 29.7.

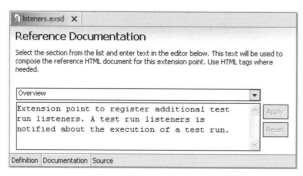

Figure 29.7

Before we close Circle Two, let's review what we did in this chapter. We

○ Updated the *plug.xml* to export all our classes to other plug-ins

○ Separated the published classes from the internal classes by moving the internal classes to `org.eclipse.contribution.junit.internal`

○ Separated UI functionality and core functionality into separate packages

○ Published our extension point by defining an extension point schema with the PDE schema editor

29.6 Forward Pointers

○ *Eclipse API ground rules*—To learn more about how to use the Eclipse API, refer to *www.eclipse.org/articles/Article-API use/eclipse-api-usage-rules.html*.

○ *Evolving Java APIs*—For guidelines about evolving Java APIs, refer to *www.eclipse.org/eclipse/development/java-api-evolution.html*.

○ *Exporting an imported plug-in*—When importing a plug-in, you can set the attribute export to `true`: `<import plugin="org.eclipse.swt" export="true"/>`. This indicates that the imported plug-in is automatically made visible to users of this plug-in. In general, explicit imports are preferred. When exporting another plug-in from your plug-in then you are making an API commitment. You should therefore not do this normally. Exporting an import can be useful when splitting a plug-in into several smaller plug-ins. Because the new plug-ins are automatically available, existing clients don't have to be changed.

CHAPTER 30

Closing Circle Two

Now we've been through two complete cycles of development on our JUnit plug-in:

1. The first cycle got the basic structure in place and the deployment infrastructure set up.

2. The second cycle added some functionality and showed all the non-coding tasks necessary to become a full-fledged enabler.

One surprise in Circle Two is the amount of non-programming work necessary to write an effective plug-in:

- ○ Internationalization
- ○ Help
- ○ Tracing
- ○ Accessibility
- ○ Plug-in schemas and documentation

This work is the difference between just adding a feature to Eclipse for personal use and really enabling other users and plug-in writers. Figure 30.1 shows all the classes we've written and how they are related.

Another surprise is how much functionality we were able to add with only a few lines of code. Eclipse really does make the extension of programming-environment-like functionality easy. That is, easy once you understand all the concepts involved.

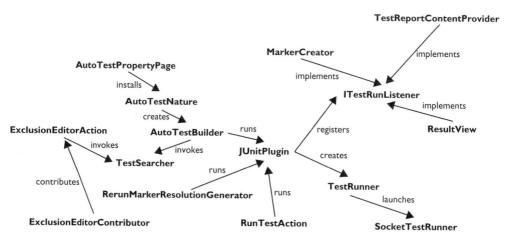

Figure 30.1   Overview of All Contributed Classes

Figure 30.2 shows the tests we wrote. They execute (on our laptops, anyway) in about 30 seconds.

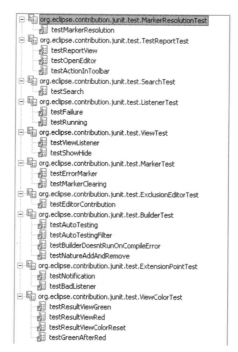

Figure 30.2   Tests Implemented for the Contributed JUnit Plug-In

30.1 Contributing

Writing and distributing our plug-in turns us into publishers. Publishing a new extension point takes us a step higher on the pyramid, turning us into enablers because others can now contribute to our contribution. To finish Circle Two, let's consider how someone might do this, extending the functionality of our test runner. The contribution will emit a short sound whenever a test fails during a test run.

We start by creating a new plug-in that we call `org.eclipse.contribution.junit.beep`. This is a simple plug-in so we don't need a plug-in class.

org.eclipse.contribution.junit.beep/plugin.xml
```
<plugin
  id="org.eclipse.contribution.junit.beep"
  name="JUnit Error Beep Plug-in"
  version="1.0.0"
  provider-name="">

  <runtime>
    <library name="junitbeep.jar"/>
  </runtime>
</plugin>
```

We don't include an export name pattern in the `runtime` element. This plug-in is not intended to be extended and therefore we need not export any classes.

`Org.eclipse.contribution.junit` has to be added as a prerequisite:

org.eclipse.contribution.junit.beep/plugin.xml
```
<requires>
  <import plugin="org.eclipse.ui"/>
  <import plugin="org.eclipse.jdt.core"/>
  <import plugin="org.eclipse.contribution.junit"/>
</requires>
```

Next we contribute to the `listeners` extension point:

org.eclipse.contribution.junit.beep/plugin.xml
```
<extension point="org.eclipse.contribution.junit.listeners">
  <listener
    class="org.eclipse.contribution.junit.beep.BeepingListener">
  </listener>
</extension>
```

Because we have defined a schema for the extension point, PDE catches a misspelling of the class attribute, as shown in Figure 30.3, where we mistyped the `class` attribute.

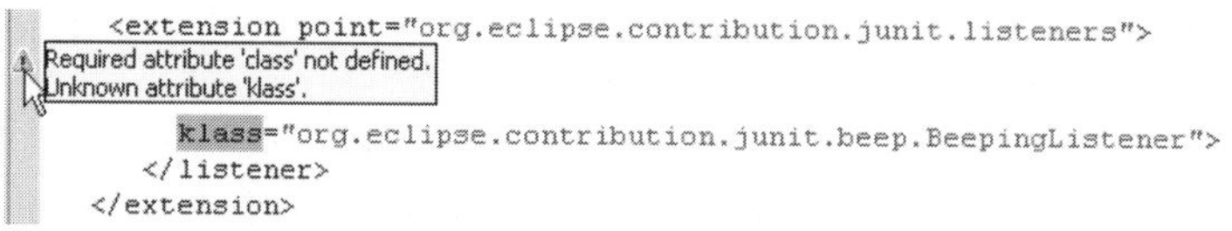

```
        <extension point="org.eclipse.contribution.junit.listeners">
Required attribute 'class' not defined.
Unknown attribute 'klass'.
            klass="org.eclipse.contribution.junit.beep.BeepingListener">
        </listener>
    </extension>
```

Figure 30.3

Finally, we define the BeepingListener. It has to conform to the ITestRun-
Listener interface. To emit a beep on a failure, the method testFailed()
is implemented; all the other listener methods do nothing.

org.eclipse.contribution.junit.beep/BeepingListener
```
public class BeepingListener implements ITestRunListener {
  public void testFailed(IJavaProject p, String klass,
      String m, String t) {
    final Display display= Display.getDefault();
    display.syncExec(new Runnable() {
      public void run() {
        if (!display.isDisposed())
          display.beep();
      }
    });
  }
  public void testsStarted(IJavaProject p, int count) {}
  public void testsFinished(IJavaProject p) {}
  public void testStarted(IJavaProject p, String klass,
      String method) {}
}
```

The beep is emitted using the SWT Display class. This class is the liaison
between SWT and the underlying operating system. The listener can be
called from a long-running operation. To avoid an illegal-thread-access exception, the beep request is posted to the UI thread.

Our contribution is finished. On the first test run the beeping plug-in is
activated and beeps when a test fails.

30.2   Redeploying the Plug-In

To finish this circle, let's redeploy and publish our enhanced version of the
plug-in. We check whether the *build.properties* file is still up-to-date to ensure
that the plug-in is properly deployed. This is the current contents:

org.eclipse.contribution.junit/build.properties
```
source.contribjunit.jar = src
bin.includes = *.jar,\
               junit.jar,\
               plugin.xml
```

The value of `source.contribjunit.jar` is correct. However, the value of `bin.includes` needs to be updated. We have added the `plugin.properties`, the externalized strings from the *plugin.xml*, an icon folder, and the help files to this plug-in. All these resources have to be included in the deployed plug-in. We therefore adjust the value as follows:

org.eclipse.contribution.junit/build.properties
```
bin.includes = *.jar,\
               junit.jar,\
               plugin.xml\
               plugin.properties,\
               icons/,\
               help.html,\
               contexts.xml,\
               toc.xml.
```

Next we increase the plug-in version number to 1.1.0 in the *plugin.xml*:

org.eclipse.contribution.junit/plugin.xml
```
<plugin
    id="org.eclipse.contribution.junit"
    name="%pluginName"
    version="1.1.0"
    class="org.eclipse.contribution.junit.internal.core.JUnitPlugin">
```

Then we propagate the version change to the *feature.xml* and update the required plug-ins. The feature manifest editor can compute the required plug-ins for us:

org.eclipse.contribution.junit-feature/feature.xml
```
<feature
  id="org.eclipse.contribution.junitfeature"
  label="org.eclipse.contribution.junit-feature"
  version="1.1.0"
  provider-name="">
  <license>
    License text goes here.
  </license>
  <requires>
    <import plugin="org.junit"/>
    <import plugin="org.eclipse.jdt.core"/>
    <import plugin="org.eclipse.jdt.launching"/>
    <import plugin="org.eclipse.debug.core"/>
    <import plugin="org.eclipse.ui"/>
    <import plugin="org.eclipse.core.resources"/>
    <import plugin="org.eclipse.jdt.ui"/>
    <import plugin="org.eclipse.help"/>
  </requires>
  <plugin
    id="org.eclipse.contribution.junit"
    download-size="0"
```

```
        install-size="0"
        version="1.1.0"/>
</feature>
```

Since we have externalized the strings from the *feature.xml* into a *feature.properties* file, we have to inform PDE about which files should be included in the deployed feature. This is done in a *build.properties* file in the same way we did for a plug-in. We add the *feature.properties* file to the `bin.includes` variable:

org.eclipse.contribution.junit-feature/build.properties
```
bin.includes = feature.xml,\
               feature.properties
```

Finally, we can rebuild the update site and add a version 1.1.0 of the feature, as shown in Figure 30.4.

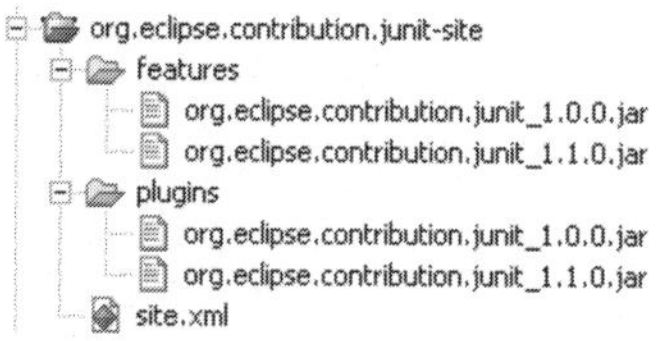

```
⊟ 🗁 org.eclipse.contribution.junit-site
    ⊟ 🗁 features
        📄 org.eclipse.contribution.junit_1.0.0.jar
        📄 org.eclipse.contribution.junit_1.1.0.jar
    ⊟ 🗁 plugins
        📄 org.eclipse.contribution.junit_1.0.0.jar
        📄 org.eclipse.contribution.junit_1.1.0.jar
    📄 site.xml
```

Figure 30.4

30.3   Where to Go Next?

No plug-in is ever done. Where would we like to go next with auto-testing?

○ Smarter rerunning of tests so we only run tests whose status might have changed based on the contents of the changes to the project

○ Automatically running our project's tests and all dependent projects' tests so we quickly identify downstream effects of our changes

○ Running tests in the background so we don't block further programming progress

○ More and better ways of understanding the relationship between tests and code under test, like coverage metrics or defect insertion

PART IV

Circle Three:
Pattern Stories

In this section we give you a cook's tour of Eclipse. We will use patterns as analytical tools to tell you compact Eclipse design stories. This will be an orthogonal view to the other circles we have traveled so far. Our goal is to give you some additional insights into Eclipse components. Once you understand the Eclipse design, you will learn more quickly how to play according to Eclipse's rules.

We assume that you know about design patterns[1] and don't have to rush to the bookshelf when you hear about Composite. You will learn some pattern variations in the discussion that follows. Patterns need to be tweaked and adapted to a particular context.

We will cover the design insight in different components. The following diagram shows pattern-story coverage of the Eclipse architecture. We have tried to cover these components in ways you will likely encounter when contributing to Eclipse.

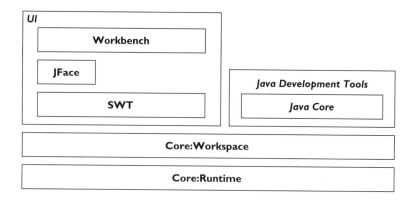

The pattern stories cover the Eclipse components from the bottom-up. We start with the Core Runtime (`org.eclipse.core.runtime`) component.

1. E. Gamma, R. Helm, R. Johnson, and J. Vlissides, *Design Patterns: Elements of Reusable Object-Oriented Software.* Addison-Wesley, Reading, MA, 1995.

CHAPTER 31

Core Runtime—IAdaptable

Our first pattern story is about the Eclipse-type extension mechanism that is provided by the Eclipse core run-time component (see Figure 31.1).

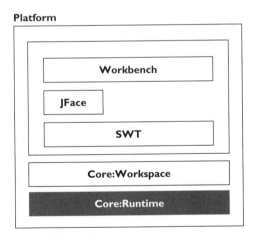

Figure 31.1   Core Runtime

Eclipse is an extensible platform. It cannot anticipate all the services its objects need to provide. As Eclipse evolves, new features will be added that will require additional services or behavior from existing classes. If we want stable APIs, we can't simply change the interface of an existing class or add a new interface. We need a mechanism to evolve the Eclipse interfaces without changing the definitions of the base interfaces. We need to be able to extend the behavior of Eclipse-provided types. The basic Java language doesn't help.

Let's see how this all got started in Eclipse. Eclipse strictly separates UI from non-UI parts. The `org.eclipse.resources` plug-in provides abstractions like `IFile`, `IFolder`, and `IProject`. Objects of these types need to be presented to the user in the UI. For example, the **Navigator** presents an icon and user label for `IFile` objects. The challenge is that the basic `IFile` interface shouldn't be "polluted" with UI details. It has to be fully UI agnostic. One solution is to add UI-specific aspects in a wrapper object. There could be an `IUIFile` type that wraps an `IFile` and adds the presentation aspects to `IFile`. This is not very elegant and adds overhead. Every time we add another `IResource`, we also have to add an `IUIResource`. Instead, we need a way to extend the behavior of `IFile`, `IProject`, `IFolder` so they can also be presented.

As a motivational example consider the Eclipse **Properties** view. The **Properties** view presents a set of properties of the currently selected object. Figure 31.2 shows the properties of the selected resource in the **Navigator**.

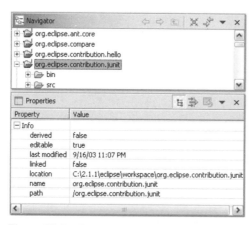

Figure 31.2   Properties View

There are two parties involved in the properties display: the **Properties** view and the selected object. The **Properties** view needs an interface to fetch the properties so that it can display them and the selected object needs to support this interface. In Eclipse, the interface required by the **Properties** view is `IPropertySource` and is defined as follows:

org.eclipse.ui.views.properties/IPropertySource
```
public interface IPropertySource {
  public Object getEditableValue();
```

```
    public IPropertyDescriptor[] getPropertyDescriptors();
    public Object getPropertyValue(Object id);
    public boolean isPropertySet(Object id);
    public void resetPropertyValue(Object id);
    public void setPropertyValue(Object id, Object value);
}
```

The selected object somehow has to surface this interface to the **Properties** view. A straightforward solution is to implement it directly in the class of the selected object:

```
public interface IFile extends IPropertySource
```

This solution has several problems:

- ❍ Adding many such service interfaces for other components to a class will result in a bloated interface.

- ❍ The fact that a class implements a service is an implementation detail that you don't want to expose if the type is API. Adding such an interface once the class is published is a breaking API change.

- ❍ An `IFile` should not have to know about the **Properties** view, which is a concept from the UI layer. This is precisely the coupling of model and user interface we want to avoid.

31.1 Extension Object/Extension Interface

We need a mechanism that allows us to

- ❍ Add a service interface to a type without exposing it in that type

- ❍ Add behavior to preexisting types such as `IFile`

The pattern is called Extension Object[1] and is also known as Extension Interface. To quote its intent: "Anticipate that an object's interface needs to be extended in the future. Extension Object lets you add interfaces to a class and lets clients query whether an object has a particular extension."

---

1. See "Extension Object" in R. Martin, *Pattern Languages of Program Design 3*. Addison-Wesley, Reading, MA, 1998. For a comprehensive description with several other implementation variations, see "Extension Interface" in D. Schmidt, M. Stal, H. Rohner, F. Buschmann, *Pattern-Oriented Software Architecture Volume 2: Patterns for Concurrent and Networked Objects*. John Wiley & Sons, 2000.

When implementing Extension Object, you have to answer several questions:

○ Do you want to extend an individual object or a class? With a class-based mechanism you add behavior to an entire class. You can only add behavior but not state, that is, no fields.

○ How is an extension described and identified?

The Eclipse extension support is class-based. That is, you can add behavior to existing classes, but not add state to its existing instances. The additional behavior is described by an interface.

The key interface of the Eclipse extension support is IAdaptable. Classes that support adaptability implement this interface. While browsing the Eclipse source, you will find that IAdaptable is a popular interface, as illustrated in the following snapshot of the **Hierarchy** view shown in Figure 31.3.

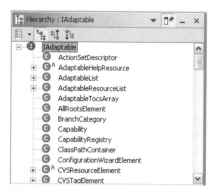

Figure 31.3   IAdaptable Type Hierarchy

What is behind the IAdaptable name? When doing some Eclipse code archeology we found the class was originally called IExtensible. This captured the idea that the mechanism existed to support extending a type with additional behavior. Over time the name got changed to IAdaptable to emphasize the fact that the mechanism enables adapting an existing class to another interface.

IAdaptable is an interface with a single method that allows clients to dynamically query whether an object supports a particular interface:

org.eclipse.core.runtime/IAdaptable
```
public interface IAdaptable {
  public Object getAdapter(Class adapter);
}
```

The `getAdapter()` method answers a particular interface. Callers of `get-Adapter()` pass in the class object corresponding to the interface (see Figure 31.4).

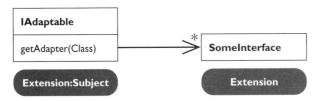

Figure 31.4   Extension Object

The class object is typically retrieved with a class literal (for example, `IPropertySource.class`). `GetAdapter()` could have taken a `String` argument instead, but then the compiler couldn't check to see whether the interface exists at compile time. `GetAdapter()` returns an object castable to the given class (or null if the interface isn't supported). Here is an example of how the **Properties** view queries the currently selected object for its `IPropertySource` interface:

org.eclipse.ui.views.properties/PropertySheetEntry
```
getPropertySource(Object object) {
  //...
  if (object instanceof IAdaptable) {
    IAdaptable a=  (IAdaptable) object;
    return (IPropertySource)a.getAdapter(IPropertySource.class);
  }
}
```

The `IAdaptable` interface is used in two different ways in Eclipse:

❍ *A class wants to provide additional interfaces without exposing them in the API*—In this case, `getAdapter()` is implemented by the class itself. Adding a new interface requires changing the implementation of `get-Adapter()`. This is useful when a class wants to support additional interfaces without changing its existing interface and thereby breaking the API.

❍ *A class is augmented from the outside to provide additional services*—In this case, no code changes to the existing class are required and the `get-Adapter()` implementation is contributed by a factory.

Let's first consider how a class can provide interfaces using `IAdaptable`.

31.2   Surfacing Interfaces Using IAdaptable

Here is an implementation of a `getAdapter()` method in a class that supports
the `IPropertySource` interface:

```
Object getAdapter(Class adapter)  {
  if (adapter.equals(IPropertySource.class)
    return new PropertySourceAdapter(this);
  return super.getAdapter(adapter);
}
```

In `PropertySourceAdapter`, you implement the `IPropertySource`:

```
public class PropertySourceAdapter implements IPropertySource {
  private Object  source;

  public PropertySourceAdapter(Object source) {
    this.source= source;
  }

  public IPropertyDescriptor[] getPropertyDescriptors() {
    // return the property descriptors.
  }
  //...
}
```

Implementing `getAdapter()` directly helps with the API evolution. If later on
the class wants to provide an additional interface, say `IShowInSource`, then
we only have to augment the `getAdapter()` method. No changes to the external interface of the class are required:

```
Object getAdapter(Class adapter)  {
  if (adapter.equals(IPropertySource.class)
    return new PropertySourceAdapter(this);
  if (adapter.equals(IShowInSource.class)
    return new ShowInSourceAdapter(this);
  return super.getAdapter(adapter);
}
```

Implementing `getAdapter()` with conditional logic is simple. But since
Extension Object is supposed to support unanticipated extension, conditional
logic isn't the final answer. The next step is externally augmenting the interfaces supported by an existing type.

31.3 AdapterFactories—Adding Interfaces to Existing Types

Let's consider how to add property-sheet support to `IFile` without having to pollute `IFile` with UI-specific behavior. A layer-preserving solution is to introduce a property-sheet *wrapper* for an `IFile`. Let's go down this path for a while to see its problems.

```
public class FileWithProperties implements IPropertySource {
  private IFile  file;

  public IPropertyDescriptor[] getPropertyDescriptors() {...}
  public Object getPropertyValue(Object id) {...}
  public boolean isPropertySet(Object id) {...}
  public void resetPropertyValue(Object id) {...}
  public void setPropertyValue(Object id, Object value) {...}

  public IFile toFile() { return file; }
}
```

The class `FileWithProperties` wraps an existing `IFile` and implements the `IPropertySource` interface. As an improvement, we could also implement the `IFile` interface (which the API contract doesn't allow) and implement the wrapper using the Decorator pattern. This would make the use of the wrapper more transparent to clients. However, there is another problem. We now end up with two different objects representing the same `IFile`. This introduces subtle complexities when it comes to testing files for equality. Life would be much simpler without any wrapping. Clients can just deal with `IFile` but extend its behavior. This is exactly the purpose of adapter factories. Here are the steps for how to extend `IFile`:

1. Implement an `AdapterFactory` with the adapters you want to add to a particular type.

2. Register the factory for a specific type with the `AdapterManager`. The `AdapterManager` is provided by the `Platform` class, a façade with static methods for general platform services.

In the implementation you have to declare which adapters the factory provides. This is done in the `getAdapterList()` method. The purpose of this declarative method is to enable a quick lookup for an adapter. With this information, Eclipse can quickly decide whether a type supports a particular adapter.

An `AdapterFactory` encapsulates the extensions you want to add for a particular type.

```
class FileAdapterFactory implements IAdapterFactory {
  public Class[] getAdapterList() {
    return new Class[] {
      IPropertySource.class
    };
  }
  //...
}
```

In our case, the factory contributes a single adapter for `IPropertySource`. The other method is `getAdapter()`. In contrast to the `IAdaptable.get-Adapter()`, it has an additional argument for the object that originally received the request:

```
public Object getAdapter(Object o, Class adapter) {
  if (adapter == IPropertySource.class)
    return new FilePropertySource((IFile)o);
  return null;
}
```

Next we have to register the factory for our desired type (`IFile`) with the `AdapterManager`. This has to occur early enough so that calls to `get-Adapter()` return the correct result. This is commonly done in a plug-in's `startup()` method or in a static initializer. Here is a a corresponding code snippet:

```
IAdapterManager manager = Platform.getAdapterManager();
IAdapterFactory factory = new FileAdapterFactory();
manager.registerAdapters(factory, IFile.class);
```

Figure 31.5 illustrates these relationships.

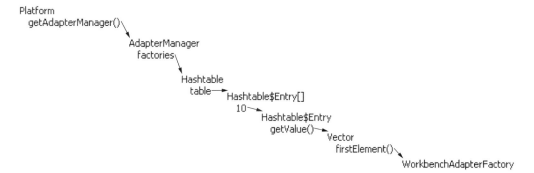

Figure 31.5   Register Adapter Factories with the Platform

Now we have added an adapter factory. However, unless it gets an opportunity to participate in the `getAdapter()` requests, we haven't made any progress. Therefore, the `getAdapter()` invoked on `IFile` objects has to enable adapter contributions from the adapter manager (the Invitation Rule). The `IFile` interface is implemented in `File`. Figure 31.6 illustrates its type hierarchy.

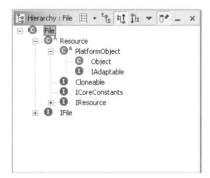

Figure 31.6   IFile Type Hierarchy

The class `File` descends from `Resource`, which descends from the class `PlatformObject`. `PlatformObject` implements `IAdaptable` and forwards `getAdapter()` invocations to the `Platform`'s adapter manager (see Figure 31.7). If you cannot derive from `PlatformObject`, you invite others to contribute adapters by calling:

```
Platform.getAdapterManager().getAdapter(this, adapter);
```

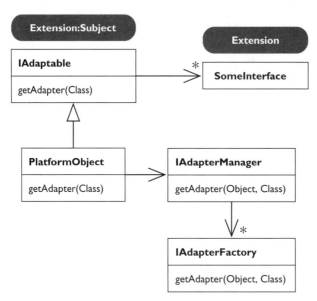

Figure 31.7 IAdapterFactory Returns Extensions for a Given Class

Once we have done all this, clients can call `getAdapter(IPropertySource. class)` without having to worry whether the interface is provided by the class itself or whether it was added externally.

Figure 31.8 shows the implementors of `IAdapterFactory` in Eclipse.

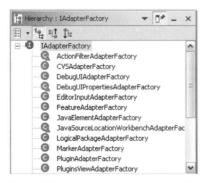

Figure 31.8 IAdapterFactory Type Hierarchy

Here are some points about the extension mechanism:

○ *Multiple adapters for the same type*—What happens when the same adapter is registered more than once in a type's hierarchy? The rule is that the most specific adapter wins. Most specific means the first adapter in the base class chain followed by a depth-first order search in the interface hierarchy.

- ○ *Stateless adapters*—Adapters that have no state are the most space-efficient and easiest to manage. You store a single instance of the adapter in a field of the adapter factory or a static variable and return it when it is requested. To reuse a single instance of the adapter for all adapted objects, the adapter methods need to support passing in the adapted object. IWorkbenchAdapter is an interface that enables a stateless implementation. IPropertySource is an interface that does not.

- ○ *Instance based extensions*—IAdaptable supports class extensions. How can you extend instances? IResource supports dynamic-state extension with properties. A property is identified by a qualified name and can be managed either per session or persistently. Refer to the API specification of IResource for more details.

- ○ *Which adapters are supported?*—You cannot determine the available adapters from just looking at a class interface. You have to read the API documentation to find out which adapters are expected by a service (see for example, org.eclipse.ui.views.properties.PropertySheet). Alternatively, search for references to IAdaptable.getAdapter() to uncover all uses of adapter interfaces.

- ○ *Adapter negotiation*—An IAdaptable client can ask for different interfaces until a suitable one is found. For example, a property sheet can be populated from an IPropertySource adapter. However, a client can also get full control over the **Property Sheet** view contents by providing an IPropertySheetPage adapter. The **Property Sheet** view first queries for an IPropertySheetPage adapter and if there isn't one then it uses a default **Property Sheet** page that queries for the IPropertySource adapter.

- ○ *Reduced programming comfort*—Programming with adapters is more bulky than programming with interfaces directly. With an adapter a direct method call is replaced by multiple statements:

```
IPropertySource source=
    (IPropertySource) object.getAdapter(IPropertySource.class);
if (source != null)
    return source.getPropertyDescriptors();
```

Extension Object—implemented as `IAdaptable`, `IAdapterManager`, and `IAdapterFactory`—furthers Eclipse's goal of supporting unanticipated extension by allowing contributors to extend the classes an object can pretend to be. While more complicated than just using objects, the extra complexity is balanced by the additional flexibility.

CHAPTER 32

Core Workspace—Resources

In Eclipse the file system rules. An Eclipse workspace is mapped to the file system directly and there is no intermediate repository. Users can either change a resource on the file system directly or from inside Eclipse. The resources plug-in provides support for managing a workspace and its resources (see Figure 32.1).

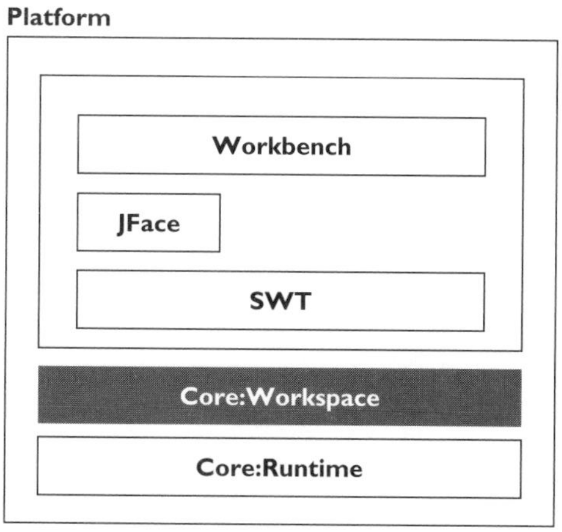

Platform

> **Workbench**
>
> **JFace**
>
> **SWT**
>
> **Core:Workspace**
>
> **Core:Runtime**

Figure 32.1   Core Workspace

32.1   Accessing File-System Resources—Proxy and Bridge

Clients need a way to track a resource in the file system. Resources change during their lifetime: they are created, their contents change, they are replaced with another version, they are deleted, and sometimes recreated. The information about a resource changes over its lifetime, but its identity doesn't. Clients need a simple way to refer to a resource independent of the resource's state in the workspace. We don't want to hold onto stale state, for example, when a file is deleted.

Eclipse addresses this problem by only giving clients access to a *handle* for a resource, not the full resource. This design is best described as the conjunction of the two structural patterns: Proxy and Bridge. Neither of the patterns alone captures the full intent of the design. The Proxy pattern tells us how to control access to an object and the Bridge pattern tells us how to separate an interface from its implementation. To quote their intent:

○ Proxy—"Provide a surrogate or place holder for another object to control access to it"

○ Bridge (also known as Handle/Body)—"Decouple an abstraction from its implementation so that the two can vary independently"

The relevant aspect from Proxy is controlling the access to an object. This is the key to avoid clients holding on to stale state. The relevant aspect from Bridge is the strong separation between an interface and its implementation. Both patterns address their problems by introducing a level of indirection. Applied to file-system resources this gives us:

○ The handle, which acts like a key for a resource.

○ An *info* object storing the representation of the file's state. There is only one implementor for each handle and it is therefore an example of a degenerate Bridge.

The handles are defined as interfaces `IFile`, `IFolder`, `IProject`, and `IWorkspaceRoot`. Figure 32.2 shows their interface hierarchy.

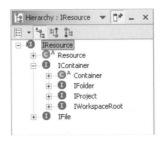

Figure 32.2   IResource Type Hierarchy

None of the resource interfaces are intended to be implemented by clients. Interfaces are used to define the API, but not so clients can implement the interfaces in different ways.

Let's verify the handle separation with the Spider (Figure 32.3) and explore the file `TestFailure.java` as presented in the Navigator (Figure 32.4).

Figure 32.3

Figure 32.4   IFile as Proxy

From the diagram we can see that a `File` handle knows only the path to the resource and its containing workspace. It acts like a key to access the file. Here are some interesting characteristics of the resource handles:

○ They are Value Objects[1]—small objects whose equality isn't based on identity. Once created, none of their fields ever change. This enables clients to store them in hashed data structures like a `Map`. More than one handle can refer to the same resource. Always use `IResource.equal()` when comparing handles.

○ Handles define the behavior of a resource, but they don't keep any resource state information.

○ A handle can refer to non-existing resources.

○ Some operations can be implemented from information stored in the handle only (handle operations). A resource need not exist to successfully execute such an operation. Examples of handle operations are: `getFullPath()`, `getParent()`, and `getProject()`. The existence of a resource can be tested with `exists()`. Operations that depend on the

---

1. M. Fowler, *Patterns of Enterprise Application Architecture*, Addison-Wesley, Boston, 2003, p. 486.

existence of the resource throw a `CoreException` when the resource doesn't exist.

○ Handles are created from a parent handle:

```
IProject project;
IFolder folder= project.getFolder("someFolder");
```

○ Handles are used to create the underlying resource:

```
folder.create(...);
```

The fixture class we used in Circle Two and shown in full in Appendix B illustrates how to use the handle-based API to create resources.

○ Since a handle is independent of the state in the file system, there is no way for the client to keep a reference to stale state, for example state about a deleted file. Every time you want state for the handle you have to fetch it anew.

Figure 32.5 illustrates the handle/body separation used for resources. In the following explanations we will use UML diagrams to illustrate the pattern stories. We annotate the UML with shaded boxes identifying the pattern being applied.

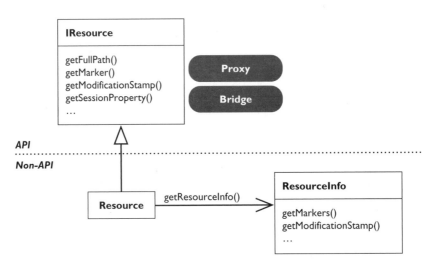

Figure 32.5   IResource Is a Proxy and a Bridge

The handle `IResource` is API and the `ResourceInfo` and `Resource` are internal classes. `ResourceInfo` is extended to store additional state for projects (`ProjectInfo`) and the workspace root. This illustrates the strong separation suggested by the Bridge pattern. Eclipse has a lot of freedom when resolving handles to find the corresponding resource state.

When an `IResource` is created, the resource information is retrieved from the workspace and the path information is stored inside the handle. Figure 32.6 illustrates how the look up is done to find the `ProjectInfo` for a project:

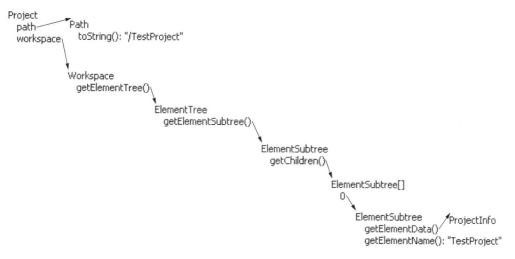

Figure 32.6   Retrieving the ProjectInfo

The Eclipse workspace stores the resource info as a complete tree in memory. This tree is referred to as the *element tree*. The resource info object corresponding to a handle is retrieved by traversing the element tree using the path stored inside the handle. A big advantage of this workspace implementation is that you can navigate the tree of files in almost no time. When you use the file system you have to make many queries to the underlying operating system (OS).

The resources plug-in not only applies handle/body separation for resources, it also applies the same separation for markers. A marker associates attributes with a resource. A marker doesn't store the attributes directly, but only stores a reference to their marker attribute info object. For markers the info object corresponds to the class `MarkerInfo`. The same coding idioms used for resources are consistently applied to markers:

❍ Markers are created from a handle.

❍ Accessing a marker attribute can throw a `CoreException`.

Now that we understand how an individual resource is represented, let's look into the representation of the resource tree.

32.2   The Workspace—Composite

The Eclipse workspace provides resources stored in the file system. A workspace consists of projects containing folders containing files, as shown in Figure 32.7.

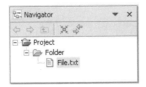

Figure 32.7

You access the Singleton workspace instance from the static accessor `ResourcesPlugin.getWorkspace()`. An `IWorkspaceRoot` represents the top of the resource hierarchy in a workspace.

The workspace is a hierarchical structure and it therefore matches the intent of the Composite pattern well: "Compose object into tree structures to represent part/whole hierarchies. Composite lets clients treat individual objects and compositions of objects uniformly." Figure 32.8 shows how the implementation of a workspace maps to Composite:

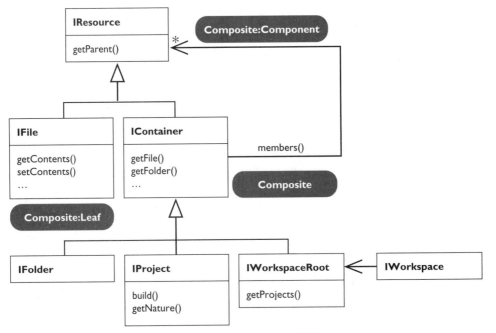

Figure 32.8   IWorkspace Is a Composite of IContainers and IFiles

Some observations on the workspace implementation:

❍ `IResource` provides access to its parent. The `getParent()` method is a handle-only operation that can derive the parent from the path stored in the handle.

❍ `IContainer` is the common base interface for the different composite classes. It provides a method `members()` that returns its children as a typed `IResource` array.

You can traverse a resource tree using the `members()` method provided by `IContainer`, but there is a better way.

32.3   Traversing the Resource Tree—Visitor

Traversing a resource tree manually using the `members()` method results in a lot of control-flow code in clients. The control flow to traverse a resource tree can be extracted with a visitor. When we check the intent of Visitor we find, "Represent an operation to be performed on the elements of an object structure. Visitor lets you define a new operation without changing the classes of the elements on which it operates." This is all correct. However, the main purpose here is to extract the common control flow and make it generally reusable.

`IResourceVisitor` is the visitor interface, which is accepted by `IResource` (see Figure 32.9).

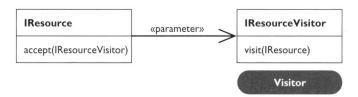

Figure 32.9   IResourceVisitor Visits IResources

The `accept()` method implements the resource traversal and calls back the visitor for each resource. The `IResourceVisitor` interface isn't type-specific; there are no separate methods for visiting a file or a folder. If you need to distinguish between the visited resource types, you can do this inside the `visit()` method using the `getType()` method. The code snippet from the Eclipse resource implementation illustrates the use of visitor.

org.eclipse.core.internal.resources/ResourceTree
```
private void addToLocalHistory(IResource root, int depth) {
  IResourceVisitor visitor = new IResourceVisitor() {
```

```
        public boolean visit(IResource resource) throws CoreException {
          if (resource.getType() == IResource.FILE)
            addToLocalHistory((IFile) resource);
          return true;
        }
      };
      try {
        root.accept(visitor, depth, false);
      } catch (CoreException e) {
      }
    }
```

Returning **true** from `visit()` indicates that the children of a resource should be visited. Returning **false** stops the traversal at the current resource.

While performance tuning, it was discovered that for some common traversals only a subset of the resource information is actually needed by the visitor. `IResourceProxyVisitor` was introduced to reduce the information fetched from the file system. It doesn't pass an `IResource` to the `visit()` method but an `IResourceProxy`.

org.eclipse.core.resources/IResourceProxyVisitor
```
public interface IResourceProxyVisitor {
  public boolean visit(IResourceProxy proxy) throws CoreException;
}
```

`IResourceProxy` is an example of a *virtual* proxy. It creates an expensive object on demand. The expensive object is in this case the full workspace path of a resource. The proxy is only valid during the call of the `visit()` method.

The Eclipse workspace has another advantage over accessing the file system directly—comprehensive support for observing changes.

32.4   Tracking Resource Changes—Observer

Resources in the workspace can change either as a result of manipulating them inside Eclipse or from resynchronizing them with the local file system. In both cases, observing clients need precise change information so that they can update themselves efficiently. To observe changes, the workspace provides a resource listener, which is an Observer variation (see Figure 32.10). Observers register with the workspace, which acts as the subject to be notified about changes.

Internally the notification mechanism is implemented by a `Notification-Manager` (see Figure 32.11).

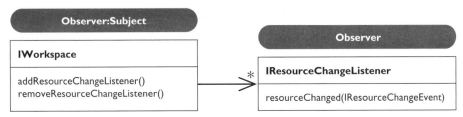

Figure 32.10   IResourceChangeListener Observes IWorkspace

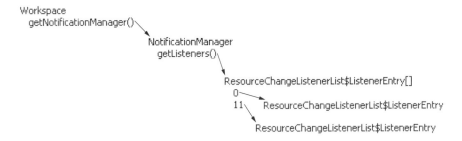

Figure 32.11   NotificationManager

Digging into the implementation of `NotificationManager`, we find that it is very careful in handling the case of modifications to the listener list during notification. By copying the listener list at the beginning of a notification, it ensures that any modifications to the listener list during the notification will have no effect on the ongoing notification. This is also referred to as making a *Safe Copy*. The internal class `ResourceChangeListenerList` implements the listener management.

org.eclipse.core.internal.events/ResourceChangeListenerList
```
public ListenerEntry[] getListeners() {
  if (size == 0)
    return EMPTY_ARRAY;
  ListenerEntry[] result = new ListenerEntry[size];
  System.arraycopy(listeners, 0, result, 0, size);
  return result;
}
```

The observer pattern asks us to decide how to provide details about a change notification. To quote the Observer pattern: "At one extreme, which we call the *push* model, the subject sends observers detailed information about the change, whether they want it or not. At the other extreme is the *pull* model; the subject sends nothing but the most minimal notification, and observers ask for details explicitly thereafter." Changes in a resource tree can be complex, so Eclipse uses the push model and provides detailed information about a change to all observers. Eclipse calls the change information *resource deltas* (see Figure 32.12).

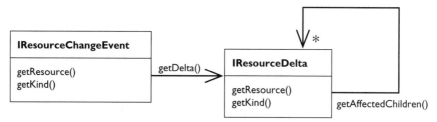

Figure 32.12 IResourceDelta Records a Tree of Changes

A resource delta describes the change between two states of the workspace tree. It is itself a tree of nodes. Each delta node describes how a resource has changed and provides delta nodes describing the changes to its children. A delta tree is rooted at the workspace root. Here is the resource delta describing a change to the file *FailTest.java* (see Figure 32.13 and Figure 32.14).

Figure 32.13

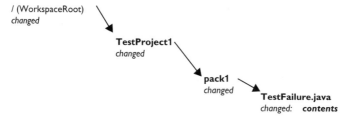

Figure 32.14 An IResourceDelta

A resource delta has several interesting properties:

○ A resource delta describes a single change and multiple changes using the same structure.

❍ A resource delta describes complete change information including information about moved resources and marker changes. The method `get-MarkerDeltas()` returns the changes to markers.

❍ It is easy to process a resource delta recursively top-down when updating an observer.

❍ Because a resource delta can be expensive, it is only valid during the call of `resourceChanged()`.

❍ Because resources are just handles to the real resources, a delta can easily describe deleted resources as well.

You can reuse the traversal logic of a resource delta with an `IResource-DeltaVisitor`:

org.eclipse.core.resources/IResourceDeltaVisitor
```
public interface IResourceDeltaVisitor {
  public boolean visit(IResourceDelta delta) throws CoreException;
}
```

32.5 Batching Changes—Execute Around Method

Any system based on change events is vulnerable to being flooded with resource change events. The common practice to avoid this flooding is to batch changes wherever possible. Changes should be grouped together so that only a single notification is sent out at the end of a single logical change. In Eclipse the batching is achieved using an `IWorkspaceRunnable` that is passed to the workspace for execution. The action specified by the runnable is then run as an atomic workspace operation. The deltas are accumulated during the operation and broadcast at the end. The snippet below illustrates how to create a marker and set its attributes with an `IWorkspaceRunnable` so that only one instead of two (creation, setting attributes) notifications are sent out:

org.eclipse.ui.texteditor/MarkerUtilities
```
public static void createMarker(final IResource resource,
    final Map attributes, final String markerType)
    throws CoreException {
  IWorkspaceRunnable r= new IWorkspaceRunnable() {
    public void run(IProgressMonitor monitor) throws CoreException{
      IMarker marker= resource.createMarker(markerType);
      marker.setAttributes(attributes);
    }
  };
  resource.getWorkspace().run(r, null);
}
```

An `IWorkspaceRunnable` is an example of the "Execute Around Method" pattern from Smalltalk[2] adapted to Java. `IWorkspace.run()` is the execute-around method. Before the runnable is executed, it informs the workspace to start batching. Then the runnable is invoked. Finally, when the runnable is done, `IWorkspace.run()` informs the workspace to end batching. Without an execute-around method, clients need to explicitly invoke the begin and end methods in the right order. This is error prone. Another benefit of an execute around method is that the begin and end batching methods do not have to be published as API.

Another example of an execute-around method in Eclipse is `Platform.run(ISafeRunnable runnable)`. It invokes the runnable in a protected mode and catches exceptions.

---

2. See "Execute Around Method" in K. Beck, *Smalltalk Best Practice Patterns.* Prentice Hall PTR, Upper Saddle River, NJ, 1997.

CHAPTER 33

Java Core

The Eclipse core workspace is programming-language agnostic. It provides API to a workspace containing projects, files, and folders. The JDT core builds on top of the workspace and provides APIs for navigating and analyzing the workspace from a Java angle (see Figure 33.1).

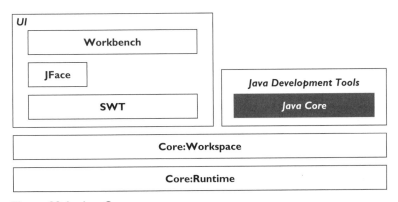

Figure 33.1 Java Core

The JDT core defines a Java nature that configures projects with an incremental Java builder. A project with a Java nature is a Java project. Each Java project maintains class-path information in a *.classpath* file. The class path captures the location of the source code, the libraries used, and the output locations for generated-class files.

33.1   From Resources to Java Elements—Adapter

The resource structure is defined in terms of files and folders. The Java-centric view on resources is defined in terms of Java elements. The Java-element-based view on resources is referred to as the Java model. The **Package Explorer** presents the structure of the Java model, as shown in Figure 33.2.

Figure 33.2

Clients navigating Java code need to have a uniform Java-centric API that is different from the resource interface. This is a typical setup for the Adapter pattern. Its intent states: "Convert an interface of a class into another interface clients expect. Adapter lets classes work together that couldn't otherwise because of incompatible interfaces." It is the first sentence of the intent that is of relevance for Java elements. `IJavaElement` plays the Adapter role and `IResource` is the adaptee (see Figure 33.3).

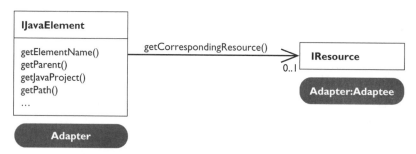

Figure 33.3   IJavaElement Adapts IResource

`IJavaElement` doesn't attempt to hide the fact that it is an adapter. It provides access to its adaptee with the accessor `getCorrespondingResource()`. Not all Java elements have a corresponding resource. The Java model also provides access to

○ Java elements that reside in JARs outside of the workspace and have no corresponding resource. An example is the JDK's *rt.jar*.

○ Java elements representing methods contained in a compilation unit. For this reason, `IJavaElement` provides additional accessor methods like `getResource()`. It returns the innermost resource enclosing this element.

`IJavaElement` allows us to navigate from Java elements to their resources. However, clients also need to be able to navigate from a resource to a corresponding Java element. Java core provides an API Façade, `JavaCore` (see Figure 33.4). It provides static factory methods to create `IJavaElements`.

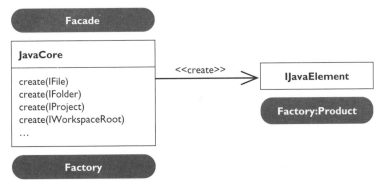

Figure 33.4   JavaCore Is a Façade and a Factory

Notice that the `create()` methods do not really create a Java project, compilation unit, or package. They only return a handle to a corresponding Java element. The handles are lightweight value objects used to reference Java elements. The Java model may create any number of handles for an element. Next, let's take a look at the handle design in more detail.

33.2   Java Elements—(Virtual) Proxy

Java elements use the same handle/body separation as is used for referencing resources (see Figure 33.5).

`IJavaElement` is the handle and `JavaElementInfo` is the body. `IJavaElement` defines the common behavior for Java elements. Several of its methods are handle-only methods, for example, `getElementName()` and `getParent()`.

Figure 33.6 illustrates the element info structure for a compilation unit.

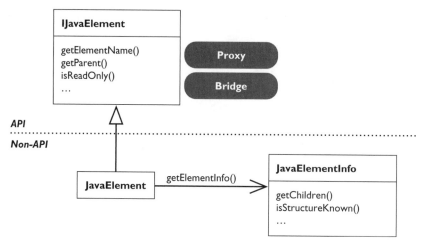

Figure 33.5   IJavaElement Is a Proxy and Bridge, Like IResource

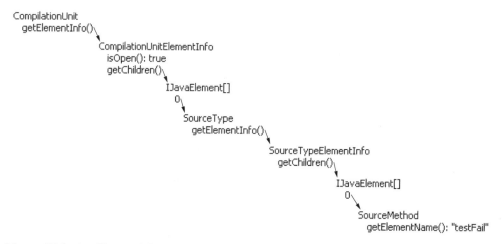

Figure 33.6   Java Element Infos

In contrast to the resource handle/body design, the one used in the Java model is much more involved. The main concern is scalability with regard to memory footprint. The Java model is much finer-grained than a resource tree. It supports navigation down to methods inside a compilation unit which requires Eclipse to parse the source of the corresponding file. Having a complete Java element tree in memory would be very expensive. The following observations help us solve the footprint problem:

   ○ Users typically only have a subset of the element tree expanded in the UI.

❍ Users only have a small number of compilation units open in an editor or expanded in a Java view.

❍ The element info can be computed based on the resource info.

It is therefore possible to consider the Java element infos as cached information for Java elements only. The implementation can maintain a bounded least-recently-used cache of element infos. The handle `IJavaElement` acts as the key into the cache. The Java model swaps out element infos to make room for other elements. Unsaved changes can never be swapped out. This might require growing the cache so isn't strictly bounded.

This, in fact, makes Java elements virtual proxies for the element info. The handle's bodies are virtualized and created on demand. In addition to all the other benefits of a handle-based design discussed above, handles naturally enable this virtualization without having to introduce yet another concept.

`JavaElementInfo`s store the cached structure and attributes for a particular Java element. There is a class hierarchy of `JavaElementInfo`s for the different kinds of Java elements, as illustrated by the following snapshot of its subclasses (see Figure 33.7).

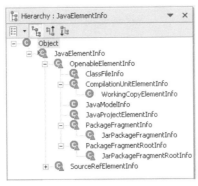

Figure 33.7   JavaElementInfo Subclasses

Elements that have their element info stored in the cache are said to be "open." The Java model transparently opens Java elements as the client navigates the element tree.

Java elements that need to be opened before they can be accessed implement the `IOpenable` interface (see Figure 33.8).

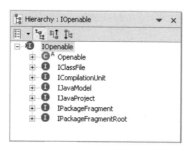

Figure 33.8   Implementors of IOpenable

The element cache is maintained by an internal singleton `JavaModelManager` (see Figure 33.9).

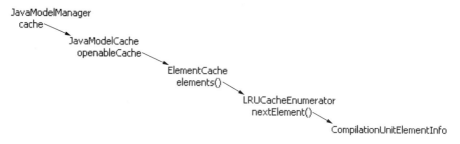

Figure 33.9   Cached ElementInfo

You can observe the opening activity by enabling a Java model tracing option, as shown in Figure 33.10. You have to enable both the `debug` and `debug/javamodel` tracing options of the `org.eclipse.jdt.core` plug-in.

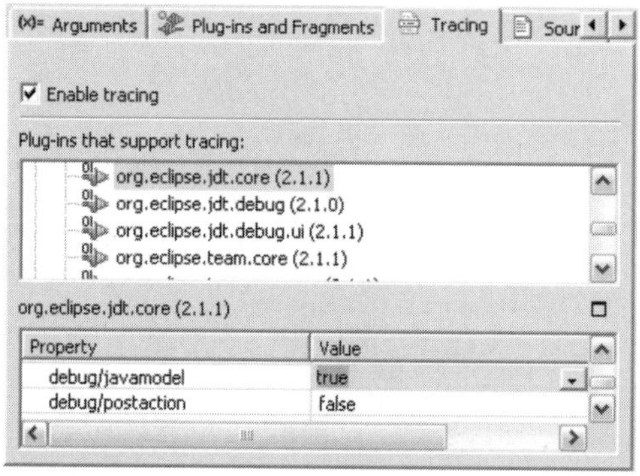

Figure 33.10

For example, when opening a source file and a class file we get the following trace:

```
OPENING Element (Thread[main,6,main]): [Working copy] Test.java [in
[default] [in [project root] [in Foo]]]
-> Package cache size = 502
-> Openable cache filling ratio = 0.35%
OPENING Element (Thread[main,6,main]): AboutDialog.class [in junit.
awtui [in C:/eclipse/ws0321/plugins/org.junit/junit.jar [in Foo]]]
-> Package cache size = 502
-> Openable cache filling ratio = 0.4%
```

Another interesting aspect of the handle/body implementation is that you can create an externalized form of a handle for an `IJavaElement`. The method `IJavaElement.getHandleIdentifier()` returns a string representation that is stable across sessions and that you can use to make persistent references to Java elements. The `JavaCore` provides a factory method, `JavaCore.create(String)`, that can recreate the corresponding handle. This is an instance of the Memento pattern.

33.3   The Java Element Tree—Composite

In contrast to the resource tree, the Java element tree is a part-whole structure with a fixed structure. It isn't just a recursive composition. Therefore, the Java element tree isn't a Composite in the pure sense. However, the composite nature of the tree can still be factored out using a Java interface `IParent`. Figure 33.11 shows the Java element tree interfaces and their structure.

All the interfaces are tagged with the same comment as `IResource`s: "This interface is not intended to be implemented by clients."

The `IParent` interface defines the composite interface with the methods `getChildren()` and `hasChildren()`. Notice that `IParent` isn't defined to extend `IJavaElement`. Peeking at the implementors of `IParent` we can see that they all implement `IJavaElement`. It would be possible therefore to have `IParent` extend `IJavaElement`, which gives the more typical Composite structure.

Why have both `getChildren()` and `hasChildren()`? The reason is performance. It is straightforward to implement `hasChildren()` in terms of `getChildren()`. However, it is often sufficient to know whether there are children at all. For example, when deciding whether a tree node should have a "+" to indicate it can be expanded, all you need to know is whether there are children, but you don't have to retrieve all of them. In particular, when it is expensive to compute the children, you can use `hasChildren()` to optimistically answer whether or not children exist.

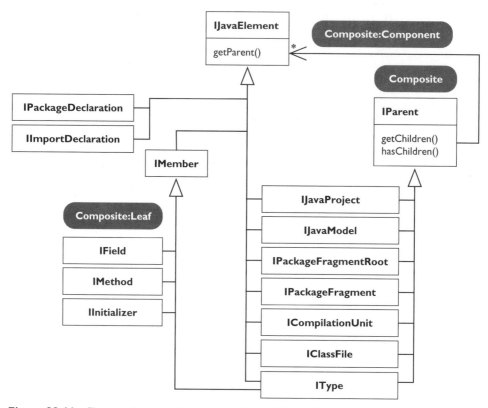

Figure 33.11   Elements Representing the Java Element Hierarchy

We have covered almost all of the key interfaces of the Java model in the above diagram. One interface we haven't mentioned yet is `ISourceReference`. `ISourceReference` is mixed into all Java elements that have associated source. It provides access to the source range of a Java element.

33.4   Type Hierarchies—Objectifying an Association

We have already discussed the motivation for separating the type hierarchy information from Java elements in Chapter 17. The sub- and supertypes define an association between types. To implement this relationship in an efficient way, and in particular to compute it only when needed, the basic pattern "Objectify Associations"[1] was applied. However, in the case of the type hier-

---

1.   See L. Rising, *The Pattern Almanac 2000*. Addison-Wesley, Boston, 2000.

archy, an entire collection of associations was reified into a separate object
(see Figure 33.12).

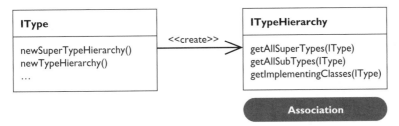

Figure 33.12   ITypeHierarchy Relates an IType with Its Supertypes and Subtypes

Having factory methods for creating either the super type hierarchy or the
complete type hierarchy allows clients to choose which association they want.
This is important because computing the super type hierarchy is much cheaper
than computing a complete hierarchy.

33.5   Traversing the Java Model

In contrast to the workspace, the Java model doesn't provide Visitors to
traverse its structure. There wasn't an urgent need to have such a visitor. More
importantly, given the lazy nature of the Java model, using a visitor is often
not the most efficient way to traverse the Java element tree. For example, finding a method by traversing the Java model starting at the root and then drill-
ing down to methods is expensive. It will fully populate the element info
caches.

You can perform search operations much faster by using Search. Search
keeps an index of the Java elements contained in compilation units. It allows
you to quickly find Java elements without having to create all of the element
infos.

A recursive traversal of the Java element tree can be done using the `IParent`
interface:

```
IJavaElement element;
IJavaElement[] children;
if (element instanceof IParent) {
    IParent parent= (IParent)element;
    children= parent.getChildren();
}
```

33.6 Tracking Java Element Changes—Observer

The support for tracking changes to Java elements is symmetrical to the workspace support for tracking changes to resources (see Figure 33.13).

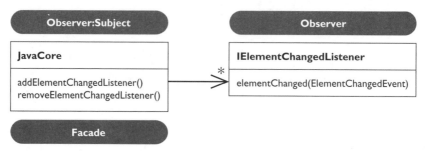

Figure 33.13 IElementChangedListener Observes the Java Model

In contrast to the workspace, clients register the listeners with the `JavaCore` Façade. A listener receives an `ElementChangedEvent`, which carries a `IJavaElementDelta` (see Figure 33.14).

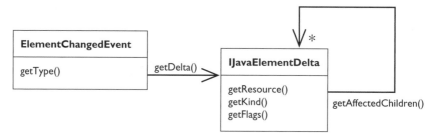

Figure 33.14 IJavaElementDelta Records a Tree of Changes, Like IResourceDelta

Resource deltas are always rooted at the top of the resource tree. Java element deltas don't make this guarantee. For example, deltas sent out while the user edits a compilation unit in the editor are rooted at the compilation unit. A Java element delta is only valid during a notification, so that its allocated resources can be freed after the event is processed.

The Java model provides the execute-around method `JavaCore.run(IWorkspaceRunnable, IProgressMonitor)` for batching change notifications. This method is the analog to `IWorkspace.run()` provided by the workspace.

Type hierarchies are not part of the element tree. To track changes in type hierarchies the Java model provides a separate change listener (see Figure 33.15). It is used when a type hierarchy is displayed in a view and needs to be updated as the source code is changing. For a type hierarchy, no detailed information about the change in the form of a delta is provided.

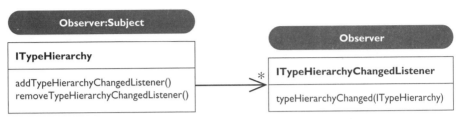

Figure 33.15 ITypeHierarchyChangedListener Observes ITypeHierarchy

Next we consider the common pattern used by the Java core to return results.

33.7 Collecting Results—Builder

The Java core provides several services that need to report their results as they are computed or discovered. However, it should be up to the clients to decide how to handle the results and how to store them. Here are some examples:

❍ The search engine accepts a search pattern and reports matches.

❍ Code assist analyzes possible completions at the current cursor location and reports them to the client.

❍ Validating a compilation unit during typing needs to report problems as they are discovered by the Java builder.

This problem of separating the process of computing a result from its representation is the intent of the Builder pattern: "Separate the construction of a complex object from its representation so that the same construction process can create different representations." Computing the result is done by what the pattern calls a Director and the handling of results is delegated to a Builder.

The Java core uses a naming convention for Builders. The corresponding interface or class names have the suffix `Requestor` or `Collector`. Let's look at two examples.

The Java core maintains an index of references and declarations to Java elements. It provides the class `SearchEngine` for searching elements matching a pattern in a specified scope (see Figure 33.16). The search pattern and the scope are created with factory methods. Using factory methods enables the hiding of the corresponding implementation classes. Search patterns can be combined to form simple logical expressions. The factory method `createOrSearchPattern()` takes two patterns and combines them into an **or** pattern.

Behind the scenes we can recognize a use of the Interpreter pattern to represent and interpret these logical expressions.

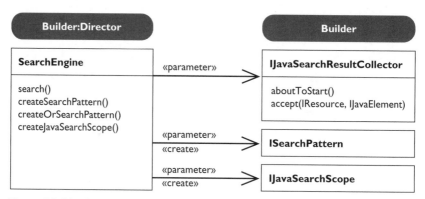

Figure 33.16   SearchEngine Builds a Search Result from Search Patterns and Search Scopes

The `SearchEngine` acts as the Director and notifies its Builder, the `IJava-SearchResultCollector`, when a match is found. Before a search starts, the `SearchEngine` informs the builder with `aboutToStart()`. The actual matches are then reported with `accept()`.

Figure 33.17 illustrates the different result collectors playing the role of a Builder.

Figure 33.17   IJavaSearchResultCollector Implementors

Code Assist follows the Builder pattern to report results as well (see Figure 33.18). Code Assist performs code completions at a given textual position inside a compilation unit.

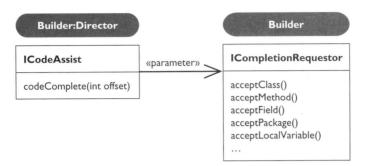

Figure 33.18   ICodeAssist Is a Builder

Code Assist reports its findings to the Builder `ICompletionRequestor`. The results are reported specifically to the type of the completion element.

33.8   Abstract Syntax Tree Analysis—Visitor

The Java model supports navigating the Java element tree. However, the model is too coarse-grained to allow for a detailed analysis of code. The Java core provides access to a compilation unit's abstract syntax tree (AST). An AST represents the result of parsing and analyzing the compilation unit. Figure 33.19 shows the AST for the following compilation unit.

TestFailure
```
import junit.framework.TestCase;

public class TestFailure extends TestCase {
  public void testFailure() {
    fail();
  }
}
```

Each node of the AST represents an element of the program and keeps track of its source range and its *bindings*. A binding represents references to named entities as seen by the compiler. The AST nodes are defined in a hierarchy descending from `ASTNode`. An AST is constructed from a compilation unit or class file with the help of the factory class AST, as shown in Figure 33.20.

There is a different AST node for each Java source-code construct (see Figure 33.21).

The reason for creating an AST is to analyze a compilation unit. To do the analysis, you traverse the AST and perform actions depending on the node

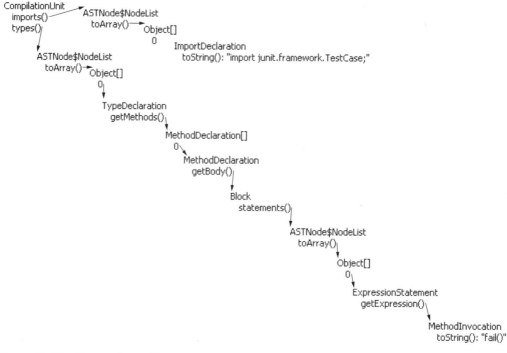

Figure 33.19   Abstract Syntax Tree

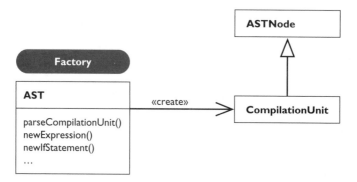

Figure 33.20   AST Creates ASTNodes

type. AST analysis is a prototypical use of Visitor. The key consideration for applying Visitor is whether the class hierarchy defining the node structure is stable. Adding a new class to the node hierarchy would make it difficult to maintain a Visitor since existing Visitors would need to be modified. The source constructs of a language are stable (at least between major releases).

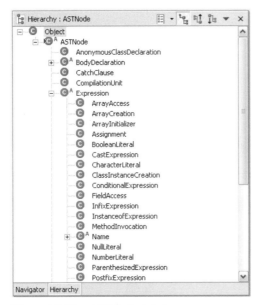

Figure 33.21 ASTNode Subclasses

Therefore the node hierarchy remains stable and Visitor is useful. The AST API provides an abstract class, `ASTVisitor`. The `ASTVisitor` defines a visit method for each node type (see Figure 33.22).

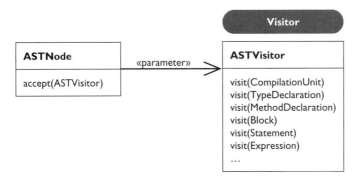

Figure 33.22 ASTVisitor Visits ASTNodes

The `ASTVisitor` provided by Java core comes with some Visitor implementation variations that are worth mentioning. Implementing a generic visitor that isn't interested in most node types is painful. A client has to override over sixty methods. For this reason the `ASTVisitor` provides two generic visit methods:

preVisit(ASTNode) and postVisit(ASTNode). Clients can override these two methods to perform a non-type-specific traversal of an AST. For example, counting all nodes in an AST can be done with the following simple visitor:

CountingVisitor
```
class CountingVisitor extends ASTVisitor {
  int count= 0;
  public void postVisit(ASTNode node) {
    count++;
  }
  public int getCount() {
    return count;
  }
}
```

It can then be called as follows:

```
CompilationUnit cu;
CountingVisitor visitor= new CountingVisitor();
cu.accept(visitor);
System.out.println(visitor.getCount());
```

The other interesting variation is that ASTVistor provides both a visit() and an endVisit() method:

○ The method visit() is called before descending into a node. Clients can return **false** from visit() when they don't want to descend into a particular node.

○ The method endVisit() is called after all the descendent nodes are visited.

Here is an example illustrating the use of visit() and endVisit(). Let's assume we want to collect a metric, the number of method invocations in each method. To simplify the example, let's further assume that no local or anonymous types are used. (Handling these types properly requires storing the method count in a stack.) Below is the visitor implementation for this simplified scenario:

```
class CallsPerMethodVisitor extends ASTVisitor {
  int callCount= 0;
  public boolean visit(MethodDeclaration node) {
    callCount= 0;
    return super.visit(node);
  }
```

```
    public void endVisit(MethodDeclaration node) {
      System.out.println("calls in "+node.getName()+":"+ callCount);
    }
    public boolean visit(MethodInvocation node) {
      callCount++;
      return true;
    }
}
```

CHAPTER 34

Standard Widget Toolkit— SWT

SWT provides a common set of widgets like buttons, menus, trees, and tables. The most succinct definition of SWT is given on the components home page:[1] *The SWT component is designed to provide efficient, portable access to the user-interface facilities of the operating systems on which it is implemented.* To achieve this goal SWT implements a thin layer on top of the operating system's native widgets. When a widget isn't available on a particular platform SWT implements the widget in Java.

SWT doesn't have any dependencies on the rest of Eclipse. You can use it independently of Eclipse (see Figure 34.1).

One general design goal of SWT is the orthogonality of the API. Once you understand a concept from SWT, you can apply it everywhere. In this chapter we will do a pattern-based analysis of how to

- ○ Compose widgets
- ○ Define a layout
- ○ Handle events

The SWT team has written articles on its internal design principles (*www.eclipse.org/articles/Article-SWT-Design-1/SWT-Design-1.html*).

---

1. *http://dev.eclipse.org/viewcvs/index.cgi/~checkout~/platform-swt-home/main.html*

Platform

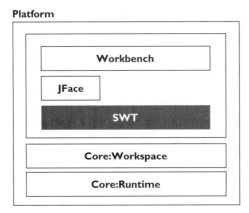

Figure 34.1   SWT

34.1   Composing Widgets—Composite

One of the most important features of a GUI toolkit is assembling widgets into more complex GUI elements. SWT distinguishes between basic and compound widgets:

❍ *Basic widgets* do not contain other widgets and are the leaves in a widget tree. Examples of basic widgets are buttons and labels.

❍ *Compound widgets* contain other widgets and are the inner nodes of a widget tree. The base class of compound widgets is `Composite`.

Let's analyze the **Find/Replace** dialog with the Spider. The **Find/Replace** dialog is shown in Figure 34.2.

Figure 34.2

Figure 34.3 shows an excerpt of the widget structure behind the **Find/Replace** dialog.

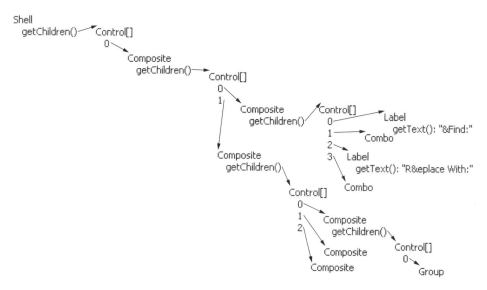

Figure 34.3   Widget Tree

The root of the widget tree is a `Shell`, which represents a window on the desktop. The rest of the widget tree is formed by composing basic widgets with `Composite` widgets. Basic widgets like the "Find" label appear as leaves.

Mapping this to the Composite pattern, we get the objects shown in Figure 34.4.

The SWT `Widget` class hierarchy has two main branches rooted at `Item` and `Control`. `Control`s represent complex and costly widgets referred to as *windowed* user interface objects in the SWT API. `Item`s are lighter-weight user interface objects contained within a `Control`. For example, a `Tree` contains `TreeItems`. You can compose `Control`s with the classical Composite patterns. Items don't participate in the Composite pattern.

SWT has to interface with the native widgets on multiple platforms. The class hierarchy is dictated by the platform limitations. Clients should therefore treat the widget class hierarchy as an implementation detail. SWT has some well-specified points where it is intended to be subclassed. Specifically, clients should only subclass `Canvas` and `Composite`. In fact, this is even checked in the code. The base class `Widget` defines a method `checkSubclass()`. Classes intended for subclassing override the method to be empty. Classes not

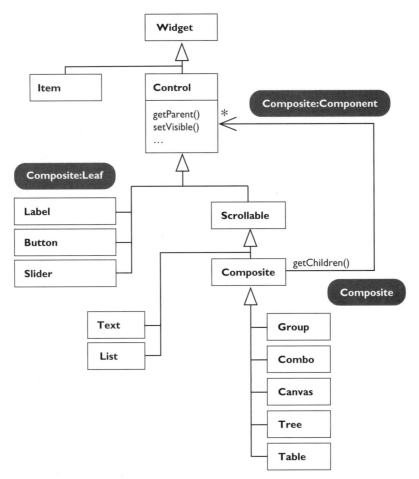

Figure 34.4 Basic and Compound Widgets

intended to be subclassed check that the class is contained inside an SWT package and throw an exception if this is not the case.

When implementing the Composite patterns there are typically `addChild()` and `removeChild()` methods. Where are these methods in SWT? Well, there aren't any! This is another interesting implementation variation of Composite. In SWT widgets are added to their parent when they are constructed. The parent is always passed to the widget's constructor. Here is an excerpt from the `AutoTestPropertyPage`:

org.eclipse.contribution.junit.ui/AutoTestPropertyPage
```
private Control addControl(Composite parent) {
  Composite composite= new Composite(parent, SWT.NONE);
  //...
```

Subclassing in the Eclipse API

Subclassing is powerful but it is also dangerous. When overriding a method, clients start to rely on implementation details of the base class. This is problematic when it comes to evolving the API. Changing a base class can break existing clients. In addition, when overriding a complex class assumptions in the base class can be violated and subtle errors can be introduced. For this reason Eclipse is very explicit in its API when it allows subclassing.

However, Eclipse doesn't go so far as to declare most of its API final. Making a class final is a strong statement. It blocks clients from fixing some problems in the future by subclassing. Eclipse therefore uses a softer flavor of final that could be called "intend final." The Javadoc API comment specifies whether a class is intended to be subclassed or not. You will therefore find comments like the following in the Eclipse API classes:

- ○ "This class may be instantiated; it is not intended to be subclassed."

- ○ "Clients may subclass."

You should have really good reasons when subclassing a class that isn't intended to be subclassed, and you have to be prepared to be broken in future releases.

```
Label label= new Label(composite, SWT.NONE);
//...
}
```

As a consequence, a widget is always parented. A common problem in other frameworks is that widgets behave differently when they are unparented, because some calls depend on having access to the parent. This is commonly addressed by introducing a notification that tells clients when a widget is parented, so that they can call methods depending on parent access. SWT avoids this complexity by completely eliminating the unparented widget state.[2]

When creating a widget, SWT uses a *style bits* idiom. Some properties of a widget can only be set at creation time and cannot be changed later in the life cycle of a widget. These properties referred to as *styles* must all be set in the constructor with flags called *style bits*. The use of style bits avoids having lengthy parameter lists in constructors.

---

2. See "Complete Constructor Method" in K. Beck, *Smalltalk Best Practice Patterns*. Prentice Hall PTR, Upper Saddle River, NJ, 1997.

A widget cannot exist outside of the widget tree. Therefore, the only way to remove a widget from the tree is to destroy it or move it to another tree. You do so by calling the widget's `dispose()` method. `Dispose()` frees the resources associated with the widget and removes it from the tree and recursively disposes its children. Clients can register a `disposeListener()` to track the disposal and clean-up additional resources.

SWT associates additional data with a widget. This corresponds to the Variable State pattern,[3] also used in JFace, which is described in the next chapter. Variable State answers the question: "How do you represent state whose presence varies from instance to instance." Variable State avoids subclassing a widget just to add some fields. The method `Widget.setData()` associates an application object with a widget. There is also `Widget.setData(String key)`, which stores the object under a particular key. You retrieve the data with the corresponding `getData()` methods.

Next let's take a closer look at how to define the layout of widgets in SWT.

34.2 Defining the Layout—Strategy

Eclipse has to run on multiple platforms using different natural languages. As a consequence it is important to support layout design independent of widget size or label length. The size of the widgets varies from platform to platform and the length of the labels varies from language to language. Therefore, SWT declaratively defines layouts without absolute positioning, similar to AWT and Swing. You define the layout of widgets with a layout manager. A layout manager determines the position and size of the children of a composite. SWT provides different layout managers implementing different layout policies. This is the Strategy pattern at work. Its intent states: "Define a family of algorithms, encapsulate each one, and make them interchangeable. Strategy lets the algorithm vary independently from clients that use it."

Each widget participating in a layout needs to be able to define its layout-specific settings. To do so, SWT `Control`s reserve a slot called `layoutData`, set by `Control.setLayoutData()`. This slot stores the settings for a particular layout manager. SWT doesn't make any assumption about commonalities among the layout settings. The type of a layout data is `Object`. Figure 34.5 shows an excerpt of the widget structure from the **Find/Replace** dialog focusing on the layout aspects.

---

3. K. Beck, *Smalltalk Best Practice Patterns*. Prentice Hall PTR, Upper Saddle River, NJ, 1997.

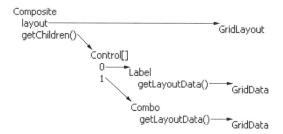

Figure 34.5 GridLayout and GridData

The composite shown in Figure 34.5 uses a `GridLayout` to define its layout. The controls participating in the layout have an associated `GridData` object. It specifies the layout attributes for the `GridLayout`. To make this more concrete, here is the corresponding code from the **FindReplace** dialog:

org.eclipse.ui.texteditor/FindReplaceDialog.createInputPanel()
```
//...
Composite panel= new Composite(parent, SWT.NULL);
GridLayout layout= new GridLayout();
layout.numColumns= 2;
panel.setLayout(layout);

Label findLabel= new Label(panel, SWT.LEFT);
findLabel.setText(EditorMessages.getString(
  "FindReplace.Find.label"));
setGridData(findLabel, GridData.BEGINNING, false,
  GridData.CENTER, false);
fFindField= new Combo(panel, SWT.DROP_DOWN | SWT.BORDER);
setGridData(fFindField, GridData.FILL, true,
  GridData.CENTER, false);
//...
```

The `GridData` is associated with the helper method `setGridData()`:

org.eclipse.ui.texteditor/FindReplaceDialog
```
private void setGridData(Control component,
    int horizontalAlignment,
    boolean grabExcessHorizontalSpace,
    int verticalAlignment,
    boolean grabExcessVerticalSpace) {
  GridData gd= new GridData();
  gd.horizontalAlignment= horizontalAlignment;
  gd.grabExcessHorizontalSpace= grabExcessHorizontalSpace;
  gd.verticalAlignment= verticalAlignment;
  gd.grabExcessVerticalSpace= grabExcessVerticalSpace;
  component.setLayoutData(gd);
}
```

Instead of setting the `GridData` values directly, SWT also provides a set of convenience style bits. Using the style bits results in more compact code and reduces the need for helper methods to initialize a `GridData`.

Finally, Figure 34.6 provides an overview of the SWT layout support. For more details on the SWT layout support refer to *www.eclipse.org/articles/ Understanding Layouts/Understanding Layouts.htm*.

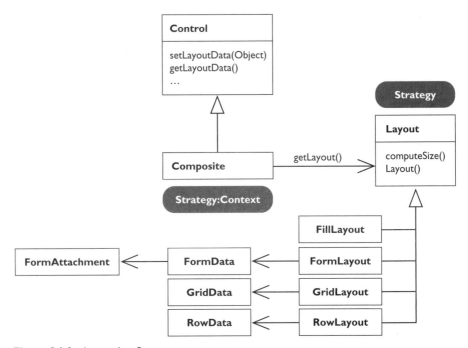

Figure 34.6 Layout Is a Strategy

SWT provides the following layout strategies:

- ❍ `FillLayout`—Arranges controls in a single row or column and all controls are given the same size. In this layout a control has no specific settings and therefore there is no corresponding layout data class.

- ❍ `GridLayout`—Arranges controls in a grid. Each control can specify its position in a grid cell using a `GridData` object.

- ❍ `RowLayout`—Arranges controls in one or more rows or columns. Controls define their layout setting using a `RowData` object.

- ❍ `FormLayout`—Arranges controls based on layout constraints specified in `FormData` objects. A `FormData` contains `FormAttachments` which specify where to attach the side of a control.

Even when you use declarative layouts you still have to test all your dialogs on all platforms with different languages to make sure they fit on the screen.

34.3   Responding to Events—Observer

SWT uses event notification patterns similar to AWT and Swing. You express interest in a particular event by registering a listener with a widget. A listener is an Observer that is notified when an event occurs. Different listeners define interfaces for handling different events. An adapter implements the listener interface and provides empty default implementations for the event handling methods. Figure 34.7 illustrates this for the `Button` widget.

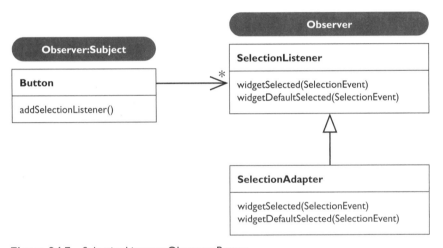

Figure 34.7   SelectionListener Observes Button

The intent of SWT is to generate events only for widget changes initiated by the user. If you change widget state programmatically, no event should be triggered. However, given the platform differences this rule cannot be strictly implemented. All SWT can do is to make the listener notification behavior consistent across platforms.

One implementation variation is that SWT offers two flavors of listeners. The `SelectionListener` is an example of a *typed* listener. A typed listener listens for a specific event and is informed with a specific event type. In the example above the event type is a `SelectionEvent`. In addition to typed listeners, SWT offers *untyped* listeners. An untyped listener implements the generic `Listener` interface:

org.eclipse.swt.widgets/Listener

```
public interface Listener {
  void handleEvent(Event event);
}
```

In the untyped case, the listener registers for an event specified by a constant. However, when it is notified it receives a generic event object (`Event`). It is up to the receiver to interpret such an event properly. Untyped listeners are useful when you want to listen to different events but handle them in a single listener class without having to implement multiple interfaces.

CHAPTER 35

JFace—User Interface Frameworks

The goal of SWT is to provide a thin and portable layer on top of the native platform widgets. SWT focuses on providing widgets, layouts, and event handling functionality. It doesn't attempt to provide any higher level application support. This is the purpose of JFace, which is intended to complement SWT (see Figure 35.1).

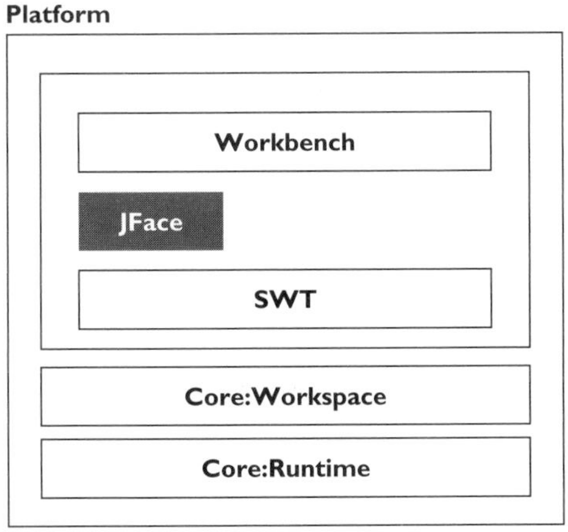

Platform

```
┌────────────────────────────────────────┐
│  ┌──────────────────────────────────┐  │
│  │            Workbench             │  │
│  │  ┌────────┐                      │  │
│  │  │ JFace  │                      │  │
│  │  └────────┘                      │  │
│  │             SWT                  │  │
│  └──────────────────────────────────┘  │
│  ┌──────────────────────────────────┐  │
│  │         Core:Workspace           │  │
│  └──────────────────────────────────┘  │
│  ┌──────────────────────────────────┐  │
│  │          Core:Runtime            │  │
│  └──────────────────────────────────┘  │
└────────────────────────────────────────┘
```

Figure 35.1   JFace

JFace is the umbrella name for a set of several smaller frameworks:

○ *Viewers*—Support using widgets with an underlying domain model

○ *Contributions/Actions*—Support handling user events independent of the widget that triggered the event

○ *Dialogs and wizards*—Higher level dialogs and dialog infrastructure

○ *Registries for images and fonts*—Support for managing UI resources

In this chapter we focus on viewers and contributions/actions.

35.1   Viewers: Connecting a Widget to a Model— Pluggable Adapter

A viewer bridges between a domain model and the SWT widget. It allows you to stay in the world of domain objects without worrying about mapping them to the SWT widgets in order to present them. JFace provides viewers for the more complex SWT widgets like trees, tables, and lists. Figure 35.2 illustrates the viewer class hierarchy.

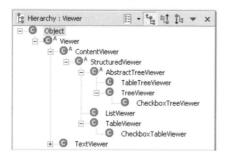

Figure 35.2   Viewer Class Hierarchy

A viewer's main responsibility is to populate a widget from a domain model. For example, the **Navigator** shows the workspace contents in a `Tree` widget. It uses a `TreeViewer` to populate the `Tree` widget with items representing, for example, projects, files, and folders. To populate the widget, a viewer needs to traverse the domain model and convert domain objects into strings and icons the tree widget can present.

How can a viewer access the domain objects without making any assumptions about the domain itself? For example, the `TreeViewer` needs to be able to call some kind of `getChildren()` method to drill down into the domain model.

Solving this problem requires support for adapting interfaces. This is a case for the Adapter pattern (not to be confused with the IAdaptable mechanism described in Chapter 31) and its "Pluggable Adapter" variant. The idea behind a Pluggable Adapter is to make a class more general by building interface adaptation into the class. The Adapter pattern sketches different flavors for implementing a Pluggable Adapter:

○ *Using abstract methods*—The class defines abstract methods to access the domain. Clients need to subclass and implement these abstract methods.

○ *Using delegate objects*—The methods to access the domain are forwarded to a separate delegate object, which defines a method like `getChildren()`.

Having separate delegate objects has several benefits. First, they can be reused in other contexts and second, clients don't need to subclass a complex viewer class. For this reason JFace viewers took the delegate objects route. Viewers use two separate delegate objects—one for traversing the domain structure and another one for presenting a domain object:

○ `IContentProvider`—Given an input object, returns a set of corresponding domain objects.

○ `ILabelProvider`—Returns an icon and string for presenting a domain object.

Both providers do not make any assumption about the domain model and therefore define their API in terms of the type `Object`. Implementations of the providers know the domain and can cast the arguments to the corresponding domain types. Figure 35.3 illustrates the Pluggable Adapter solution for the `TreeViewer` implementation. In JFace the actual provider interfaces are factored into multiple interfaces. For illustration purposes we have flattened them into single `ILabelProvider` and `ITreeContentProvider` interfaces.

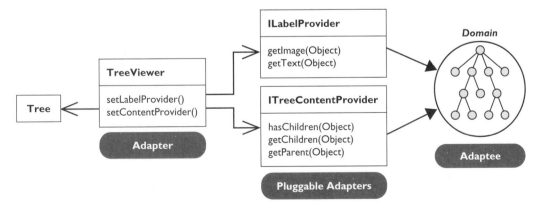

Figure 35.3   ILabelProvider and ITreeContentProvider Are Pluggable Adapters

Given the interface of the `ITreeContentProvider`, the `TreeViewer` can populate the `Tree` widget lazily as the user expands the nodes. Why are there two separate adapters and not just a single one? Having two separate adapters, one for presenting a domain object and another one for accessing the domain model, allows you to reuse them independently. For example, you can reuse the same label provider implementation across the different structured viewers—`TreeViewer`, `TableViewer`, and `ListViewer`.

Figure 35.4 illustrates how the Resource Navigator uses the `TreeViewer` and adapts it for the workbench.

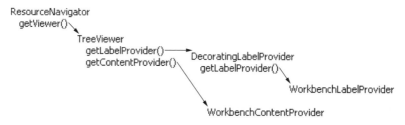

Figure 35.4   The Navigator Implemented with a TreeViewer

The label provider is a *decorating label provider* to enable label decorations.

Label Decorations

A label shown in a structured view can be enriched by additional decorations which give additional status information for an element. The following label is a Java element label enriched by a CVS label decoration:

>Platform.java 1.1

The CVS label decoration indicates that *Platform.java* has an outgoing change. A label decoration can enrich both the image and the text of a label.

To make a label decoration appear requires the collaboration of the user, a plug-in contributing a decorator, and the viewer that owns the label provider.

Users enable and disable label decorations on the **Windows > Preferences > Workbench > Label Decorations** preference page. Multiple decorations are applicable for a single element and users choose which one they want to see.

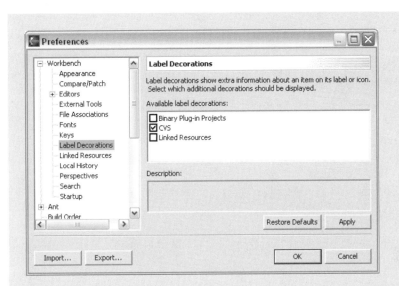

This is an example of the User Arbitration Rule. The user needs to decide which contributions out of many possible should be active.

Plug-ins contribute label decorators with the `org.eclipse.ui.decorators` extension point. A label decorator is contributed for a particular object class. A label decorator implements the `ILabelDecorator` interface.

A viewer supports label decorations by decorating its base label provider with a `DecoratingLabelProvider`. The `DecoratingLabelProvider` is an instance of the Decorator pattern. Using the Decorator pattern is handy since it allows transparently adding this feature to any label provider. To enable decorations, we configure the viewer with a decorating label provider.

```
IWorkbench wb= getSite().getWorkbenchWindow().getWorkbench();
viewer.setLabelProvider(
  new DecoratingLabelProvider(
    new BaseLabelProvider(),
    wb.getDecoratorManager().getLabelDecorator()));
```

The `DecoratingLabelProvider` takes a base label provider and a label decorator as arguments. The workbench provides access to a label decorator that manages the decorations contributed via the `org.eclipse.ui.decorators` extension point.

In addition to providing access to the domain, the content provider is responsible for keeping the viewer synchronized when the domain changes. The content provider registers as a listener with the domain model. For example, the `WorkbenchContentProvider` registers as an `IResourceChangedListener` with the workspace. When the domain changes the content provider is notified. Then the content provider informs the viewer about the changes by calling corresponding update methods. For example, the `TreeViewer` provides the following update methods:

- `add(Object parent, Object element)`—Adds the element as a child of the given parent

- `remove(Object element)`—Removes the element from the viewer

- `refresh(Object element)`—Refreshes the viewer's content starting at the given element

- `update(Object element, String[] properties)`—Updates a single element's presentation.

These update methods should only be called from the content provider in response to changes to the domain model. Once more, all the interaction with the viewer can be done in terms of domain objects. It is the viewer's responsibility to map the domain objects to the corresponding SWT widgets.

Spider shows how this mapping between domain objects and SWT widgets is done (see Figure 35.5). A spider click on **TestFailure.java** in the **Navigator** setup shown in Figure 35.6 shows that JFace viewers leverage the widget's extension data slot to keep track of the corresponding domain object. This is just an implementation detail on which you should never rely. To know about this implementation detail is helpful when debugging and when using Spider clicks. A Spider click allows you to navigate quickly to an SWT widget; expanding the widget's data slot allows you to get to the underlying domain object.

Figure 35.5

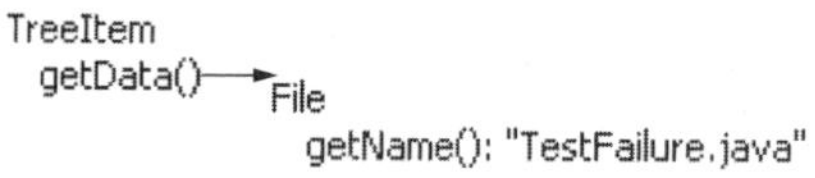

```
TreeItem
   getData()──►
               File
                getName(): "TestFailure.java"
```

Figure 35.6   Mapping Between SWT Widgets and the Underlying Domain Objects

35.2   Viewers: Customizing a Viewer without Subclassing— Strategy

When using a viewer, you typically want to customize some of its behavior:

○ Sorting—How the elements in a viewer are sorted

○ Filtering—Which elements should be filtered out in a viewer

Viewers are complex classes and it is desirable to not rely on subclassing to enable these customizations. In addition, you might want to reuse both the filtering and sorting behavior for different viewers. For these reasons, JFace viewers use the Strategy pattern to forward these behaviors to separate objects. This enables viewer customization by configuration instead of subclassing (see Figure 35.7).

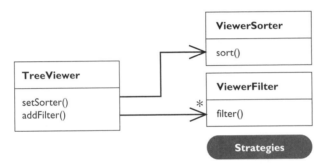

Figure 35.7   ViewerSorter and ViewerFilter Are Strategies

Figure 35.8 illustrates how the **Navigator** uses the filtering and sorting support.

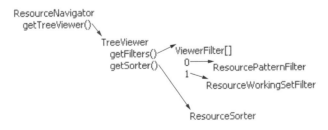

Figure 35.8   TreeViewer with Filtering and Sorting

The **Navigator** registers two filters: one to filter out resources matching a pattern and another one to filter out resources not in the active working set.

Given that both Pluggable Adapters and Strategies are provided to customize a viewer, you can often reuse a viewer without any subclassing. Viewers are therefore an example of *black-box reuse*: reuse based on composition and not on inheritance.

As a historical side note, in an earlier incarnation of JFace it was possible to specify a viewer configuration and even the viewer's layout in XML. For a developer it is simpler to configure a viewer in code. In particular it is simple to set a breakpoint in Java code to track down a problem, which isn't easy to do with an XML-based specification.

35.3   Actions—Command

SWT allows listeners to register for events when the user clicks a button, menu, or toolbar item. However, as an application developer you want to define the logic for handling a user event independent of the widget that has triggered it. For example, a *save* operation should do the same operation independent of whether it was triggered through a menu selection or by clicking a toolbar item.

This smells like a case for introducing an object, as recommended by the Command pattern. The Command pattern's intent states: "Encapsulate a request as an object, thereby letting you parameterize clients with different requests, queue or log requests, and support for undoable operations." Only the first part is relevant here: We need a way to define what should happen when the user clicks a menu item, toolbar item, or a button.

In JFace a command is called an *action*. IAction defines a run() method to be called to execute the request. IAction also

○ Stores all the information required to present the action in a menu, toolbar, or button. This includes the action's label, icon, tooltip, and enablement state. JFace internally uses this information to create and initialize the SWT widget when presenting the action in the UI.

○ Fires a property change event when an action's state changes. This allows JFace to keep the state of the widget in sync with the action.

○ Can be used from multiple widgets at the same time. You can create an Action once and share it among menu items, toolbar items, or buttons.

Figure 35.9 illustrates the IAction interface.

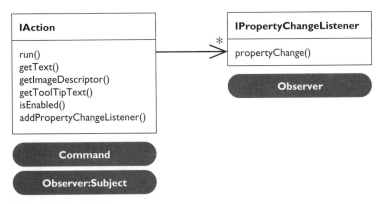

Figure 35.9 IAction

The connection of an action with an SWT widget is shown in Figure 35.10. It shows how the workbench offers the Save action from both a menu item (**File > Save**) and from the toolbar.

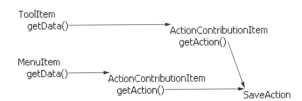

Figure 35.10 Toolbar and Menu Share an Action

JFace uses the data extension slots to associate an `ActionContributionItem` with the toolbar and menu items. The `ActionContributionItem` belongs to the JFace contribution framework. JFace contribution managers like `IMenu-Manager` or the `IToolBarManager` manage contribution items and not actions directly. The managers provide convenient methods for adding an `IAction` which they wrap in an `ActionContributionItem`. The `Action-ContributionItem` populates the SWT widget from the `Action`'s state and registers as an event listener with the widget. When an event notification arrives, the action contribution item invokes the action's `run()` method. The contribution item also registers as a property change listener with the action in order to update the widget—for example, its label or enabled state—when the action changes.

When clients implement an action, all they have to define is its user interface state like name, icon, or tooltip and implement the `run()` method. The JFace action support handles the SWT widget interactions for them.

CHAPTER 36

UI Workbench

The workbench defines the Eclipse UI paradigm—editors, views, and perspectives. It builds on top of SWT and JFace (see Figure 36.1).

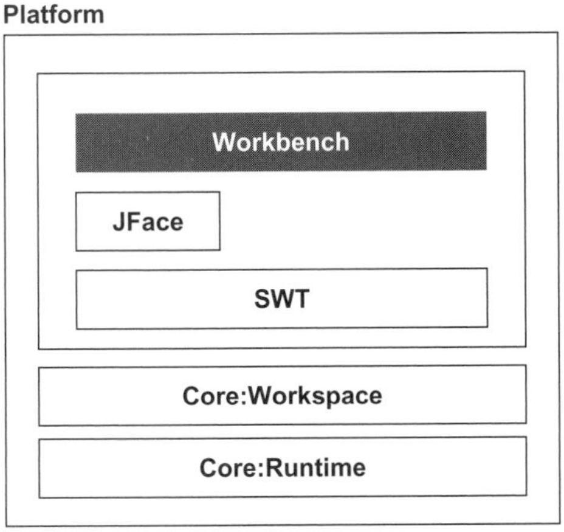

Platform

```
┌─────────────────────────────────────────────┐
│  ┌─────────────────────────────────────────┐ │
│  │         Workbench                       │ │
│  │  ┌───────────┐                          │ │
│  │  │  JFace    │                          │ │
│  │  │   ┌─────────────────────────────┐    │ │
│  │  │   │          SWT                │    │ │
│  │  └───┴─────────────────────────────┘    │ │
│  └─────────────────────────────────────────┘ │
│  ┌─────────────────────────────────────────┐ │
│  │         Core:Workspace                  │ │
│  └─────────────────────────────────────────┘ │
│  ┌─────────────────────────────────────────┐ │
│  │         Core:Runtime                    │ │
│  └─────────────────────────────────────────┘ │
└─────────────────────────────────────────────┘
```

Figure 36.1 Workbench

In this chapter we peek into the implementation of the workbench and focus on

- ○ How the workbench implements the Lazy Loading Rule
- ○ How the workbench saves and restores the state of the user interface
- ○ How the workbench uses the `IAdaptable` mechanism to provide its user interfaces services

36.1   Implementing the Lazy Loading Rule—Virtual Proxies

The workbench defines many extension points. It is therefore the prime example for how to comply with the Lazy Loading Rule. Let's take a look at the **Add CVS Repository** action (see Figure 36.2).

Figure 36.2   Add CVS Repository Action

The **Add CVS Repository** action is contributed by the CVS UI plug-in with the following declaration:

org.eclipse.team.cvs.ui/plugin.xml
```
<extension point="org.eclipse.ui.actionSets">
  <actionSet
  ...
    <action
      toolbarPath="Normal/CVS"
      label="%CVSActionSet.newLabel"
      tooltip="%CVSActionSet.newTooltip"
      icon="icons/full/wizards/newconnect_wiz.gif"
      class="org.eclipse.team.internal.ccvs.ui.actions.
        NewRepositoryAction"
      id="org.eclipse.team.cvs.ui.actions.NewRepositoryAction"
      definitionId="org.eclipse.team.cvs.ui.new.location">
    </action>
  </actionSet>
</extension>
```

The NewRepositoryAction is defined in an action set containing a single action that allows the user to create a new repository location. At runtime the workbench creates the object structure around the action, as shown in Figure 36.3. Figure 36.3 is a snapshot that was taken after the user clicked the toolbar item, which triggered the loading of the extension class.

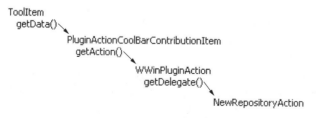

Figure 36.3   Workbench Loads a Contributed Action

The toolbar item for the **New Repository** action is associated with a contribution item. The contribution constructs an action representation in an SWT toolbar. The WWinPluginAction extends a class PluginAction. PluginAction turns an Action into a proxy for a real action. The Eclipse workbench populates a PluginAction from the information in the manifest (title, icon, tooltip). The only thing it cannot do is actually perform the action. When the toolbar button is pressed, the PluginAction loads the extension class and forwards the run() request to it. Figure 36.4 illustrates these relationships at the class level.

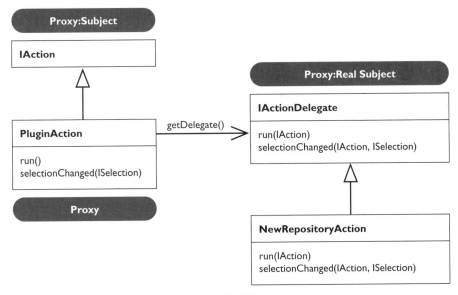

Figure 36.4   PluginAction Lazily Loads the Real Action

The forwarding of the run() action is done using Self Delegation.[1] The proxy action is passed as an argument to the action delegate. In this way the delegate can get at the action's state. The same is done with the selectionChanged() method.

36.2   Persisting UI State—Memento

One goal of the Eclipse UI is to preserve the illusion of continuity across sessions. The workbench saves the current configuration and contents of a workbench

---

1. See K. Beck, *Smalltalk Best Practice Patterns*. Prentice Hall PTR, Upper Saddle River, NJ, 1997.

window when a session ends and restores that state when a new session starts. This leads us to the User Continuity Rule:

USER CONTINUITY RULE   Preserve the user interface state across sessions.

Establishing this rule requires some basic infrastructure to store and retrieve the objects representing important UI state.

36.2.1   Memento

Here are some requirements for the storage mechanism:

○ The storage format needs to be robust in the face of changes. A new version of a class needs to be able to restore the data from an older version. In particular the class might not be available at all in a later session.

○ The storage mechanism needs to support complex structures.

○ The storage mechanism needs to be able to save and restore arbitrary objects.

Java's built-in object serialization and externalization support comes close to addressing these requirements. However, using serialized objects as a long-term storage format is fragile. Eclipse avoids using Java object serialization because of this fragility.

The storage mechanism needs to preserve the object's encapsulation. This leads us to the Memento pattern. The intent of Memento states: "Without violating encapsulation, capture and externalize an object's internal state so that the object can be restored to this state later." A memento stores a snapshot of the internal state of another object. The workbench provides a general memento interface, IMemento:

org.eclipse.ui/IMemento
```
public interface IMemento {
  void putString(String key, String value);
  String getString(String key);

  void putInteger(String key, int value);
  Integer getInteger(String key);

  IMemento createChild(String type);
  IMemento[] getChildren(String type);
  //...
}
```

An IMemento stores key-value pairs of primitive types. It stores a structure by creating a tree of mementos. The memento structure is backed by an XML-based storage format.

How is the IMemento revealed to clients? Here is an excerpt from the implementation of the **Navigator** view that illustrates how it saves the current selection:

org.eclipse.ui.views/ResourceNavigator
```
private static final String TAG_SELECTION = "selection";
private static final String TAG_ELEMENT = "element";
public void saveState(IMemento memento) {
  //...
  //save selection
  Object elements[] =
    ((IStructuredSelection)viewer.getSelection()).toArray();
  if (elements.length > 0) {
    IMemento selectionMem = memento.createChild(TAG_SELECTION);
    for (int i = 0; i < elements.length; i++) {
      IMemento elementMem = selectionMem.createChild(TAG_ELEMENT);
      elementMem.putString(
        TAG_PATH,
        ((IResource) elements[i]).getFullPath().toString());
    }
  }
}
```

The workbench passes an IMemento to saveState() and clients fill the memento with the state that needs to be preserved. Restoring the state isn't symmetrical, as there is no restoreState() method called by the workbench. Instead, clients receive a view's memento in init(). The view typically stores the memento in a field so it can be accessed when the view's widgets are created.

org.eclipse.ui.views/ResourceNavigator
```
IMemento memento;
public void init(IViewSite site, IMemento memento)
    throws PartInitException {
  super.init(site, memento);
  this.memento = memento;
}
```

The workbench also needs to store arbitrary objects polymorphically. Support for saving and restoring arbitrary objects uses IAdaptable. When the workbench needs to save an object to preserve UI state, it asks it for an IPersistable-Element adapter:

org.eclipse.ui/IPersistableElement
```
public interface IPersistableElement {
  void saveState(IMemento memento);
  String getFactoryId();
}
```

Using the IPersistableElement adapter the workbench can ask the object to record its state in a memento. The method getFactoryId() identifies the factory that can resurrect the object from the memento again. A factory has to conform to the IElementFactory interface and is registered with the workbench via the org.eclipse.ui.elementFactories extension point.

org.eclipse.ui/IElementFactory
```
public interface IElementFactory {
  public IAdaptable createElement(IMemento memento);
}
```

36.2.2 Restoring Many Open Views and Editors

A workbench page can have many open views and editors, but editors and views can be stacked on top of each other. As a consequence, only a subset of them is visible at a given time. If all the views and editors inside a workbench window were immediately activated when Eclipse started up, many plug-ins would be activated. To enable lazy loading of visible parts, the workbench uses the Proxy pattern again. However, in this case, clients have to cooperate a little. When asking a workbench page for its views or editors, a well-behaved client asks for the view references and editor references only. References are proxies for the real workbench parts. A reference provides a method to retrieve the real part. Figure 36.5 illustrates how a workbench page provides access to editor and view references.

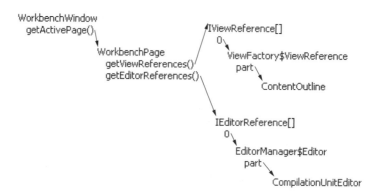

Figure 36.5 Workbench Page Indirectly References Views and Editors

Figure 36.6 illustrates reference/part relationship for editors at the class level.

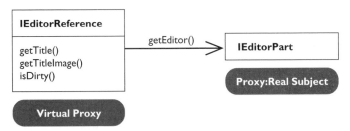

Figure 36.6   IEditorReference Is a Proxy for IEditorPart

36.3   **Workbench Services—IAdaptable**

The workbench provides general UI services. These UI services need to be available for different models such as the workspace. To achieve this flexibility the workbench uses `IAdaptable` as described in Chapter 31.

36.3.1   *IWorkbenchAdapter*

How can you provide a visual presentation for an element without knowing its concrete type? This is the purpose of the `IWorkbenchAdapter`. You can ask an object for its `IWorkbenchAdapter`. Then you can present it with a label and image in the user interface or get access to an element's hierarchical structure. Here is an example for how to retrieve the label for some arbitrary object:

```
public static String getTextLabel(Object obj) {
  if (obj instanceof IAdaptable) {
    IWorkbenchAdapter wa=
      (IWorkbenchAdapter)((IAdaptable)obj).getAdapter(
        IWorkbenchAdapter.class);
    if (wa != null)
      return wa.getLabel(obj);
  }
  return "<no label>";
}
```

36.3.2   *IResource Adapter*

Consider the following scenario. You have selected a compilation unit in the **Package Explorer** and you want to add a bookmark. The add bookmark action adds bookmarks to files. The problem is that the **Package Explorer** presents `IJavaElement`s and not resources or files. `IJavaElement`s provide a Java-specific view of a resource tree. An `IJavaElement` isn't a resource, but it has an underlying resource. It could therefore serve as a fine target for the add bookmark action (see Figure 36.7).

Figure 36.7   Java Element Has an Underlying Resource

As it currently stands, one either has to provide a separate add bookmark action for IJavaElements or the add bookmark action is just disabled in the **Package Explorer**. Neither solution is appealing.

   A better solution is to generalize the add bookmark action so that it can also operate on elements that have a corresponding resource, even if the element isn't a resource. This is done using the adapter mechanism. IResource serves as the adapter interface and an element can bring its underlying resource to the surface when queried for the IResource interface. The add bookmark action can then be generalized to not only operate on files, but on any object providing an IResource adapter. Here is the corresponding code from the class AddBookMarkAction:

org.eclipse.ui/AddBookmarkAction
```
void createMarker(String markerType) {
  IStructuredSelection selection = getStructuredSelection();
  for (Iterator i = selection.iterator(); i.hasNext();) {
    Object o = i.next();
    if (o instanceof IAdaptable) {
      Object resource =
        ((IAdaptable) o).getAdapter(IResource.class);
      if (resource instanceof IFile)
        // create bookmark
    }
  }
}
```

Java elements provide an IResource adapter. When you want to work with an Object as an IResource, you should adapt it to IResource, not just cast it or check its type with instanceof.

```
if (object instanceof IAdaptable) {
  IResource r=
    (IResource)((IAdaptable)object).getAdapter(IResource.class);
  if (r != null)
    // there is an underlying resource
```

36.3.3   Object Contributions

The fact that an object has an underlying resource but isn't itself an
`IResource` causes problems for object contributions. Object contributions
are based on the type of the selected object. For example, the following action
intends to contribute a compare action to all `IResources`. Again we have the
problem that the **Package Explorer** shows Java elements. Java elements are
not `IResources`, but can deliver one using the `IResource` adapter. With the
declaration below the compare action will not be available for compilation
units shown in the **Package Explorer**.

org.eclipse.compare/plugin.xml
```
<objectContribution
  id="org.eclipse.compare.CompareAction"
  objectClass="org.eclipse.core.resources.IResource">
```

This problem is addressed in the object contribution mechanism using adapters. In the definition of an object contribution, you can declare whether the
adapter should be considered as well. Here is the definition of the compare
action that enables the `IResource` adapter:

org.eclipse.compare/plugin.xml
```
<objectContribution
  id="org.eclipse.compare.CompareAction"
  objectClass="org.eclipse.core.resources.IResource"
  adaptable="true">
  ...
```

The fact that many actions operate on the "least common dominator" of
`IResource` leads us to another rule when you introduce new domain objects.
To enable existing contributions for `IResource` for your domain object, make
the domain object an `IAdaptable` and implement the `IResource` adapter.
This is the Adapt to `IResource` Rule.

> **ADAPT TO `IResource` RULE**   Whenever possible, define an IResource
> adapter for your domain objects.

36.3.4   Overview of Workbench-Provided Adapters

The Eclipse workbench introduces a set of adapters for its services and its
views:

  ❍ `IPropertySource`—Returns the properties displayed in the **Properties**
     view. The **Properties** view also supports an `IPropertySheetPage`

adapter. If you provide this adapter, you have control of the entire **Properties** view contents.

○ IContentOutlinePage—Finds the content outline associated with an editor part. Given the tight coupling between an editor part and its outline, it may be surprising that there are no explicit methods in IEditorPart to get at the **Outline** view. However, this would be a violation of the Fair Play Rule. All plug-ins must use the same mechanisms. A new kind of **Outline** view contributed by a client doesn't have the option to add methods directly to IEditorPart, so the Eclipse workbench uses an adapter.

○ IPersistableElement—Used for objects that need to be consistent across sessions in a memento.

○ ITaskListResourceAdapter—This adapter exists to allow more specific adaptation in the context of the **Tasks** view rather than simply looking for an IResource adaptable.

○ IShowInTarget, IShowInSource, IShowInTargetList—Supports the implementation of the **Navigate > Show In >** actions.

○ IActionFilter—Supports filtering on arbitrary attributes of an object. This appears in the declaration of a contribution and gives you more precise control over the visibility of your action (Relevance Rule).

All these workbench services are primarily used by the standard views that are included in the Eclipse platform: **Properties** view, **Outline** view, **Navigator**, and **Task** view. The adapter mechanism helps make these views generally usable. Therefore, when you intend to contribute a view to Eclipse, you should consider using these adapters.

CHAPTER 37

Closing Circle Three

When reviewing the pattern stories, we can make the following observations:

○ When using the patterns as an analytical tool we can cover significant portions of the design with patterns.

○ Several Eclipse components make use of the Composite pattern. Once you understand the structure of the composite, you understand a significant portion of the component.

We began this book with an apparent contradiction—the simultaneous need to be supported while programming and the need to support others. Along the way we have encountered many other apparent contradictions resolved by the design and implementation of Eclipse. Here are a handful:

○ *Loosely coupled versus tightly integrated.* We would like our tools to be tightly integrated with each other, but loosely enough coupled that we can mix and match tools. The explicit declaration of extension points provides a balance between the clear and explicit interfaces and decoupling.

○ *Flexibility of lots of pieces versus performance.* The need to be able to start up the system independent of the number of plug-ins is a theme running through Eclipse. The plug-in manifest file provides a way to rapidly load the user-visible appearance of a plug-in without incurring the cost of loading all the code.

○ *Big project versus need for coherent design* (to enable contribution). Eclipse is a substantial piece of software. The Eclipse team has a clear and mostly consistent vision of what constitutes good software. You see this in the clear separation of layers—core versus UI and language-specific versus language-neutral. There are exceptions to rigid consistency, like SWT's use of abstract classes to define APIs instead of interfaces, but even these exceptions are internally consistent.

○ *IDE versus general platform.* The first goal of Eclipse is to be an effective general purpose platform for software development. The Java tooling is only one aspect of that. Where necessary, the platform has remained simple and general while the specific applications have grown their own functionality; for example, the similar-but-different implementations of listening for resource changes between the platform and Java.

Although it seems to us that we have dug deep into Eclipse with this book, in truth we have only scratched the surface. We'll leave you with an interesting and useful grab-bag of topics to explore as you continue to contribute to Eclipse.

37.1   Final Forward Pointers

Until now we have primarily focused on extending the Eclipse platform with the Java development tools APIs. In addition, we have also used the Help component. However, Eclipse provides many other components like Debug, Compare, Search, and Team to support building integrated development tools. All these components follow a common layering structure that leads us to the Strata Rule:

> **STRATA RULE**   Separate language-neutral functionality from language-specific functionality and separate core functionality from UI functionality.

The Debug component illustrates the Strata Rule. Figure 37.1 shows the four Debug plug-ins and their layering and prerequisites.

Understanding the Strata Rule helps you explore these components. When you implement support for a new language or a new set of functionality, consider following the Strata Rule. As usual, there are trade-offs. You can decide to fold some layers into a single plug-in. For example, the smaller components like Search and Compare fold language-neutral support into a single plug-in. As a plug-in grows you will often separate its functionality according to the Strata Rule. We have observed this for the Text component. The Search component will likely evolve in a similar fashion.

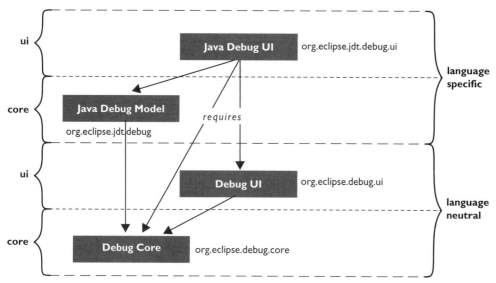

Figure 37.1   Separate Language-Specific from Language-Neutral and Core from UI

37.1.1   *Additional Eclipse Components Overview*

Here is a brief overview of additional components provided by Eclipse. For each component we give some pointers to source code for further exploration:

○ **Debug**—The Debugger defines a common debugger UI that is shown in the Debug Perspective. The common debugger UI builds on top of a language-neutral Debug Model API. The Model API defines interfaces for common debug artifacts (threads, stacks frames) and actions (step, resume, terminate). To support debugging a new language, you implement the debug model interfaces. Once you have done that, the rest of the debugger just works. You can then extend the debugger UI using the standard extension mechanisms. For example, you can contribute menu items or toolbar items to the predefined views. The debugger component includes a launching framework. A *launch configuration* captures the settings for starting a particular program. You can contribute new launch configuration types and contribute additional tabs to the launch dialog (**Run > Run...** or **Run > Debug...**).

Pointers to examples: Eclipse includes a Java debugger. The debugger is implemented on top of the standard Java Platform Debugger Architecture (JPDA) in the plug-ins `org.eclipse.jdt.debug` and `org.eclipse.jdt.debug.ui`. The debugger plug-ins contribute launch configurations for Java programs, applets, and a launch configuration to attach to a remote Java VM.

○ **Team**—The Team component supports sharing resources with a team via a repository. Users associate a project with a particular repository. The Team component provides APIs and extension points (`org.eclipse.team.core.repository`) for defining new kinds of repositories. There are some companion extension points to define how a repository handles file modifications and moving and deleting files (`org.eclipse.core.resources.fileModificationValidator` and `org.eclipse.core.resources.moveDeleteHook`).

Pointers to examples: Eclipse includes a CVS repository provider. The corresponding plug-ins are `org.eclipse.cvs.core` and `org.eclipse.cvs.ui`. This separation is another example of the Strata Rule. There is also an example plug-in project `org.eclipse.team.examples.filesystem`. It implements a simple repository provider that uses a location on the file system as a repository.

○ **Search**—The Search component defines the **Search** dialog and the search result view. You contribute new searches in form of additional search pages. Search provides an API to populate the search results view with your matches.

Pointers to examples: The `org.eclipse.search` plug-in contributes support for textual searching. The Java development tools contribute a Java-specific search in the `org.eclipse.jdt.ui` plug-in and the package is `org.eclipse.jdt.internal.search`.

○ **Compare**—The Compare component contributes viewers to perform two- and three-way comparing and merging of textual and hierarchical structures. It includes differencing engines for both text and trees. The definition of the structure to be used for a comparison is pluggable and contributed with the `org.eclipse.compare.structureCreator` extension point.

Pointers to examples: the JDT plug-in `org.eclipse.jdt.ui` leverages the compare component and implements structural comparisons of Java compilation units at the method level. See the package `org.eclipse.jdt.internal.ui.compare`. You can also find a simpler example that illustrates structural comparisons for files storing key-value pairs. The code is available in the example plug-in: `org.eclipse.compare.examples`.

○ **JFace text**—JFace text provides a framework for editing source documents. The framework includes support for syntax highlighting, content assist, formatting, annotations, and much more.

Pointers to Examples: The Java editor (`org.eclipse.jdt.internal.ui.javaeditor.*`) contributed by the `org.eclipse.jdt.ui` plug-in is a comprehensive example of how to use JFace text. A simpler editor illustrating all the standard features for a custom editor is provided in the example plug-in `org.eclipse.ui.examples.javaeditor`.

37.1.2   Example Plug-Ins and Sample Code

The example plug-ins referred to above are not part of the Eclipse SDK. You can download them separately by visiting *www.eclipse.org/downloads/* and navigating to the section **Example Plug-ins**.

Additional example code for SWT is available from the SWT component pages: *dev.eclipse.org/viewcvs/index.cgi/~checkout~/platform-swt-home/ dev.html#snippets*. This page refers to a collection of useful code snippets that were posted over time to the Eclipse news group.

37.1.3   Eclipse Articles

The list of forwarding pointers would not be complete without pointing you to the collection of articles available on *www.eclipse.org/articles*. These articles were written by Eclipse developers and other members of the community. They cover the various Eclipse components and provide you with in-depth information about how to use and extend them.

37.2   An Invitation to Contribute

The primary goal of this book is to help you find your way when you parachute into Eclipse. We have succeeded if we have sparked your desire to extend Eclipse with your own contributions. However, implementing plug-ins is not the only way you can contribute to the Eclipse project:

❍ *Use it and report bugs*—Use Eclipse any way you like, learn about the open source tools like Bugzilla and enter bugs and feature requests. Vote for bugs you think are important to fix.

❍ *Track progress*—Download and validate the milestone builds as they become available. Don't wait for major releases. Eclipse gets better with each milestone.

❍ *Help others*—Show what you already learned about Eclipse by participating in news groups and answering questions.

○ *Fix bugs*—Attach fixes to bug reports in the form of patches. If you also attach broken test cases, you increase your chances of the resulting fix doing exactly what you want.

○ *Grow Eclipse*—Publish your plug-ins and ship products on top of Eclipse.

PART V

Appendices

APPENDIX A

TestRunner Details

How do we run tests? We could run our tests in the host Eclipse directly. While this is simple, it has the drawback that side effects of a test can impact the development environment. Consider a test that gets out of control and consumes all CPU cycles. You would have to shutdown your host Eclipse to recover, just because of a test. Moreover, running tests inside the host Eclipse instance makes it difficult to debug test failures.

Therefore, we want to execute the tests in a separate virtual machine. Figure A.1 illustrates the setup. Our contributed JUnit plug-in contains a test runner that launches a `SocketTestRunner` in a separate VM to execute the tests. The `SocketTestRunner` reports the results back via a socket connection. The tests to be run are contained in a project inside the Eclipse development workspace, and the `SocketTestRunner` runs them from there.

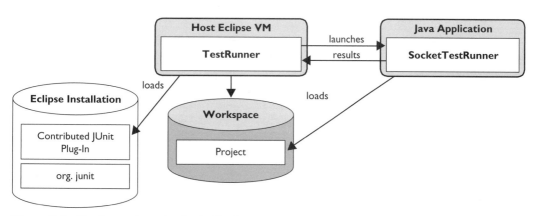

Figure A.1   TestRunner Launches SocketTestRunner and Reads Results

A.1   TestRunner

The class `TestRunner` is responsible for running tests. It is invoked from our contributed `JUnitPlugin` as follows:

org.eclipse.contribution.junit/JUnitPlugin
```
public void run(IType type) throws CoreException {
  //...
  new TestRunner().run(type);
}
```

In Circle Two we refactored the test runner to support passing in a project and to also support running multiple test cases.

[Circle-2] org.eclipse.contribution.junit/JUnitPlugin
```
public void run(IType[] types, IJavaProject project)
    throws CoreException {
  //...
  new TestRunner(project).run(types);
}
```

Behind the scenes the `TestRunner` launches a second VM that runs the `Socket-TestRunner`. The `TestRunner` performs two main tasks:

❍ Constructing the command line to launch a VM that executes the `Socket-TestRunner` class

❍ Listening to messages communicated back from the `SocketTestRunner` via a socket and notifying the registered `ITestRunListeners`

Most of the complexity of the `TestRunner` is in the construction of the command line, in particular, the class path. For example, the command line to run the test `pack1.TestFailure` stored in the project *Project-1* is shown in Table A.1.

Table A.1

`java.exe`	The Java VM to be started

`-classpath`
`c:/eclipse/plugins/org.eclipse.contribution.`
`junit/contribjunit.jar;`
`c:/eclipse/plugins/org.junit/junit.jar;`
`c:/eclipse/workspace/`**`Project-1`**`/bin`
	The classpath

`org.eclipse.contribution.junit.SocketTestRunner`	The main class
`14026`	The port to be used for creating the socket
`pack1.TestFailure`	The test's class name

SocketTestRunner is contained in the org.eclipse.contribution.junit plug-in. Therefore we have to include *org.eclipse.contribution.junit/contribjunit. jar* on the class path.

In the above example the test is contained in the project *Project-1*. We include the output folder of this project on the class path as well. That's why we need *workspace/Project-1/bin*. Finally, the JUnit classes need to be accessible, so we add *junit.jar* from the org.junit plug-in in the Eclipse installation to the class path.

Here is the code of TestRunner. We also show the changes that we introduced in Circle Two and tag the lines with //c2.

org.eclipse.contribution.junit/TestRunner

```
package org.eclipse.contribution.junit;
//c2 package org.eclipse.contribution.junit.internal.core;

// imports...

public class TestRunner {
  static final String MAIN_CLASS=
    "org.eclipse.contribution.junit.SocketTestRunner";
//c2"org.eclipse.contribution.junit.internal.core.SocketTestRunner";

  private int port;
  private IJavaProject project;
  private BufferedReader reader;

  public TestRunner() {
  }

//c2    public TestRunner(IJavaProject project) {
//c2      this.project= project;
//c2    }

  public void run(IType type) throws CoreException {
    project= type.getJavaProject();
    run(new IType[] {type});
  }

  public void run(IType[] classes) throws CoreException {
    IVMInstall vmInstall= getVMInstall();
    if (vmInstall == null)
      return;
    IVMRunner vmRunner= vmInstall.getVMRunner(
    ILaunchManager.RUN_MODE);
    if (vmRunner == null)
      return;

    String[] classPath= computeClasspath();
    VMRunnerConfiguration vmConfig=
      new VMRunnerConfiguration(MAIN_CLASS, classPath);
```

```
    String[] args= new String[classes.length + 1];
    port= SocketUtil.findUnusedLocalPort("localhost",
      10000, 15000);
    args[0]= Integer.toString(port);

    for (int i= 0; i < classes.length; i++)
      args[i + 1]= classes[i].getFullyQualifiedName();
    vmConfig.setProgramArguments(args);

    ILaunch launch= new Launch(null, ILaunchManager.RUN_MODE,
      null);
    vmRunner.run(vmConfig, launch, null);
    DebugPlugin.getDefault().getLaunchManager().addLaunch(launch);
    connect();
}

private String[] computeClasspath() throws CoreException {
  String[] defaultPath=
    JavaRuntime.computeDefaultRuntimeClassPath(project);
  String[] classPath= new String[defaultPath.length + 2];
  System.arraycopy(defaultPath, 0, classPath, 2,
    defaultPath.length);
  JUnitPlugin plugin= JUnitPlugin.getPlugin();
  URL url= plugin.getDescriptor().getInstallURL();
  try {
    classPath[0]= Platform.asLocalURL(
      new URL(url, "bin")).getFile();
    classPath[1]= Platform.asLocalURL(
      new URL(url, "contribjunit.jar")).getFile();
  } catch (IOException e) {
    IStatus status= new Status(IStatus.ERROR,
      plugin.getDescriptor().getUniqueIdentifier(),
      IStatus.OK, "Could not determine path", e);
    throw new CoreException(status);
  }
  return classPath;
}

private void connect() {
  try {
    ServerSocket server;
    server= new ServerSocket(port);
    try {
      Socket socket= server.accept();
      try {
        readMessage(socket);
      } finally {
        socket.close();
      }
    } finally {
      server.close();
    }
  } catch (IOException e) {
```

```
      //TODO unhandled exception
      e.printStackTrace();
    }
  }

  private void readMessage(Socket socket) throws IOException {
    reader= new BufferedReader(
      new InputStreamReader(socket.getInputStream()));
    try {
      String line= null;
      while ((line= reader.readLine()) != null) {
        parseMessage(line);
      }
    } finally {
      reader.close();
    }
  }

  private void parseMessage(String line) {
    JUnitPlugin plugin= JUnitPlugin.getPlugin();
    if (line.startsWith("starting tests ")) {
      int start= "starting tests ".length();
      int count= Integer.parseInt(line.substring(start));
      plugin.fireTestsStarted(count);
//c2     plugin.fireTestsStarted(project, count);
    }

    if (line.startsWith("ending tests")) {
      plugin.fireTestsFinished();
//c2     plugin.fireTestsFinished(project);
    }

    if (line.startsWith("starting test ")) {
      int start= "starting test ".length();
      String method= line.substring(start, line.indexOf("("));
      String klass= line.substring(line.indexOf("(") + 1,
        line.indexOf(")"));
      plugin.fireTestStarted(klass, method);
//c2     plugin.fireTestStarted(project, klass, method);
    }

    if (line.startsWith("failing test ")) {
      int start= "failing test ".length();
      String method= line.substring(start, line.indexOf("("));
      String klass= line.substring(line.indexOf("(") + 1,
        line.indexOf(")"));
      StringWriter buffer= new StringWriter();
      PrintWriter writer= new PrintWriter(buffer);
      String frame= null;
      try {
        while ((frame= reader.readLine()) != null &&
          (!frame.equals("END TRACE")))
```

```
        writer.println(frame);
      } catch (IOException e) {
       // TODO Log later
       e.printStackTrace();
      }
      String trace= buffer.getBuffer().toString();
      plugin.fireTestFailed(klass, method, trace);
//c2      plugin.fireTestFailed(project, klass, method, trace);
    }
  }

  private IVMInstall getVMInstall() throws CoreException {
    IVMInstall vmInstall= JavaRuntime.getVMInstall(project);
    if (vmInstall == null)
      vmInstall= JavaRuntime.getDefaultVMInstall();
    return vmInstall;
  }
}
```

To launch the VM we use the launching support provided by the `org.eclipse.jdt.launching` plug-in. This plug-in shields us from the details of launching a VM. `IVMInstall` represents a particular VM installation. From an installation we request an `IVMRunner` that can run an installed VM. The arguments for launching the VM are captured in a `VMRunnerConfiguration`. We create a `Launch` object that we register with the launching infrastructure. Once the `VMRunner` is set up we run it. This creates a new process for the VM. In the above code we have ignored limitations on the maximum number of arguments that can be passed on the command line. A more defensive solution would store the test names in a file and only pass the name of the file on the command line.

The rest of the code handles the communication with the `SocketTestRunner`. When a `TestRunner` receives a message from the `SocketTestRunner`, it translates the message into a `ITestRunListener` notification.

A.2   SocketTestRunner

The `SocketTestRunner` is a JUnit test runner variation. It is very similar to the JUnit's text test runner. Instead of printing the results of a test run to the console, it writes the results to a socket connection using a simple string-based protocol, as shown in Table A.2.

Table A.2

`"starting tests "+number`	Test run started with the given number of tests.
`"ending tests "`	Test run ended.
`"starting test " + testmethod+"("+classname+")"`	The given test has started. A test is identified by the method name followed by the class name.
`"failing test " + testmethod+"("classname+")"`	The given test has failed. The stack trace follows in subsequent lines terminated by "END TRACE".

org.eclipse.contribution.junit/SocketTestRunner

```
package org.eclipse.contribution.junit;
//c2: package org.eclipse.contribution.junit.internal.core;

public class SocketTestRunner implements TestListener {
  private int port;
  private Socket socket;
  private PrintWriter writer;
  /**
   * The entry point for the test runner.
   * The arguments are:
   * args[0]: the port number to connect to
   * args[1-n]: the name of test classes
   */
  public static void main(String[] args) {
    new SocketTestRunner().runTests(args);
  }

  private void runTests(String[] args) {
    port= Integer.parseInt(args[0]);
    openClientSocket();
    try {
      TestSuite suite= new TestSuite();
      for (int i= 1; i < args.length; i++)
        suite.addTestSuite(Class.forName(args[i]));

      writer.println("starting tests " + suite.countTestCases());
      TestResult result= new TestResult();
      result.addListener(this);
      suite.run(result);

      writer.println("ending tests");
    } catch (ClassNotFoundException e) {
      System.out.println("Not a class: " + args[1]);
    } finally {
      closeClientSocket();
    }
  }
```

```java
    private void openClientSocket() {
      for (int i= 0; i < 10; i++) {
        try {
          socket= new Socket("localhost", port);
          writer= new PrintWriter(socket.getOutputStream(), true);
          return;
        } catch (UnknownHostException e) {
          e.printStackTrace();
        } catch (IOException e) {
          e.printStackTrace();
        }
        try {
          Thread.sleep(500);
        } catch (InterruptedException e1) {
        }
      }
    }

    private void closeClientSocket() {
      writer.close();
      try {
        socket.close();
      } catch (IOException e) {
        e.printStackTrace();
      }
    }

    public void addError(Test test, Throwable t) {
      writer.println("failing test " + test);
      t.printStackTrace(writer);
      writer.println("END TRACE");
    }

    public void addFailure(Test test, AssertionFailedError t) {
      addError(test, t);
    }

    public void endTest(Test test) {
    }

    public void startTest(Test test) {
      writer.println("starting test " + test);
    }
}
```

The JUnit framework supports listening to a TestResult with a TestListener. The SocketTestRunner registers itself as a listener for the current test result and translates test listener notifications into messages written to the socket connection.

APPENDIX B

The TestProject Fixture

This appendix lists the full source code of the `TestProject` fixture class that we used to implement the tests.

org.eclipse.contribution.junit.test/TestProject

```java
public class TestProject {
  public IProject project;
  public IJavaProject javaProject;
  private IPackageFragmentRoot sourceFolder;

  public TestProject() throws CoreException {
    IWorkspaceRoot root= ResourcesPlugin.getWorkspace().getRoot();
    project= root.getProject("Project-1");
    project.create(null);
    project.open(null);

    javaProject= JavaCore.create(project);
    IFolder binFolder= createBinFolder();
    setJavaNature();
    javaProject.setRawClasspath(new IClasspathEntry[0], null);
    createOutputFolder(binFolder);
    addSystemLibraries();
  }
  public IProject getProject() {
    return project;
  }

  public IJavaProject getJavaProject() {
    return javaProject;
  }
```

```java
public void addJar(String plugin, String jar)
  throws MalformedURLException, IOException, JavaModelException {
  Path result= findFileInPlugin(plugin, jar);
  IClasspathEntry[] oldEntries= javaProject.getRawClasspath();
  IClasspathEntry[] newEntries=
    new IClasspathEntry[oldEntries.length + 1];
  System.arraycopy(oldEntries, 0, newEntries, 0,
    oldEntries.length);
  newEntries[oldEntries.length]=
    JavaCore.newLibraryEntry(result, null, null);
  javaProject.setRawClasspath(newEntries, null);
}

public IPackageFragment createPackage(String name)
    throws CoreException {
  if (sourceFolder == null)
    sourceFolder= createSourceFolder();
  return sourceFolder.createPackageFragment(name, false, null);
}

public IType createType(IPackageFragment pack,
    String cuName, String source) throws JavaModelException {
  StringBuffer buf= new StringBuffer();
  buf.append("package " + pack.getElementName() + ";\n");
  buf.append("\n");
  buf.append(source);
  ICompilationUnit cu= pack.createCompilationUnit(cuName,
    buf.toString(), false, null);
  return cu.getTypes()[0];
}

public void dispose() throws CoreException {
  waitForIndexer();
  project.delete(true, true, null);
}

private IFolder createBinFolder() throws CoreException {
  IFolder binFolder= project.getFolder("bin");
  binFolder.create(false, true, null);
  return binFolder;
}

private void setJavaNature() throws CoreException {
  IProjectDescription description= project.getDescription();
  description.setNatureIds(new String[] { JavaCore.NATURE_ID });
  project.setDescription(description, null);
}

private void createOutputFolder(IFolder binFolder)
    throws JavaModelException {
  IPath outputLocation= binFolder.getFullPath();
  javaProject.setOutputLocation(outputLocation, null);
}
```

```
    private IPackageFragmentRoot createSourceFolder()
        throws CoreException {
      IFolder folder= project.getFolder("src");
      folder.create(false, true, null);
      IPackageFragmentRoot root=
        javaProject.getPackageFragmentRoot(folder);

      IClasspathEntry[] oldEntries= javaProject.getRawClasspath();
      IClasspathEntry[] newEntries=
        new IClasspathEntry[oldEntries.length + 1];
      System.arraycopy(oldEntries, 0, newEntries, 0,
        oldEntries.length);
      newEntries[oldEntries.length]=
        JavaCore.newSourceEntry(root.getPath());
      javaProject.setRawClasspath(newEntries, null);
      return root;
    }

    private void addSystemLibraries() throws JavaModelException {
      IClasspathEntry[] oldEntries= javaProject.getRawClasspath();
      IClasspathEntry[] newEntries=
        new IClasspathEntry[oldEntries.length + 1];
      System.arraycopy(oldEntries, 0, newEntries, 0,
        oldEntries.length);
      newEntries[oldEntries.length]=
        JavaRuntime.getDefaultJREContainerEntry();
      javaProject.setRawClasspath(newEntries, null);
    }

    private Path findFileInPlugin(String plugin, String file)
        throws MalformedURLException, IOException {
      IPluginRegistry registry= Platform.getPluginRegistry();
      IPluginDescriptor descriptor=
        registry.getPluginDescriptor(plugin);
      URL pluginURL= descriptor.getInstallURL();
      URL jarURL= new URL(pluginURL, file);
      URL localJarURL= Platform.asLocalURL(jarURL);
      return new Path(localJarURL.getPath());
    }

    private void waitForIndexer() throws JavaModelException {
      new SearchEngine()
        .searchAllTypeNames(
          ResourcesPlugin.getWorkspace(),
          null,
          null,
          IJavaSearchConstants.EXACT_MATCH,
          IJavaSearchConstants.CASE_SENSITIVE,
          IJavaSearchConstants.CLASS,
          SearchEngine.createJavaSearchScope(new IJavaElement[0]),
          new ITypeNameRequestor() {
        public void acceptClass(char[] packageName,
          char[] simpleTypeName, char[][] enclosingTypeNames,
          String path) {
        }
```

```
      public void acceptInterface(char[] packageName,
        char[] simpleTypeName, char[][] enclosingTypeNames,
        String path) {
      }
    }, IJavaSearchConstants.WAIT_UNTIL_READY_TO_SEARCH, null);
  }
}
```

The method `waitForIndexer()` deserves some additional explanation. Deleting a project requires a non-obvious step. The Java search infrastructure uses an index to perform precise and efficient declaration and reference searches. The indexer is updated in a background thread whenever the contents of a project change. To avoid the indexer interfering with deleting (for example, trying to delete a file the indexer just opened), we wait until the indexer is finished. This is done by performing a dummy search query. The query specifies that it should wait until the indexer is up-to-date and ready. Before deleting a project we call `waitForIndexer()`.

APPENDIX C

AutoTestBuilder with Exclusion Support

This is the version of the `AutoTestBuilder` with exclusion support. Before each test run, the exclusion file *test.exclusions* is read and applied to the list of available types.

org.eclipse.contribution.junit/AutoTestBuilder

```
public class AutoTestBuilder extends IncrementalProjectBuilder {
  private static boolean enabled= true;
  private static boolean trace= false;

  public AutoTestBuilder() {
  }

  protected IProject[] build(int kind, Map args,
      IProgressMonitor pm) throws CoreException {
    if (hasBuildErrors() || !AutoTestBuilder.enabled)
      return null;
    IJavaProject javaProject= JavaCore.create(getProject());
    IType[] types= new TestSearcher().findAll(javaProject, pm);
    types= exclude(types);
    if (trace)
      printTestTypes(types);
    JUnitPlugin.getPlugin().run(types, javaProject);
    return null;
  }

  public static void setEnabled(boolean isEnabled) {
    AutoTestBuilder.enabled= isEnabled;
  }

  private boolean hasBuildErrors() throws CoreException {
    IMarker[] markers= getProject().findMarkers(
      IJavaModelMarker.JAVA_MODEL_PROBLEM_MARKER, false,
```

```
        IResource.DEPTH_INFINITE);
      for (int i= 0; i < markers.length; i++) {
        IMarker marker= markers[i];
        if (marker.getAttribute(
            IMarker.SEVERITY, 0) == IMarker.SEVERITY_ERROR)
          return true;
      }
      return false;
    }

    static {
      String value= Platform.getDebugOption(
        "org.eclipse.contribution.junit/trace/testfinding");
      if (value != null && value.equalsIgnoreCase("true"))
        trace= true;
    }

    private static void printTestTypes(IType[] tests) {
      System.out.println("Auto Test: "); //$NON-NLS-1$
      for (int i= 0; i < tests.length; i++) {
        System.out.println("\t"+tests[i].getFullyQualifiedName());
      }
    }

    private IType[] exclude(IType[] types) {
      try {
        Set exclusions= readExclusions(getProject().getFile(
          new Path("test.exclusions")));
        List result= new ArrayList(types.length);
        for (int i= 0; i < types.length; i++) {
          IType type= types[i];
          String typeName= type.getFullyQualifiedName();
          if (!exclusions.contains(typeName))
            result.add(type);
          return (IType[])(result.toArray(
            new IType[result.size()]));
        }
      } catch (Exception e) {
        // fall through
      }
      return types;
    }

    private Set readExclusions(IFile file)
        throws IOException, CoreException {
      Set result= new HashSet();
      BufferedReader br= new BufferedReader(
        new InputStreamReader(file.getContents()));
      try {
        String line;
        while ((line= br.readLine()) != null) {
          line= line.trim();
          if (line.length() > 0)
            result.add(line);
        }
      } finally {
```

```
            br.close();
        }
        return result;
    }
}
```

References

○ K. Beck, *Smalltalk Best Practice Patterns*. Prentice Hall PTR, Upper Saddle River, NJ, 1997, ISBN: 013476904X.

Basic reference for implementation patterns.

○ K. Beck, *Test-Driven Development: By Example*. Addison-Wesley, Boston, 2003, ISBN: 0321146530.

Introduction to TDD.

○ M. Fowler, *Patterns of Enterprise Application Architecture*. Addison-Wesley, Boston, 2003, ISBN: 0321127420.

Basic reference for large-scale design patterns, with some interesting smaller patterns also.

○ E. Gamma, R. Helm, R. Johnson, and J. Vlissides. *Design Patterns: Elements of Reusable Object-Oriented Software*. Addison-Wesley, Reading, MA, 1995, ISBN: 0201633612.

Basic reference for design patterns.

○ R. Martin, editor, *Pattern Languages of Program Design 3*. Addison-Wesley, Reading, MA, 1998, ISBN: 0201310112.

Collected patterns on a variety of topics.

○ L. Rising, editor, *The Pattern Almanac 2000*. Addison-Wesley, Boston, 2000, ISBN: 0201615673.

A comprehensive reference for patterns.

○ D. Schmidt, M. Stal, H. Rohner, F. Buschmann, *Pattern-Oriented Software Architecture Volume 2: Patterns for Concurrent and Networked Objects*. John Wiley & Sons, 2000, ISBN: 0471606952.

Patterns for distributed systems.

Index